Praise for
Star-Spangled Jesus

"*Star-Spangled Jesus* is the Rosetta Stone for understanding white Christian Nationalism. Behind all the stats and the polling are the people who subscribe to this ideology, and few will even come close to April Ajoy's firsthand experience in the movement... *Star-Spangled Jesus* will help you understand white Christian Nationalism's hold on so many people and the danger it poses to democracy and the church."

—Jemar Tisby, PhD, professor of history at Simmons College of Kentucky and *New York Times* bestselling author of *The Color of Compromise* and *The Spirit of Justice*

"An insightful and hilarious journey out of Christian Nationalism... both timely and timeless, challenging readers to rethink beliefs while providing plenty of laughs along the way. This is the guidebook for finding a faith that's true to its roots and open to the future."

—Mary Katherine Backstrom, author of *Holy Hot Mess*

"Who knew Christian Nationalism could be so funny?! This was exactly the kind of transparent, hysterical storytelling that I needed to make me start believing again."

—Tyler Merritt, author of *I Take My Coffee Black*

"This book is not preaching to the choir... It is the breadcrumbs to help lead millions out of the forest of lies they were taught from inception... how we were all groomed to become warriors for the kingdom, not citizens of this world. My only hope... is that we can get enough copies into the hands of those who need this salvation."

—Father Nathan Monk

"A courageous call to reimagine faith. With defiant joy and her characteristic humor, April Ajoy offers us all an invitation to stubbornly refuse to let the patriotic pastors and prosperity preachers steal our faith. . . . For many people, rejecting the star-spangled Jesus is not the end of faith—it is a new beginning."

—Shane Claiborne, author, activist, and founder of Red Letter Christians

"If you only have time to read one book on the state of American Christianity this year, it should be *Star-Spangled Jesus*."

—Jonathan Merritt, critically acclaimed author and columnist

"April shares her story using wit and humor . . . You'll hear what only someone who lived through it can share and why it's so important for Christians to rise up and resist Christian Nationalism."

—Tim Whitaker, founder of The New Evangelicals

STAR-SPANGLED JESUS

LEAVING CHRISTIAN NATIONALISM AND FINDING A TRUE FAITH

APRIL AJOY

WORTHY PUBLISHING

Nashville • New York

Worthy
Hachette Book Group
1290 Avenue of the Americas, New York, NY 10104
worthypublishing.com
@WorthyPub

First Edition: October 2024

Worthy is a division of Hachette Book Group, Inc. The Worthy name and logo are registered trademarks of Hachette Book Group, Inc.

The publisher is not responsible for websites (or their content) that are not owned by the publisher.

The Hachette Speakers Bureau provides a wide range of authors for speaking events. To find out more, go to hachettespeakersbureau.com or email HachetteSpeakers@hbgusa.com.

Worthy books may be purchased in bulk for business, educational, or promotional use. For information, please contact your local bookseller or the Hachette Book Group Special Markets Department at special.markets@hbgusa.com.

Print book interior design by Kristen Andrews.

Library of Congress Cataloging-in-Publication Data
Names: Ajoy, April, author.
Title: Star-spangled Jesus : leaving Christian nationalism and
finding a true faith / April Ajoy.
Description: First edition. | Nashville : Worthy Books, 2024.
Identifiers: LCCN 2024012044 | ISBN 9781546006688 (hardcover) |
ISBN 9781546006701 (ebook)
Subjects: LCSH: Evangelicalism—United States—History—21st century. |
Religious right—United States—History—21st century. |
Christianity and politics—United States—History—21st century.
Classification: LCC BR1642.U5 A38 2024 | DDC 320.55—dc23/eng/20240517
LC record available at https://lccn.loc.gov/2024012044

ISBNs: 978-1-5460-0668-8 (hardcover), 978-1-5460-0670-1 (ebook)

Printed in the United States of America

LSC-C

Printing 1, 2024

For my dad.
For instilling in me a passion to always stand up for what I believe is right.

Contents

PART FOUR
FRONTLINES OF CHRISTIAN NATIONALISM

Introduction

The crowds gathered in the frigid January air in the Ellipse in Washington DC. As speaker after speaker addressed the masses, the energy in the park began to build. Former New York City Mayor Rudy Giuliani called for "trial by combat."[1] Representative Mo Brooks of Alabama said, "Now, our ancestors sacrificed their blood, their sweat, their tears, their fortunes, and sometimes their lives to give us, their descendants, an America that is the greatest nation in world history. So I have a question for you—are you willing to do the same?"[2]

When President Trump, who had just lost an election but refused to accept defeat, finally stood and addressed the people, he was greeted by deafening cheers. He got up and told them, "We fight like hell. And if you don't fight like hell, you're not going to have a country anymore."[3]

These patriotic Americans weren't fighting off a foreign terrorist threat or trying to stop a looming war that day. No, the enemy they were facing was far worse. These politicians needed to save America from a true threat—from President-elect Joe Biden and his posse of godless Democrats because...something about Antifa, or maybe Marxists? Who were maybe working with the global elite to ruin our forever perfect, God-blessed Christian nation?

It was all a little unclear. But that didn't make what happened next any less disturbing. America watched in horror as the crowd marched to the Capitol Building. Then they climbed the walls, fought through security, and breached the building, aiming for the Senate chamber, with plans to stop Vice President Mike Pence from certifying the election.

Newscasters, journalists, and most of the American public were shocked to see this violence unfold live on national television.

I wasn't shocked. I had heard plenty of rumblings inside conservative Christian Facebook groups leading up to this event. I had seen people claiming, "This is our 1776 moment." Others posted about their travel plans to DC or the signs they were making. Some even showed pictures of the bullets they were buying in preparation for the day.

Just months before, I had gotten into an argument over the looming potential danger with my spouse, Beecher. I had grown up in the Church. My father was the pastor of a conservative evangelical church, and we traveled around the world preaching the gospel. I went to Christian schools, Christian college, and a Christian grad school. I even worked in conservative Christian media. I knew the conservative world well, and based on the conversations I was hearing, I was convinced something bad was going to happen regardless of who won the 2020 election.

Beecher, the optimistic one in our marriage, tried to encourage me. "It will be okay," Beecher said, insisting my doom-and-gloom perspective was an overreaction. But I knew better. After a lengthy and intense discussion, I eventually convinced my spouse that we were in trouble no matter the outcome. I went to sleep easily that night, satisfied that I had proven my point. Beecher, however, stayed up for several more anxious hours trapped in worry and quietly fuming at me while I slept soundly.

As much as I liked winning the argument, I didn't want to be right. But I saw how my fellow Christians were comparing Trump to Jesus himself. I saw how, when the votes were counted in November, many claimed a holy resurrection was coming. Believing the stolen election narrative, a lady from my former church even posted online, "They thought it was over when they nailed Jesus to the cross, this is far from over! Go Trump!"

I saw all the posts talking about "taking the country back for God" and the increasing not-so-subtle threats online, but I *still* hoped that it would all work out okay.

A knot grew in my stomach as I heard Trump encourage the thousands of people to march to the Capitol. I watched from the comfort of my living room in small-town Tennessee. Beecher was at work, teaching at a local conservative Christian college, while I anxiously paced at home. I couldn't take my eyes off the TV. I held my coffee cup in one hand and used my spare hand to take care of our two daughters, a four-year-old and an almost two-year-old. It was a multitasking kind of day.

I tried to convince myself it would be fine. *Surely no one would actually be violent over election results. This is America. We have our problems, but we have always had a peaceful transfer of power from one president to the next.*

But then the rioters broke through the security line at the Capitol. It's one thing to see threatening Facebook posts. It's another thing entirely to see people beating police officers with BLUE LIVES MATTER flags flying behind them.

Is that a noose? I thought as I heard people chanting, "Hang Mike Pence."

I stared at the television, unable to look away. Then I saw something that disturbed me even more.

Sprinkled throughout the crowd, I noticed numerous Christian signs and flags. Signs that said, JESUS IS MY SAVIOR, TRUMP IS MY PRESIDENT; JESUS SAVES; JESUS 2020. Even a picture of Jesus wearing a MAGA hat.

What does Jesus have to do with this? This was *my* Jesus. The same Jesus who told Peter to lay down his sword and taught his followers to turn the other cheek. What did Trump have to do with *him*?

I had been a conservative evangelical for most of my life. Despite that, I felt so disconnected from the people on that screen. These were not people I recognized. This was not a Christianity I had ever followed. I could not wrap my head around why this group was committing such horrible acts for a man who seemed only in it for himself.

Beecher arrived home just as the dust from the attack began to settle. I still had the television on. News channels were calling it an insurrection. They showed horrific scenes from inside the Capitol Building and talked about the people who had been injured and died in the attacks. Then they started releasing photos identifying people who had participated.

The news station flashed a photo of the infamous "Zip Tie Guy" on-screen. Remember him? The guy who had carried zip ties into the Senate Chamber so he could allegedly tie up members of Congress?[4]

"Uhhh, I know him," Beecher said in disbelief.

Beecher knew "Zip Tie Guy" as a youth group kid named Eric. They had gone to the same small Baptist church in middle-of-nowhere Georgia while they were in high school.

While we were still reeling from that discovery, another picture on the TV caught my attention.

"Oh my gosh...that's Jenna!" Jenna was a Dallas Realtor who had gone to my dad's church. *My* church. I had worshipped with her, talked with her at events, and eaten church casseroles beside her.

That's when it hit home. The people breaching the Capitol were not some extremist sect that I had never interacted with before. I knew them. These were my people.

An unsettling thought popped into my head: *If my life had gone differently, I could've been there with them.*

This was quickly followed by a realization that rocked my world:

Oh crap. I was a Christian Nationalist!

Now, I wouldn't have called myself a Christian Nationalist back then. I didn't even know the term at the time. I thought I was just doing what every good Christian was supposed to do: love God, love people,[5] and vote red. Republican-ness was close to godliness, and based on that criterion, I was a very godly girl.

I guess you could say I came by it honestly. I saw my dad devote his life to winning souls and turning America back to Jesus. Dad was a world-renowned traveling evangelist and took our family with him on the road most of the time. My mom, my brothers, and I would all take turns singing onstage before Dad would preach in churches and stadiums all around the world. We were incredibly close-knit, with my dad as the clear leader of the pack. The purpose of all our traveling and ministry was to lead as many people to Christ as possible. To save souls. We believed in what we were doing with an all-encompassing passion.

When we were in the States, we often traveled in our 40-foot motor home, driving from church to church. Our permanent home was in Dallas, Texas, where my dad co-pastored a large church with my grandfather, who was the founding pastor. My dad was often featured on Christian television and had his own radio show. I don't mean to brag, but in certain Pentecostal evangelical circles, my dad was kind of a big deal, and I wanted nothing more than to follow in his footsteps.

He also dabbled in politics and was loyal to the Republican Party. I remember having deep talks with him about government policies and the importance of keeping America a Christian nation. Dad had a large, specially designed decal with the words AMERICA SAY JESUS put on all sides of the RV we traveled in. His faith was loudly interconnected with his political beliefs, and as a daddy's girl, I made sure to be just as bold.

When I was seventeen, I created a Myspace group titled "I'm a Christian, therefore I'm a Republican." A year later, I performed a song I wrote called "America Say Jesus" on national Christian television's *The Jim Bakker Show*. Yes, it was as cringey as it sounds. I'll tell you more about that later.

At the all-knowing age of nineteen, I wrote a book called *A Dying Breed*. It was about how young Christians like me—those of us who were willing to stand up for God's truth against culture—were few and far between. This literary masterpiece included sentences like, "I have a passion for my generation to be freed of this liberal brainwash." It also included chapters that railed against the gay agenda, the ACLU, and Christians who are too nice. This wasn't bigotry, though; I was just fighting for Jesus.

This mentality stayed with me into my twenties as I campaigned for Mitt Romney and left my corporate job to be a TV producer at Pat Robertson's Christian Broadcasting Network. The pay cut was worth it, because it would allow me to further the Kingdom of God and work to make America more godly. It was just what good Christians did. Not only did we need to save souls from Satan's grasp, but we needed to save America from something just as sinister: Democrats.

Hello, Christian Nationalism.

Christian Nationalism is not new. It is an ideology that has been around since the beginning of our country, but it has only recently been given a name and gained traction as a major political force. But what is it, and why do we need to be paying attention to it?

In short, it's a belief that America was founded as a Christian nation, and that we should do whatever it takes to return America to its Christian roots so that God will continue to bless our nation. But what that looks like and how it plays out are different depending on who you ask.

Christian Nationalism has been getting a lot of extra attention since the storming of the Capitol, and even more so since, in late 2023, Republicans elected a new Speaker of the House who is pretty much Exhibit A[6] (looking at you, Mike Johnson!). But it can be hard to pinpoint exactly *what* it is and *who* actually is a Christian Nationalist.

That's where I come in. I make funny videos on TikTok about different cringey aspects of Christian Nationalism, which obviously makes me an expert on the topic. But also, as someone who spent the majority of my life as a diehard Christian Nationalist but didn't know it, I have quite a bit of firsthand information about what Christian Nationalism is, what it looks like, what its goals are, and why we need to resist it.

In this book, I'm going to dive into my past, sharing personal stories from my time inside the ideology-turned-movement. I'll examine the central *tenets* of Christian Nationalism, the *tactics* Nationalists use, and the *issues* its leaders rally supporters around. Each story will connect the Christian Nationalism of my past with historical or current context, to help us figure out how we got here.

Now, a warning: At times, it may seem like the stories I share relate more closely to conservative evangelical culture in America than just straight Christian Nationalism. That's because the two have become so intertwined that it can be really hard to spot the differences. It's one of the more difficult things about stopping Christian Nationalism—it hides in plain sight as regular old American Christianity. Positioning itself as the one and only *true* form of Christianity is actually one of the tenets that we will get into later.

For now, just know that Christian Nationalism uses so much of evangelicalism to further its own power-hungry agenda: from White supremacy to end times eschatology to proselytizing to gender roles and so much more. Conservative Christianity and today's Christian Nationalism have become pretty hard to separate, but they are not the same thing. There's a lot of overlap, but differences do exist.

How are they different? you ask. Well, there's enough nuance to require a book on the subject. And, hey, lucky for you, you're reading one.

Hopefully by the end of this book, you'll be able to understand where cultural Christianity and Christian Nationalism overlap and where they differ, and how Nationalists use issues Christians care about to further their own agendas. I hope you'll also have a few laughs along the way, too, because what's funnier than a fringe group trying to destroy democracy in the name of Jesus?

I mean, a lot. But humor is how I cope.

There are lots of reasons you might have picked up this book. Maybe you've seen some of the videos I've posted online making fun of this stuff and want to have a good laugh. Hopefully you'll do plenty of that in these pages. Maybe you are an outsider who wants to understand what all the fuss is about. Maybe you are reading for academic purposes, to understand how something like January 6th could have happened. Maybe someone gave you this book as a passive-aggressive gift. If that's the case, you may want to consider the possibility that someone's trying to tell you that you might be a Christian Nationalist.

After reading this far, are you worried that you might be a Nationalist? No problem. I have created this handy quiz to help you determine right off the bat where you fall on the Christian Nationalist spectrum. Simply answer each question and give yourself the number of points listed in parentheses for that answer.

1. At your religious gatherings, which of the following have you done? Check all that apply.

   ____ Honored Veterans (0)

   ____ Recited the Pledge of Allegiance (1)

____ Sung "God Bless America" (1)
____ Chanted "Let's Go Brandon" (3)
____ Stormed the Capitol waving Jesus-themed signs and American flags (5)

2. How do you view America in comparison with the rest of the world? Check all that apply.
____ It's just like any other country, with good and bad parts (0)
____ It's better than most because of its economy and world impact (1)
____ It's the best because God blesses us the most (2)
____ It's currently bad because of leftist woke sheep but true America is the best country in the world, and godly men will make her great again (5)

3. How many of the following products or companies have you boycotted in your life? Check all that apply.
____ Bud Light (1)
____ *Barbie* movie (1)
____ Starbucks (1)
____ Target (1)
____ Chick-fil-A (1)
____ Disney (1)
____ It would be faster to name the things I have *not* boycotted (5)

4. How many of the following groups are not true Christians? Check all that apply.
____ Muslims (0)
____ Buddhists (0)
____ Catholics (1)
____ Pentecostals (they speak in tongues and dance occasionally) (1)

____ Baptists (they stand still during worship and never raise their hands) (1)
____ Universalists (they believe hell doesn't exist) (1)
____ Affirming Denominations (they believe LGBTQ people can be Christians) (1)

5. What do you think is Jesus' most defining act?
   ____ Flipping the tables angrily at the temple (2)
   ____ Telling Peter to lay down his sword (0)
   ____ Willingly being crucified without fighting back (0)
   ____ Returning at the second coming like a lion to annihilate everyone who doesn't believe in him (5)

6. What is a Christian's main calling in life?
   ____ Take care of orphans and widows (0)
   ____ Convince others to follow Jesus so they can spend an eternity in heaven (0)
   ____ Keep everyone in line with God's morality (2)
   ____ Take over the government to make America the godliest nation on earth (5)

7. How many of the following groups do you consider real threats to American life?
   ____ White supremacists (0)
   ____ Antifa (1)
   ____ LGBTQ people (3)
   ____ Reptilian Shape-Shifting Satanists in high government positions (5)

8. How many of the following are examples of religious persecution?
   ____ Christians being beheaded in other countries for following Jesus (0)

____ A baker being forced to make a wedding cake for a same-sex couple (1)
____ A former president being ordered to pay $80 million for being found liable for assaulting and defaming a woman (3)
____ A person going to prison for merely taking a peaceful walk around the Capitol with weapons while searching for Mike Pence (5)

9. What should be done with a book that has content in it you don't like?

____ Nothing. Don't read it and leave it be. (0)
____ Burn it in a church bonfire and boycott the author (2)
____ Ban it and all books that go against Christian beliefs—save the children! (3)
____ Send the author to jail for treason (5)

10. When you hear of wars happening across the world, how do you feel?

____ Sad for the people involved (0)
____ Happy because this is a sign that Jesus is coming back soon (2)
____ Believe America should get involved and end it (we have bombs for a reason!) (2)
____ Indifferent—they aren't Christian nations so of course they're going to do stupid things (2)

Now add up your points and see where you fall.

0–5 **ANTIFA Super Soldier Level.** If you finished in this range, this means you are probably NOT a Christian Nationalist. But this also means that the Christian Nationalism movement is now against you and has labeled you an anarchist set to destroy America as we know it. Welcome to the dark side.

5–10 **Evangelical Pastor Level.** If you fall in this group, you are more than likely an evangelical who has managed to avoid the harsher aspects of Christian Nationalism. But watch out because it's still lurking around the edges of your faith. This could be a very helpful book for you as you sort things out.

10–20 **Billy Graham Level.** *That* Billy Graham? The one who saved millions and made the gospel his main mission? Yes, because *that* Billy Graham also assisted in making America as Christian as possible, from a personal and governmental level. If you are here, you probably don't identify as a Christian Nationalist, but I bet it's hard to determine where your political affiliation ends, and your theology begins. This book can help you sort that out.

20–30 **Lauren Boebert Level.** You may not understand what Christian Nationalism is enough to celebrate or deny it, but there's enough here to put you on the fringes of the ideology at a minimum. You want a godly country first and foremost and are probably quite outspoken about it. This might not be your favorite book, but I have a hunch that it will give you more perspective and insight to help you explain your thoughts better.

30–40 **Marjorie Taylor Greene Level.** I imagine you are fine with being called a Christian Nationalist. You may even wear a shirt claiming to be one as you read this book and laugh at me. You may not be actively storming the Capitol or anything, but you also aren't afraid to cheer on those who are. If you keep reading this book, you probably won't be triggered too much, because you can just write off what I say by believing that George Soros is paying me with eternal youth from his space lasers.

40+ **Proud Boys Level.** Welp, congrats. You are definitely a Christian Nationalist, and probably a violent one at that. I am totally good if you don't want to read this book any further.

> You've already gotten through most of the intro. That's the best part. No reason to keep reading! I'm just a nobody and you should totally not focus on me. Please forget I exist. And please stop posting death threats on my videos.

Okay, so how'd you do? Were you surprised by the results? Well, so was I when I started looking into it. It's not like I had a part of my life that was the Christian Nationalism section. The ideology was intertwined into my entire existence. My faith. My politics. My fears. My family. My hopes. My livelihood. Christian Nationalism was the almonds inside my White conservative Christian brownie.

That's because Christian Nationalism is not something you enroll in. It's not a moniker used openly in many church services. You don't get an ID card and a welcome party where you are handed an AR-15. One day, you are just a Bible-believing Christian in a sanctuary and the next you are at a political rally with a Jesus flag. It happens quite slowly and under the surface. That is by design.

Welcome to my wild journey of leaving Christian Nationalism behind and my plea for America to leave it behind, too.

PART ONE

TENETS OF CHRISTIAN NATIONALISM

Every movement has a set of core underlying beliefs at its heart. These beliefs are the reason why people do what they do, and understanding these core principles helps outsiders make sense of what can seem to be confounding behavior.

Before we take a deep dive into the Christian Nationalist playbook and look at the ways people in the movement are changing our schools, courts, and culture in the name of God, let's look at the why. Understanding the logic (such as it is) and reasoning driving the movement will help readers not only spot Christian Nationalism in the wild, but also help us make sense of what's at stake here.

I believe there are three main tenets that drive followers of Christian Nationalism in their mission to make America a Christian nation, and I'll explore each of those in the following chapters. Keep in mind that there is no official organized list of rules and beliefs for this group, so I can't cite a source document or article of incorporation here, but these tenets are things that stick out to me based on my time in the movement and my understanding of where things stand today.

So come with me as we peek behind the curtain of Christian Nationalism.

We'll look at the good, the bad, and the very, very ugly.

CHAPTER 1

America Is the Best

Once upon a time, a group of the greatest, strongest, handsomest, and manliest men set out on a holy quest. These men fled the tyrannical country of England to start a new country, where they would have the freedom to worship Jesus how they wanted. These great men, who were basically Christ's disciples 2.0, embarked on a journey to fight for their religious freedom.

They loaded up on ships that sailed across the ocean on this God-ordained mission. Sure, some may have *technically* brought enslaved people with them, but it was a different time. And they treated them with the utmost respect, kindness, and love.

And sure, *some* people technically already inhabited the new land, but they didn't really count because they weren't Christians. They needed Jesus. And the people in the colonies, set up by the righteous men from England, helped these native people have a much better life—because they now had Jesus to comfort them on the Trail of Tears (we don't really need to talk about that, though, because again, it was a different time).

Then the big bad godless British people wanted to stake their claim on the new land. But God would not stand for such evil in his new country, so he declared war through his chosen one, George Washington. God supernaturally blessed his troops to defeat the British. Yeah, some people died, and a lot of the British were *sort of* Christian, too, but it was the price of freedom. And the greatest country the world would ever know was born: the United States of America.

Okay, so maybe some bad people in the southern part of the country refused to stop owning people and tried to repeat what Americans had just done to the British, but they failed! Because God was on the side of the holiest president of all, *Republican* Abraham Lincoln, who signed the Emancipation Proclamation and ended racism forever.

Over the next 150 years, America spread this gospel message of hope and freedom all over the world. God blessed our country in every war we ever fought. The Axis Powers of World War I? We beat 'em. Nazis? Really beat them. Vietnam? Uh... not sure but I think we probably won. The Cold War? Tear down that wall. The War on Terror? Mission accomplished. All these victories occurred because America was founded as a Christian nation, and as long as it stayed the most Christian nation on earth, it would continue to be supernaturally blessed. Hallelujah, the Great I Am and Uncle Sam were quite the team!

This—almost exactly this— is what I wholeheartedly believed about American history for most of my life. I was taught that I was on the side of good, and everything I did was done with the goal of keeping that goodness going for generations to come.

No one told me about the true, brutal history of Native American displacement and genocide. I vaguely knew about slavery, Jim Crow, and the KKK—whose members were largely Christians—and the fuzzy morality of using nuclear bombs. None of that fit the narrative I was taught. The message I received was very simple: America is the best. Period.

I know now this belief is literally the definition of "nationalism," which *Merriam-Webster's Collegiate Dictionary* defines as "loyalty and devotion to a nation," especially with "a sense of national consciousness exalting one nation above all others and placing primary emphasis on promotion of its culture and interests as opposed to those of other nations."

So... pretty much exactly what I grew up believing.

Of course, we never used the term "Nationalist." It was simply called patriotism, and it ranked just below holiness. This is the first tenet of Christian Nationalism: The belief that America has been specially selected by God, and that it has a special place in God's plan for redemption.

Now, I've already told you that when I was growing up, our family had a 40-foot motor home covered with the words AMERICA SAY JESUS, which we drove across the country as we ministered in churches. We had that sign made because, in 2005, my dad wrote a book called *America Say Jesus*, which was all about how America was founded as a Christian nation and should get back to that. A lot of the book examines the Christian beliefs and writings of the Founding Fathers. On the front of the book, he included this prophetic warning:

> Unless America defines her God (which is Jesus Christ), God the Father will lift the veil of protection that is over this country, and America will experience bloodshed and devastation in unprecedented ways. That's why our president and every Christian must confess Jesus Christ publicly!

To throw my support behind my dad's book, I wrote and performed an original song called "America Say Jesus" on *The Jim Bakker Show*. At the time, I didn't know much about Jim Bakker, other than he was once a prominent televangelist who went to jail over financial issues. It turns out, he defrauded donors out of $158 million, which came to light after a woman accused him of sexual misconduct and it came out his ministry had given her funds, seemingly as hush money.[1, 2] But I didn't know most of that when I went to sing on his show. What I did know was that Christianity is about forgiveness, and Jim had written a book in prison about how he was wrong, so everyone was morally cleared to support his ministry again. Those crimes were washed by the blood, and it was now part of his testimony.

Bakker's new show wanted to feature my dad's latest book *and* my song of the same title. It felt like God opening a door, and who were we to say no? The episode fell right before Father's Day, so they asked our whole family to be on the show.

I was eighteen, had just graduated from high school, and was ready to leave my mark on the world. Backstage, I drenched my wet, curly hair in Aussie long-lasting hair gel. I cupped my locks into my hands and scrunched, repeating this process until every strand was frozen in a fresh-out-of-the-shower look that made my hair hard as a rock. I applied lots of blush, mascara, and light pink lipstick.

I was ready for my close-up.

The producer walked toward us and yelled, "Fifteen seconds out!" before beginning the countdown. He mouthed the last five seconds before the red camera light turned on.

We were on the air.

The show mostly consisted of Jim and my dad talking about the book, the state of America, and why we needed to put God back in it. Sometimes Lori, Jim's wife, chimed in. They were both kind and threw a couple questions to my mom and us kids, but we mostly just sat there, feigning excitement over talking points we'd heard a million times.

Jim talked about Father's Day and gifted my dad a real sword he called "Solomon's Sword" live on the show. This was a product he was selling to his viewers that day. But before I could question why my dad was receiving a sharpened weapon as a gift on a Christian show, I heard Jim cue the song.

"Now sing with her! Her original song, she wrote it. Here's April!"

I started tapping my feet, nodding my head, and clapping my hands to get the audience involved. The crowd of mostly White senior citizens seemed to clap on fifty-seven different beats, but I focused on nailing my song.

I belted out the first verse.

"They tell us that we're wrong for telling them that's what they are
They say we can't define sin and that we've gone too far
We can worship as we please
And choose how we believe
As long as we don't say the name of Jesus publicly

They're always on our necks and I am downright sick
of them demanding me to be politically correct."

The audience was with me as I rolled into the chorus.

"America Say Jesus
He makes our nation free
Jesus gives us life and liberty
We can't ignore our history
And how God gave us our country
And yet his name we're not supposed to speak?
America Say Jesus, America Say Jesus
Jesus makes our nation great
Let's all publicly say his name
America Say Jesus"

As I began singing the second verse, the background singers came out behind me, smiling and clapping. I finished out with the bridge and a couple more choruses, and the song ended. The show then cut to a commercial for the *Revelation Generation Emergency Backpack*. Dark, edgy music played as the narrator talked about the impending end of days, and the visuals depicted the struggle of a post-apocalyptic life. Then they showed a backpack that would help Christian families be "prepared for the disasters that are looming on the horizon."

Even then, it seemed a bit extra to me, but I remained unfazed. After all, we shared an end-goal with Jim Bakker: to turn America back to God.

Patriotism was an increasing part of my dad's ministry in those days. When I was fifteen, after traveling to countries all over the world, my family had shifted its focus from worldwide evangelism to the spiritual battle at home. We believed America was a Christian nation, but it was slipping away from a righteous path, so my dad planted a new church called *America's Church*. To emphasize America being a Christian nation and our church being American, the church's branding included

American flags. My dad even bought a billboard with Old Glory flying behind the Church's name to invite the community to join our Sunday services. *America's Church* was part of our attempt to set the nation back on a holy track.

If you were to go back and listen to my dad's sermons or read his books now, you would find that Jesus was always the most important thing to him. Saving individuals from eternal damnation was his main priority. And while he preferred one-on-one conversions, he also believed that a way to save souls was to keep America Christian. A Christian America would lead to a Christian world. So we all rooted for America like she was our favorite sports team.

When, in 2000, President George W. Bush spoke about the nation's divine blessing, saying, "Our nation is chosen by God and commissioned by history to be a model to the world,"[3] his words resonated deep within my bones. I believed this completely.

But W, of course, was not the first person to espouse this belief. Far from it. While the concept has morphed some over the centuries, it originally can be traced back to the Doctrine of Discovery issued in the Papal Bull by Pope Alexander VI in 1493. The document supported Spain's subjugation of the New World and claimed that any land inhabited by non-Christians was fair game, declaring that "the Christian religion be exalted and be everywhere increased and spread, that the health of souls be cared for and that barbarous nations be overthrown and brought to the faith itself."[4] In other words, White European countries and Western Christianity were superior to all other religions and cultures,[5] so it didn't matter what they did to everyone else.

In 1630, the Puritans believed their success in the New World was evidence of God's favor. On the ship on their way over, John Winthrop gave a sermon that referred to their religious settlements as "a city upon a hill," in reference to Jesus' Sermon on the Mount, when he said, "You are the light of the world. A city set on a hill cannot be hidden" (Matthew 5:14 ESV). This became the basis for what would become known as Manifest Destiny, or the belief that America was destined by God to spread Christianity across North America.[6]

The phrase "a city on a hill" was reclaimed by Ronald Reagan to emphasize American exceptionalism, and it has continued to be used to this day. It was even referenced in a question to GOP candidates at the Republican presidential primary debate in August 2023. Former Vice President Mike Pence answered, "God is not done with America yet, and if we will renew our faith in him who has ever guided this nation since we arrived on these wilderness shores, I know the best days for the greatest nation on earth are yet to come."[7]

It's Christian Nationalism math:

God + America = Greatest Nation on Earth

This was just a fact I accepted growing up. While my family spent time traveling overseas to spread the gospel, very little of my time in Christian Nationalism was spent focusing on other countries. Wherever we went, we told them about our faith and our way of life but didn't really learn about theirs.

The most quoted verse in all of evangelical American Christianity is John 3:16 (ESV), which says, "For God so loved the world, that he gave his only Son, that whoever believes in him should not perish but have eternal life." This verse was used to explain salvation and convince people to turn to Jesus. The part that wasn't highlighted nearly as much was the opening, where God "loves the *world*." Kinda like how grandparents say they love *all* their grandchildren the same, but everyone knows they have a favorite. America was God's unspoken favorite.

We believed America was exceptionally blessed by God. God shedding his grace on us was what made our nation the best. So when we saw liberals, atheists, and Democrats allowing decadence to creep into the nation, we viewed that as a threat. It would destroy God's favor on our country. For America to stay the best, she had to keep the Christian identity we believed she was founded on. We needed to get America back on the holy, righteous track to stay in God's good graces and ultimately help the world.

This all sounds strange in hindsight... especially realizing the horrors of slavery, racial genocide of indigenous people, and war crimes our nation committed throughout history. And God was... supposedly guiding that bloodshed?

But we didn't ask that question back in the day. America was blessed by God. Period. It wasn't White supremacy or our nation's violent past that would put us at risk of losing God's favor; it was the sin of feminists and leftists who would be America's downfall.

But when we weren't terrified of losing our divine favor, we were really proud of our country. We were proud to be American and proud to be Christian. And in my family, we were extra obnoxious because we were also Texan. When you're born in Texas, you come out of the womb clapping to "Deep in the Heart of Texas" and your first words are "Don't mess with Texas." I knew Texas was better than the other states because we were a Republic before we joined the Union, and we loved to bring that up any time the Democrats did stupid things at the federal level. "Well, we could just secede. America needs Texas, but we don't need those loons in Washington." It was a sentiment I brought up a lot.

As I look back on this, it strikes me as odd to believe that America is the best but also be so willing to leave it. Kinda like how some conservatives I know have accused President Joe Biden of being both senile *and* an evil mastermind colluding with China to completely take over America. Pick a struggle, please. It gives similar vibes to Southern Americans flying Confederate flags. Like, if you believe America is so amazing, why are you flying a flag reminding us your ancestors tried to leave it once?

Anywho, I spent most of my life as an outspoken, proud Texan, Christian, conservative, and American. I wore all the labels proudly. Sure, Proverbs 16:18 (ESV) says, "Pride goes before destruction," but that verse really only got brought up in June when we were discussing Pride Parades. Our pride was not only allowed, it was warranted. America was the best.

What's wrong with loving your country, you might ask? Nothing, in theory. Patriotism can be good when it's directed at making the country better for *all* people. The problem arises when it assumes that what's best for all people regardless of their belief is whatever lines up with a narrowly defined Christian worldview. And that's what happens when a movement's goal is to get its own people into positions of power to shape the laws and culture to fit their viewpoint. We'll get into that more later.

Looking back, I have a hard time coming up with more than a handful of names of evangelicals I knew who didn't espouse Nationalism in some way. Which is both saddening and alarming, actually. One does not need to wear the Christian Nationalist label to spread the ideology. Christian Nationalism is a disease that has spread undetected in many churches for decades.

Of course, there were a few conservative Christians who felt differently. I remember meeting a pastor who became close friends with my dad in his final years. This friend was conservative but occasionally said things that didn't sound very Republican.

"You know, they never found weapons of mass destruction. Our country killed lots of innocent people for something that wasn't true," I overheard him tell my dad. *Whose side is he on?*

Another time I overheard a conversation between him and my dad where he said something positive about Barack Obama. Yes, *that* Barack Obama. I was still figuring out if he was the Antichrist or not and this pastor was complimenting him? His salvation was suddenly suspect.

This pastor was a walking conundrum to me. He believed all the same things we did but didn't seem to hold America in the same superior regard. To him, it seemed like America was just another country, with good and bad all mixed in. This man's life exhibited loving thy neighbor. All his neighbors.

He didn't care if his insurance premiums or taxes were raised if it helped his less fortunate neighbors afford health care or other basic needs. He still shared conservative ideals, but he never equated someone's salvation or Christianity with how they voted. That was politics. Jesus was love.

It took me years to understand his perspective. This is because I hadn't yet come to understand that conservative Christianity and patriotism were not one and the same. I hadn't yet been introduced to the idea that you could be a Christian, an earnest, God-fearing Christian, and *not* vote Republican, or not support unlimited gun rights, or not believe that America is the most exceptional country in the history of the world. I hadn't yet come to understand that, at its core, Christianity wasn't about America at all. Eventually, I came to meet Christians who saw the world differently, and to be honest, at first I thought they were probably doomed for hell.

And a lot of these Christians were *gasp* Democrats. But not all of them. Some believed they were following Jesus by voting red, but they also embraced *all* of John 3:16, even the part about the rest of the world. They didn't put America on a pedestal or believe she has a higher calling than the rest of the world. They might still have had pride in their nation and wished her well, but not at the expense of other nations or people.

By contrast, I was willing to help the world so long as it wasn't at the expense of my country or my rights. I wanted refugees and asylum seekers to find safety and refuge, but I didn't understand why they needed to sneak across the Mexico-Texas border to find it. That was *my* state, and Fox News told me these "illegal aliens" were ruining my country and taking away the job I didn't even have yet.

It reminds me of a joke my dad used to tell.

Two people are chatting, and one man says, "I love you so much that if I ever have two houses, I will give you one."

"Wow, you're a great friend," the friend replies.

Feeling good, the man continues, "If I ever have two cars, I'll even give you one of the cars."

The other friend says, "Wow, you are so kind... what about if you have two goats?"

"No," the man says emphatically.

"Why not?" the friend asks quizzically.

The first man replies, "Because I have two goats."

And such went our compassion until our rights or privileges were at stake.

My kindness had limits. My love had conditions.

But Jesus' love didn't.

And eventually, after meeting people in the crosshairs of our culture war, I began to realize that in my quest to take America back for Jesus, I had become a pretty terrible Christ follower.

It's taken over a decade of getting to know the people Christian Nationalism demonized and wrestling with a belief system that didn't always line up with Jesus' teaching to get here— and I'll get into more of that journey in this book. Now I see that this love for *all* people in *all* places of the world without judgment is beautiful. It's what I believe Jesus wanted. But I've discovered that this posture can be hard to find in American churches today. More and more, it seems like Christianity and patriotism are conflated from our pulpits.

We used to sing "America the Beautiful" or other patriotic songs in church to celebrate Memorial Day, Veterans Day, or the Christian Nationalism holy day, the Fourth of July. Not great, but that was child's play compared to the annual "Freedom Sunday" at First Baptist Church in Dallas, Texas, where "patriotic worship" is sung in the Sanctuary once a year to celebrate our freedom as both Americans and Christians.[8] Or John Hagee's Cornerstone Church hosting the "ReAwaken America" conference that pushed conspiracies about the 2020 election and had attendees chanting "Let's Go Brandon" from church pews.[9] After backlash, Cornerstone released a statement saying that, while they hosted the event, their church did "not endorse their views."[10]

This stuff can get pretty weird. One time my spouse, Beecher, ran camera for a Christian conference where, at one of the services, a youth group performed a crucifixion scene that included a White male teenager playing Jesus. As the large wooden cross was raised up on the stage, a giant American flag fell behind him. This cued the room to sing "God

Bless America" as a teenage Jesus hung on the cross, like it was the most normal thing in the world.

Maybe the verse should have been, "By his red, white, and blue stripes we are healed."

This conflation of religion and politics is one reason the "America First" messaging works so effectively within American evangelical communities today. Underpinning so much of American evangelicalism is the belief that God really loves America the most (only possibly tied with Israel). So it's okay if we are first.

The irony is not lost on me that Christian Nationalism worships the same man who humbled himself and refused to accept power in favor of helping individuals. A man who often chose people over beliefs, like healing on the Sabbath, to the dismay of some religious leaders of his day.

When Jesus walked the earth, many people saw him as a messiah who would deliver freedom to Israel. He rode in on a donkey on Palm Sunday surrounded by people who wanted to crown him king of a nation with borders and citizens. But what did Jesus do during his time on earth? He told people there is a kingdom beyond that is far more important than any nation here and handed himself over to the Romans.

He didn't claim the vote was rigged when the crowd chose to crucify him over Barabbas. He didn't encourage his followers to storm Rome's Capitol Building and demand different results.

His life rejected nationalism. His followers should, too.

CHAPTER 2

Christian = Evangelical

Jesus lived and died on the earth about 2,000 years ago. When he died, he left very specific, very clear instructions for how his followers were to act, what they should believe, and how they should interact with the world around them. That's why all Christians have always agreed on every aspect of their faith and have worked together in peace and harmony to share Christ's message with the world ever since.

Lol. Just kidding. Jesus' followers were fighting about what it meant to be a Christian since the Resurrection. Some thought only Jews were included in Christ's redemption, while others believed it was for everyone. Some believed you had to act or worship or dress or eat a certain way to be a Christian, while others thought Christ's death got rid of those rules. Some believed Jesus was fully divine, while others said that was a lie from the pit of hell and he was just human, thankyouverymuch. Centuries went by and various church councils debated Christ's human versus divine nature. In AD 451, the Council of Chalcedon decreed that he was fully both.[1] Of course, debates continued, but any other belief was considered heretical thereafter. Kinda like Michael Scott in *The Office* declaring bankruptcy. "I declare heresy!" the Church said of anyone they disagreed with.

One of my favorite fights in the early church occurred in Acts 15, when Christian men argued about their penises. They debated whether or not salvation depended on a man's crotch turtle shedding its shell. I mean, naturally the men thought it all came down to their penises, right? Christ may have busted open the gates of heaven (or not, depending on who you asked) but men were still men. I always wonder what the women were doing while the men theologically discussed their privates. Like, *Do we not exist?* Maybe the men wanted women quiet because vaginas would just confuse their theology.

Docetism, an early church doctrine that was thrown around, believed Jesus' body was actually just a phantom. That's right. Only Jesus' ghost-like illusion was crucified while the real Jesus was chilling in heaven.[2] Sounds like something out of a scary campfire story.

In the sixteenth century, there was supposedly a German sect of Anabaptists called the Abecedarians. Central to their belief was the rejection of *all* forms of learning. This included the alphabet, believing that man's quest for knowledge undercut their need to rely on a higher power. Instead, they claimed God would teach the elect from within themselves.[3] I guess for the Abecedarians, ignorance really was bliss.

In the eighteenth century, there was this thing called "sin-eating" for a while, where some Christians believed if they prepared a meal near or sometimes *inside* a corpse, they could posthumously take on the sins of that deceased person as Jesus did in his death.[4] Listen, I'm all for a good sermon illustration, but this one's a little too morbidly creative for me. I love my dad and all, but dining among his remains just isn't happening.

The end of the eighteenth century also saw the formation of the Shakers, who lived simply and communally. Unfortunately, they also didn't believe in having sex—even in marriage. The lack of childbearing didn't bode well for their growth and they eventually all but died out.[5]

I could go on and on, but I'll end the list with a more recent one.

In the 1990s, a denomination known as the Church of the Almighty God believed that Christ was reincarnated as a middle-aged woman from central China called Lightning Deng.[6] The group was eventually banned from China, but you can apparently still find Lightning Deng living in New York City's Chinatown.[7] No word on if she's healing people on the streets or not.

This stuff is strange, but it's only a fraction of the stories that tell the weird history of Christianity. Through the ages, there have been about as many ways of understanding what it means to be Christian as there are people, and we're no different today. Dr. Seuss could have easily written a poem based on the wide range of beliefs and denominations within the Big capital-C Church. I imagine it might go something like this:

One Church
Two Church
Red Church
Blue Church
Loud Church
Quiet Church
Cowboy Church
Riot Church
Juice church. Wine church.
Literal blood of the divine church.
This one speaks in wild tongues.
This one handles snakes for fun.
Say! Look how many churches there are!

Yes, some are Mega. And some are small.
If you lay hands on some, back they fall.
Some leaders wear collars. Others skinny jeans.
Some are kind and some are mean.
This church bans dancing. That church bans dating.
Some pray for the end times while others stay waiting.
They're all different, unlike another.
But don't ask me why.
Just ask your mother (but not Mother Mary, because that's blasphemy).

From all my in-depth studies into these different sects and churches, I've found that there are two ideas they universally share: They all call themselves Christians, and they each wholeheartedly believe that they are the ones following Jesus the *right* way.

Today, there are over 45,000 denominations worldwide that fall under the Christian umbrella.[8] Forty. Five. THOUSAND. I spent most of my life deeply embedded in Christian evangelical culture and I could have listed maybe fifteen denominations total.

In fact, I was sheltered from just how big the Christian umbrella is. My family and I didn't need to know or talk about the thousands of other denominations. Because they didn't matter. They all believed slightly different things, but *we* were the ones who had it right. The Bible was clear about that. All the long and glorious history of Christianity had led up to our very church, with its unique ability to intuit and practice the faith exactly as God intended.

We were nondenominational Pentecostals and everyone around me assured me that we had all the answers for everything. Any Christian who said otherwise, or had slight theological differences, was just sadly misinformed. We could bless their little hearts for trying, though. Unless they were a Democrat. Then there was a good chance they were in cahoots with demonic forces to purposely throw us off.

Today, the term "narrow-minded" is mostly meant as an insult, but we wore that term like a badge of honor. My dad regularly touted from the pulpit, "People call us narrow-minded. Maybe that's true, but we can afford to be because we're right!" He used that one a lot, and congregations around the country always roared at it.

I included the same sentiment in one of the verses in my "America Say Jesus" song:

"They say we're narrow minded always trusting in God's might,
But they can argue all they want because we know we're right!"

It makes me cringe now, but I believed every word. And in the self-published book I wrote when I was nineteen, I said one of Satan's most dangerous tactics was convincing people to be open-minded.

When I was a junior in college, I accidentally became good friends with a Catholic girl. We were at a Baptist college, so I assumed I was surrounded by Protestant evangelicals. She was nice, tall like me, with blond hair that she curled with a flatiron (a trick she taught me). She wore Hollister shirts, was funny and cool, and I loved hanging out with her. We had several conversations about God and faith, and there was nothing out of the ordinary in her answers. The snake, the apple, and nakedness in the Garden of Eden? Check. David, the giant-slaying king of Israel? Check. The Virgin Mary? Check. Jesus dying on the cross? Check. Then, a few months into our friendship, she referenced going to Mass.

"Mass?!" I asked in horror.

She nodded.

"Wait, are you Catholic?"

While I was iffy on the eternal destination of some denominations, I just knew Catholics had it wrong. Why would you pray to saints when you could just pray to God? Mary was cool and all, but I heard Catholics worshipped her, which was blatant blasphemy. I also thought there was a 20 percent chance the Pope was the Antichrist the Bible warned us about. (I didn't make that up, for the record. In my circles, the Pope was always brought up when we debated who the Antichrist might be, second only to whichever Democrat was currently making a bid for the White House.)

She confirmed my suspicions, and for the first time in my life, I had to face the fact that her Catholic faith seemed so . . . normal. It was not at all what I thought Catholics were like. Eventually, after I talked with her and wrestled with it for a while, I decided that *maybe* Catholics weren't as devilish as I had been told. They had moved up to the same iffy plane as Methodists now.

Even within our own congregation—the one place where we were sure we had it right—there was infighting about the right way to do things. One time some church board members left because the drummer didn't have a proper sound cage. Another time people left because they didn't like the new worship pastor. Or once, the new pastor wanted to pray with the choir before the service and the worship pastor didn't like it, so she quit. You know—big, important theological debates.

I remember hearing about an associate pastor secretly recording one of the Sunday school teachers when I was a kid. He hid the tape recorder in the classroom before the service because there were rumors that the teacher wanted to start his own church, and the associate pastor wanted to catch the teacher in the act of bad-mouthing the lead pastor, who was my dad. Sure enough, the teacher did say bad things about my dad during his Sunday school lesson, and it was caught on tape. The drama this caused led to a small church split.

The point is that Christians have *never* agreed on one consistent, all-encompassing belief system or faith practice. Yet when I was growing up, everyone around me brushed all that aside consistently by claiming that the Bible is very clear about, well, everything. We alone understood how it was meant to be interpreted, and anyone who disagreed with us was wrong.

Honestly, it never even occurred to me that *I* could be the one who had it wrong. Not once. I knew I was right, and I had the assurance of salvation beyond a shadow of a doubt. I was proud of my beliefs. Doubts were for wussies.

Which leads me back to Christian Nationalism. While there are a lot of ways to be Christian, Christian Nationalism is predicated on believing that you and you alone are practicing the Christian faith the right way. And that one right way, coincidentally, looks a lot like one particular version of Christianity.

What I'm trying to say is that the "Christian" in Christian Nationalism of today means the White evangelical sect of Christianity in America. This is another tenet of Christian Nationalism: Christianity = their specific, conservative version. Any Christianity outside of their belief is mere "Christianity." We always put it in quotes because it was false, heretical, even laughable.

Merriam-Webster's Collegiate Dictionary defines "evangelical" as "of, relating to, or being in agreement with the Christian gospel especially as it is presented in the four Gospels." But as history shows us, even saying you believe the gospel can mean you might hold a wide range of beliefs.

So let's narrow down what it means to be evangelical in America. The word comes from the Greek word *euangelion*, which means "good news" or "gospel."[9] Practically speaking, it's generally an identity held by those who hold a more fundamentalist, literal view of Scripture and believe in a personal conversion experience, the authority of the Bible as God's Holy Word, and the Resurrection and deity of Christ.

Most Protestant denominations in America would be considered evangelical. Most preachers on TV and radio are as well. Billy Graham. Steven Furtick. Joel Osteen. Joyce Meyer. Jimmy Swaggart. Kenneth Copeland. They're all shades of evangelical. If someone uses the term "born-again" to describe their faith, they're probably evangelical.

Nowadays, the term "evangelical" isn't just a religious term; it also has an automatic political association attached to it. That's because in the last forty years, politicians have recognized just how potent the evangelical vote can be. Ronald Reagan seemed to tap into this power first, winning the White House in 1980 with two-thirds of the White evangelical vote.[10] In 2020, White evangelicals made up 14 percent of the American population. This doesn't sound too powerful at first, but when you consider that this equals over 46 million people who vote pretty uniformly, it can make or break an election.[11] Donald Trump won 85 percent of the White evangelical vote in 2020.[12] While other religious groups seemed splintered on their presidential picks, White evangelicals voted cohesively.

Growing up, we didn't use the term "evangelical" very much, even though we fit that definition. We just referred to everyone who received our stamp of approval as "Bible-believing Christians," or "born-again." I think if I'd been growing up now, my church would have embraced the term enthusiastically. And as I've already told you, I knew that America had been founded by God to be a Christian nation and needed to stay that way.

So when I turned eighteen, I was ready to put my evangelical values to the ultimate test: voting. I passed with flying colors when I turned in my straight Republican ballot. A+ for voting like a good Christian, aka evangelical. Of course, Satan was working against us, which was made clear when Democrat Barack Obama beat Republican John McCain in the 2008 presidential election. I cried for two days. America had slipped a little further from her Christian roots.

When we called America a Christian nation, we really meant an evangelical nation. When we told stories of our Founding Fathers being Christians, we pictured them as evangelicals like us. I honestly believed Benjamin Franklin probably dipped his pen in anointing oil before signing the Declaration of Independence. I imagined George Washington singing a 1776 version of Hillsong United's "Oceans" when he crossed the Delaware River. When someone told me that Thomas Jefferson was a Deist who cut all the miracles out of the Bible, I believed that was revisionist history.

In other words, when I say we sought to move the nation back closer to God, what I mean is that we were really trying to make America more evangelical.

Now, there are different denominations (even some Catholics, despite the reputation) and varying theological stances represented within Christian Nationalism. But they agree on the evangelical essentials enough to come together for the mutual goal of making America Christian.

I don't think it's an accident that evangelicalism and Christian Nationalism are so often intertwined. The cohesion and groupthink that unites most evangelicals behind common ideals, political movements, and candidates also make it the perfect soil to be exploited by nationalist ideals. To be in the cool club of evangelical culture, you have to believe the same things as everyone else around you. This makes evangelicals primed and ready to be swept up by Christian Nationalism.

A recent survey found that nearly two-thirds of White evangelicals were Christian Nationalists or sympathizers of the ideology. To be classified as Christian Nationalists in this survey, respondents had to agree with statements like these: "The U.S. should be declared a Christian nation," and "God has called Christians to exercise dominion over all areas of American society." The study also found a strong correlation between church attendance and the likelihood of being a Christian Nationalist. Attending church weekly greatly upped your chances of succumbing to nationalist ideals[13]—remember, church was how Beecher and I knew two people convicted in the infamous January 6th riot.

All of this is why it can be very hard to separate being evangelical from being a Christian Nationalist, even though they're different beasts. The Nationalist ideology cleverly hides itself among so many aspects of evangelicalism that sometimes it can be hard to separate the faith from the political movement. Sometimes they can be interconnected so closely that you can go thirty years before you wake up one day with the horrid realization that you were a Christian Nationalist all along. (Can I get a witness? No? Just me? Okay, moving on.)

We see the same narrow-mindedness that I once espoused in Christian Nationalism today. When Representative Mike Johnson was elected Speaker of the House in October 2023, he quickly equated the political moment with Christianity. "I believe that scripture, the Bible, is very clear that God is the one that raises up those in authority.... And I believe that God has ordained and allowed us to be brought here to this specific moment and time." But that belief seems to dissipate when it's a Democrat who is elected, as Johnson was a pivotal player in trying to overturn the 2020 election.[14] Even though Joe Biden is also a Christian, God apparently got it wrong ordaining him as president.

Because Biden is not the evangelical brand of Christian that Christian Nationalism needed.

Johnson has touted the importance of America being a Christian Nation and said he's been profoundly influenced by Christian-right activist David Barton. Barton claims the separation of church and state is a myth and advised that Johnson's staff should be "people with his worldview."[15]

By worldview, we know he means a conservative evangelical lens.

In defending Mike Johnson's anti-LGBTQ stance, conservative

reporter for *The Daily Wire* Megan Basham referred to their beliefs as "True Christianity."[16] In fact, Christian Nationalism has intentionally tied several key political issues to faith issues, like espousing the idea that true Christians want full access to gun ownership so we can defend our freedom of worship or that true Christians are against LGBTQ rights and abortion. Later, we'll dive more into these frontline issues and how Christian Nationalists manipulate them to gain power.

Leading up to the 2020 election, evangelist Franklin Graham (Billy Graham's son) sent out a special *Decision Magazine* Election Guide. In his article titled "Blessed Is the Nation Whose God Is the Lord," Graham wrote, "History teaches us that if the progressive, socialist left can seize power, Christians especially will be targeted."[17] When he says "Christian," he doesn't mean a social justice–focused faith. Or one that affirms LGBTQ people. Or one that wants universal health care. No. He means conservative evangelical Christians. Progressive Christians are not even a consideration.

To be clear—while the "Christian" in Christian Nationalism today means evangelical, the term "evangelical" does not necessarily mean Christian Nationalist.

Someone can absolutely be a conservative evangelical in America without being a Christian Nationalist. I know many conservative Christians who embrace their faith with a big-tent approach. They believe in Jesus, the inerrancy of Scripture, and the importance of sharing the gospel, but they don't necessarily believe that America needs to elect *only* Christian leaders who will return the country to its evangelical roots. They believe they are right in the way they worship God, but are open to learning new things, new ideas, and do not believe they hold exclusive access to truth.

I know Pentecostals who attend charismatic churches because that form of worship is how they feel closer to God. They don't hate Baptists or think they are better than them. They realize their denomination is right for them, but they don't necessarily believe everybody else is doing it wrong. This open-mindedness makes it much harder for Christian

Nationalism to take root. If someone already values people who think differently than they do and understands their perspectives might be equally valid, it makes it much harder to paint those differences in an evil light. That openness makes it much harder to demonize people outside your circle.

Romans 12:2 (ESV) says, "Do not be conformed to this world, but be transformed by the renewal of your mind, that by testing you may discern what is the will of God, what is good and acceptable and perfect."

Renewing our minds allows us an openness to transformation and keeps us from being stuck in our ways. It gives us the ability to approach new information and people with less judgment and more discernment. Instead of thinking what the loud man from the pulpit is telling me to do, I can think and pray for myself and make up my own mind.

Jesus did this often. There was no place and no person who was off limits. He met with tax collectors, prostitutes, the sick and blind, and he did it without judgment.

Looking at the life of Jesus in the Gospels, it makes sense why there are so many denominations and so many beliefs about what it means to be a Christian. Jesus never made belief a main focus of his ministry. There was no creed he dictated informing everyone on what to think in order to get to heaven. Instead, he focused far more on action, behavior, and how to treat our fellow humans.

Reverend Robin Meyers put it this way in his book, *Saving Jesus from the Church*: "There is not a single word in that sermon [the Sermon on the Mount] about what to believe, only words about what to do.... Yet three centuries later, when the Nicene Creed became the official oath of Christendom, there was not a single word in it about what to do, only words about what to believe!"[18]

The emphasis on belief was pivotal when I was growing up. Looking back, I can see I judged someone's Christianity more on what they believed than how they behaved. I thought someone was a good Christian if they thought just like I did. I didn't really consider how they loved their neighbor or lived their life.

I started to realize many years ago that my passion to take America back for Christ was often at odds with the teachings of Jesus. I could only carry that cognitive dissonance for so long.

Because Jesus didn't say, "Blessed are those who believe all the exact, right things."

He said blessed are the poor in spirit, those who mourn, the meek, the merciful, the pure in heart, the peacemakers.

To follow these teachings, I had to lay down my need to be right. After all, what is the point of having faith if you already know everything? I had to leave my *beliefs* of Christian Nationalism behind before I could *live* out a truer faith.

CHAPTER 3

Morality Should Be Mandated

My earliest memory is of saying the sinner's prayer at just three years old. I had heard my dad's sermons and watched him pray with people enough that I wondered if sin was something I also needed forgiveness for. I went to my dad and asked if I could have Jesus in my heart, too. Overjoyed by my question, he took my hand, and I repeated the sinner's prayer after him.

"Dear Jesus. I believe you died on the cross and rose again. Come into my heart and forgive me of my sins. Amen," I said, repeating after my dad.

I remember my dad called Nanny and Bobo, my grandparents on his side. They were pastors themselves, so they, too, were thrilled. I recall how good it felt to make them proud.

My three-year-old soul was officially saved. After that moment, I tried really hard to follow my dad's example. For as long as I can remember, I wanted to win as many people to Christ as I could. Partly because I wanted people to accept Christ so they'd be happy, but also because I desperately wanted to make my dad proud.

When we ate at restaurants, my brothers and I would often argue over whose turn it was to witness to the waitstaff. Witnessing for us then was just about which of us kids got to say, "Jesus loves you." If that was received well, then my dad would ask to pray with the waiter by the end of the meal. If it went really well, then my brothers or I could lead the prayer. The better the interaction, the more likely the story would be told by my dad from the pulpit. We never talked about it in that way then, but there was validation that came from getting a sermon shout-out.

I remember one time my brother Matt, who was five at the time, surprised us all by going straight for the prayer—or as we called it, "closing the deal."

"Excuse me, miss. Can I pray with you?" He looked at our waitress with his pouty baby-blue eyes.

The waitress looked confused for a moment, but I think she realized she couldn't say no to this adorable kid with a bowl cut.

"Sure," she replied.

Matt gave a huge smile and reached for her as he repeated what he had heard my dad say countless times. "Take my hand."

She grabbed his tiny hand as my brother said, "Now repeat after me. Dear Jesus."

"Dear Jesus," she repeated.

"I am a very bad person." Matt blurted it out like it was a totally normal thing to say. I peeked through my closed eyes to see how she would respond. My parents also peeked and gave the waitress an apologetic look, trying not to laugh.

The waitress hesitated for a beat but then smiled and said, "I am a very bad person."

Matt seamlessly continued. "Forgive me of my sins."

"Forgive me of my sins."

"In Jesus' name..."

"In Jesus' name..."

"Amen."

"Amen," all of us said in unison.

The waitress was a good sport and smiled as my parents thanked her. She took our order, and the rest of the meal went on as if Matt hadn't called this complete stranger a very bad person. But Matt was beaming, and so was my dad. Matt had closed the deal! To be fair, we all doubted the effectiveness of that particular conversion, but it made for a great story my dad would use in his sermons for the rest of his life.

As we grew up, it became a bit of a competition as we started counting how many people got saved because of our witnessing. But at a certain point, the excitement of witnessing faded as my social awareness kicked in and I realized it wasn't really a cool thing to do. My love for Jesus and not wanting anyone to go to hell usually forced me to witness anyway, but sometimes I didn't have the energy to do it.

And the guilt of *not witnessing* would eat me alive.

Her blood is on my hands, I'd think to myself. I tried to focus on all the times I *did* witness to offset the people who slipped through the cracks. But as I got older, more and more slipped through. I still witnessed more than most Christians I knew, but not like before.

Witness to some. Euphoria. Don't witness to some. Guilt.

Rinse and repeat.

But I didn't see that inward battle with my dad.

I know proselytizing gets a bad rap, and it's usually with good reason. Most people think about street corner preachers with megaphones, condemning everyone around them to hell while yelling "Repent" or "Turn or Burn." But that wasn't really our style.

My dad used to say, "If people don't like you, they won't like your Jesus." As it turned out, most people liked my dad, and he made witnessing look easy. He had a way of making anyone feel special. When he looked you in the eyes to ask about your life, you felt seen. Complete strangers would pour out their hearts to him and he listened.

He would pray with anyone, anywhere. Bank tellers, gas station clerks, hotel staff, neighbors, taxi drivers, flight attendants, construction workers. There was even a hairdresser he continually went back to because she was going through a hard time. Even though he didn't really want the perm she had convinced him to get, he kept going back to encourage her. He ended up leading her to Christ, and then everyone else in that hair salon followed suit. He even led a Bible study with them during their lunch break.

Once in the late seventies, he preached in a movie theater. He'd just watched a film about Biblical prophecy and the end times called *The Late*

Great Planet Earth. As the credits rolled, he got up and said, "Nobody leave this theater! I can give you hope on how you can escape this terrible end!" He told the room about Jesus and led the room in the sinner's prayer.

I saw him spend hours talking with homeless people who everyone else ignored. He would find out their name, story, give them money, and *then* pray with them. He was able to help a lot of people find employment and buy them clothing for job interviews.

I went with him into underprivileged neighborhoods to pray with people, help them buy groceries, and invite them to church, where we served breakfast for free each week. If people wanted to come but didn't have a ride, my dad found a way to get them there, whether it was giving them bus money or sending someone to pick them up.

My dad's quest to win souls was born out of a genuine desire to help them. He believed with all his heart that, without Jesus, people would experience an eternity of suffering in hell when they died. He often cried at the thought of it.

And he believed the more Christian our county was, the more people would be led to Christ. One of the books he wrote was titled *I Can Win Your City to Christ in One Month.* In it, he laid out a plan that included door-to-door witnessing, nightly services, Jesus marches, and other citywide events to convert the majority of any city to Christianity. He believed America could become a fully Christian nation again by convincing individuals of the goodness of God and the joy of salvation.

We wanted a government that honored God in all its ways. My dad preached about electing people of faith into roles of authority. He preached against social policies that he thought went against the Bible. We were convinced that living godly was what was best for the country and every citizen within it.

And this is where the line between conservative Christianity and Christian Nationalism gets fuzzy. Both generally want—as my father did—to see more Christians in leadership positions in the government. But if you want your congressman to be an evangelical, someone with your same worldview, because you want someone in government who truly represents you at the table, I'd say that's basic conservative Christianity. This sounds like just wanting your voice heard and accounted for as the country makes decisions. We all vote for people who line up with our values in some way, after all.

But if you want *all* governmental leaders to have the exact same evangelical worldview as you do and want them to make laws and policies that line up with your particular beliefs, while ignoring other voices or opinions, this... feels very much like you've entered Christian Nationalist territory.

Think about it. In 2020, only 14% of America classified themselves as White evangelicals.[1] By the ideas put forth by democracy, the government should roughly match that number with only 14% of those in Congress also being White evangelicals.

But in 2023, 87% of Congress identified as Christian, with 57% considering themselves Protestant.[2] Now, I'm not sure how many of these consider themselves evangelical, but I'm guessing it's over 14%. And with 75% of Congress being White Americans, this means White evangelicals are overrepresented in government.[3] It's almost as if this power imbalance is intentional.

Which it is.

Some Christian Nationalists believe taking control of the nation is actually mandated by God. Those who adhere to the Seven Mountain Mandate believe Christians are called by God to have dominion over not just America, but eventually the world.

I suppose this is a good time to tell you about the Seven Mountain Mandate. The Seven Mountain Mandate is a global strategy that seeks to spread Christianity to all corners of the world and often focuses on America as the vessel to do this. It's the belief that the best way to expand the Kingdom of God is for Christians to take control of the world, bringing heaven to earth through the seven main spheres or "mountains" of influence in the world: education, religion, family, business, government/military, entertainment, and media (though there's slight variation on this list depending on who you ask).[4] Those who adhere to this ideology believe Christians must prepare the earth for Christ's return by controlling these mountains. Only when all seven have been conquered will Jesus roll out the end times.

The Seven Mountains idea was apparently started in the seventies by Youth with a Mission (YWAM) founder Loren Cunningham, Campus Crusade for Christ founder Bill Bright, and evangelist Francis Schaeffer, all of whom claimed they received the same message from God for Christians to go after these seven spheres. Bethel Church of Redding, California, a large and prominent institution, is one of many churches to openly promote it.[5] Many evangelical leaders who prophesied a Trump victory in 2020 adhere to the Seven Mountain Mandate, including Paula White, who was a spiritual adviser to Donald Trump. In February 2022, Lance Wallnau, a vocal Christian Nationalist and 7MMer, appeared on *FlashPoint* (a TV show that airs on Kenneth Copeland's Victory Channel network) and said, "We want souls and we want nations! Jesus was promised nations for his inheritance, not just churches!"[6]

The Seven Mountain Mandate gives a clear road map to converting everyone in America, and eventually the world, into Christians. The ultimate goal is for Christians to have dominion over the globe, creating what they believe would be heaven on earth. It's inspiring to those who adhere to it since it's believed to be a mandate given directly by God.

While those who believe in the Seven Mountain Mandate want to take over all seven spheres—and we'll explore some of the others later—it's the government mountain that I want to focus on here. Filling the government with people who follow Christian Nationalism is a primary goal of the movement to ultimately lead to Christian theocracies.

Theocracy was not really something I heard about a lot growing up, except when our Sunday school teachers were trying to explain the Old Testament and the nation of Israel. Then they talked about how Moses was given the Ten Commandments from God and how God led the Israelites by pillars of fire around the desert. At this point, Israel didn't have a king or a president, just... God. They were led directly by God, which is a theocracy in the most literal sense. In Greek, *theo* means "god," and *cracy* means "rule" or "government."[7] For early Israel, God was their only government.

[Sidenote: Does that mean when God fed all of Israel manna from heaven for forty years, it was a form of communism? I mean, everyone was getting everything they needed from the governmental authority of the time... I think we can agree, it's at very least a very large handout. Moving on.]

Today, when people refer to theocracies, they are not referring to a literal deity leading a country. Instead, a theocracy is a form of government where leaders rule in the name of God. They make decisions based on what their religion or deity tells them to do. Science, economics, and citizens' opinions take a back seat to "God told me to do it this way."

When I was a Christian Nationalist, I wouldn't have said I wanted a theocracy. I would have said I was a Christian and, as such, wanted Christians in office that represented my values. I would have merely insisted that implementing Biblical morality through laws would be good. Totally not a theocracy. Because I believed making America more Christian meant saving souls, which, to me, was the point.

A lot of Christian Nationalists today don't even pretend that making America more Christian is for the purpose of saving souls. The love of Christ has been put on the backburner. When I listen to Marjorie Taylor Greene or Michael Flynn talk about the nation turning back to God, I don't hear them calling on people to love their neighbor and share Jesus with them. I hear them calling on Christians to prepare for battle. People they disagree with aren't depicted as fellow humans worthy of salvation, but as enemies deserving of defeat.

Congresswoman Greene has openly embraced the Christian Nationalism label and said that her fellow Republicans "should be Christian nationalists."[8]

Pastor Greg Locke has notoriously called Democrats "God-denying demons" and stated you could not be a Christian if you voted Democrat.[9] To be fair, that's a sentiment I fully believed at one time, too.

Once my friend said something nice about Bill Clinton and I doubted her salvation.

Michael Flynn, a former Trump adviser, has regularly talked about the "spiritual war" going on in America during his ReAwaken America tour. At a church in Texas, Flynn touted the importance of making Christianity the faith of the nation. "If we are going to have one nation under God, which we must, we have to have one religion. One nation under God, and one religion under God, right?"[10] This was the same event that featured a lovely church-wide chant of "Let's Go Brandon."[11] Christ's love just oozed out of that tour.

At another ReAwaken event, Flynn said that pastors should be "talking about the Constitution from the pulpit as much as the Bible."[12] You know, because the Bible says, "In the beginning was the constitution," or something.

Of course, making one religion the primary religion of our country would have unfortunate consequences for people who hold other beliefs. But there's nothing to be done about that, sadly. In his book *The Case for Christian Nationalism*, Stephen Wolfe wrote, "Crafting policy (and ethics generally) in a fallen world requires us to consider unpleasant trade-offs, and magistrates must have the fortitude to enact and enforce the greatest good, despite unfortunate costs involved, and Christians should recognize the *necessity* of such choice and shun the moralism that limits action."[13]

And this is where I see my dad's ministry and our version of Christian Nationalism being different from today's. Both wanted America to be a holier nation in the eyes of God. My dad saw the clearest path to do that was by convincing individual citizens to turn to God. Current Christian Nationalists see the best path as taking over the government and mandating morality. Persuasion versus force.

Both approaches have been used before. The most obvious example I know of that used persuasion is Saint Patrick in Ireland. According to tradition, Saint Patrick was a missionary who converted the entire pagan culture of Ireland to Christianity without an army or bloodshed. He just arrived on the island with a very convincing argument, and the supernatural presence of the Holy Spirit did the rest.

On the flip side, the Crusades are probably the clearest example of the use of force. The Crusades were a series of wars spanning over two centuries. They were fought in the name of Jesus and consisted of killing those who didn't convert and submit to Christianity.

My dad was the Saint Patrick type. He was going to bring the country back to God one person at a time by influencing their spiritual life and leading them to live more righteously. Yes, he openly voted for Republicans who wanted to enact Christian laws across the country, but he did that mainly because those candidates publicly professed Jesus in their personal lives. He wanted Christian leaders because he believed they would make decisions based on the Holy Spirit's guidance. When you believe all morality comes from God, it makes sense to include God in your laws and lawmakers.

The forceful version of this is electing an all-evangelical government to enact authoritative morality laws on all citizens, regardless of their beliefs. This is a central goal of Christian Nationalism and another main tenet: to mandate *their* idea of morality on all citizens.

Worship leader Sean Feucht, who infamously held worship "protests" during the pandemic, seemed to insinuate that morality by force is the goal. "We wouldn't be a disciple of Jesus if we didn't believe that," he said at a church in Oklahoma in April 2023. "We want God to be in control of everything! We want believers to be the ones writing the laws! Yes! Guilty as charged."[14]

Honestly, saying that you want God to be in control kind of sounds okay on paper, if you're talking about classic Jesus. You know, the one who wanted to take care of the poor and sick, who emphasized justice and mercy and taught radical, inclusive love of all people. A nation based on those teachings doesn't sound terrible, but sadly that is not the focus of today's Christian Nationalism.

Today's Christian Nationalists are more focused on gaining political power by enforcing specific, conservative ideals based on a narrow, fundamentalist interpretation of the Bible. This includes enacting strict laws around abortion, LGBTQ rights, and access to books and education (tactics and issues we will get into later). The aim is to make their own beliefs about these topics the law of the land. It's not really about saving souls or spreading God's love. There is no freedom in Christ under Christian Nationalism. Heck, there's no freedom in general.

What does the movement's goal of mandating morality have to do with God? The short answer is it really doesn't. Not the big God with a capital G anyway. This is a confusing goal for a movement that also says God gives us free will and wants us to *choose* him (or not). (Unless you're a Calvinist and believe in predestination. In which case, I was destined to leave Christian Nationalism, and nothing I do matters at all. So stop DMing me the verses about women being quiet. I know them already, thanks.)

But the Christian Nationalism god is small, placed in a box of a White, American evangelical worldview. This god cares far more about the genitals of our neighbor than the humanity of the world. The "force" part coming in hot.

And I think what we know of Jesus shows mandating morality isn't what he'd want done in his name. The religious leaders were the ones constantly obsessed with strict rules. One of their favorite topics they brought up to Jesus was around the Sabbath. This was one day a week when all Jewish people were supposed to rest.

In Mark 2:23–27 (ESV), religious leaders questioned why Jesus allowed his disciples to pick heads of grain on the Sabbath. Jesus responded, "The Sabbath was made for man, not man for the Sabbath."

In Matthew 12:9–13 (NIV), Jesus healed a man with a shriveled hand on the Sabbath. The religious leaders grew mad and questioned him, to which Jesus replied, "If any of you has a sheep and it falls into a pit on the Sabbath, will you not take hold of it and lift it out? How much more valuable is a person than a sheep!"

That's the thing. Jesus' biggest adversaries were constantly trying to enact morality laws. Perhaps they believed forcing people to obey their rules would bring everyone closer to God.

Jesus, though? He regularly bucked the laws the religious leaders tried to enforce. And I don't think it's because he was in his rebel phase. I think Jesus knew forcing people to follow your own version of morality isn't right. Jesus was people focused. Love always came before the law.

I feel like the question Jesus would ask Christian Nationalists today would be: How much more valuable is a person than a political seat?

PART TWO

HISTORY OF CHRISTIAN NATIONALISM

How did a group of Christ followers turn a faith based on forgiveness into a machine stoking anger over forgiving student loans? How did churches that profess a faith of peace start boasting about how many guns they have? How did pastors who claim to love everyone start demonizing half the country from the pulpit for how they voted?

The actual history of Christian Nationalism would be an entire book on its own—probably several books. Those books exist, and if you want more info on the exhaustive history of it, I highly recommend reading those. This is not that book. Those books are written by academics who probably didn't live in a Jesus-themed RV as a teenager.

I am not a historian, but I didn't think I could, in good faith, talk to you about what it's like inside Christian Nationalism without giving some history of the movement. I felt like we needed some background, a road map to show how on earth we got to this crazy town.

Buckle up.

CHAPTER 4

Racial Reconciliation Sunday

The screen fades in from black. An American flag flaps in the wind as an airplane flies across the blue sky behind it. Scenes from Washington DC flash across the screen—the White House, the Capitol, the Mall—and then three different voices speak.

Voice 1: "I'm voting as a student."
Voice 2: "I'm voting as a woman."
Voice 3: "I'm voting as a minority."
All 3 in unison: "I'm voting as an American."

A twenty-something, blond version of myself appears on-screen, the Lincoln Memorial behind me. Earnestly looking into a camera, I plead, "As a grad student, please don't end my future before I have a chance to get started."

The scourge that was about to decimate my world, erasing any hope of a future? It wasn't the threat of climate change or nuclear war or terrorism. No, it was even worse.

It was Barack Obama.

And I knew the best way to fight back against his ruinous ways was to make a YouTube video.

"I grew up with the view of a bright future and the belief that I could accomplish the American Dream," I stoically recited as a flash of Martin

Luther King Jr.'s "I Have a Dream" marker in DC appeared on the screen. "But as of right now, that dream is fading."

Y'all, I fully believed my words.

It was fall of 2012 and the presidential race between President Barack Obama and Mitt Romney was heating up. My two friends and I from my graduate school decided we had to do something. We took it upon ourselves to drive the three hours from Virginia Beach to Washington DC to film a Romney campaign video. To be clear: We weren't hired to do this. We just thought we were doing our part. We honestly believed a two-minute ad posted on a YouTube channel with six subscribers was really going to make a difference.

We titled the video *Women, Students and Minorities for Romney* and posted it. All three of us who made the video were students, two of us were women, and one of us was South Korean—so our title was *almost* accurate. But *Women, Students and a Minority for Romney* didn't have the same ring to it.

The cringe is not lost on me now. We really turned to our friend who had more color than us and had him say the line, "I'm voting as a minority." That really happened.

But we were all so outraged after watching Dinesh D'Souza's propaganda film *2016: Obama's America* in theaters that no tactic seemed off limits. We had to pull out all the stops because we were convinced socialism was one Obama term away from being fully implemented in America. Right after I watched the film, I shared the movie poster on my Instagram page and captioned it: "I am so fired up right now. If you don't want a future for yourself, vote for Obama. If you value freedom and what our founding fathers stood for, you will NOT vote for Obama. Romney 2012. Let's end this anti-American president's term."

In our quest to elect Romney, a Mormon (but we were willing to look past that in these desperate times), we knew we were at a disadvantage with People of Color. This wasn't anything new. As a lifelong Republican, I knew most Black people voted Democrat. I also knew a lot of them considered themselves Christians, which was a hard pill for me to swallow. Conservative talk radio told me that many People of Color voted blue because of all the handouts Democrats gave, and I didn't know enough to fight that explanation. Because we knew Romney needed as much color as we could muster, we used our friend's minority status to try to persuade the masses—or at least the whopping ninety-one people who watched our YouTube video.

And that was how I had dealt with racial issues for most of my life. I believed proximity to someone of a different race could fix the racial divide. Showing non-White people as a part of your church, movement, or political party was enough to sway people. See? No racism here!

If anything, we thought affirmative action was the real racism. I'd hear fellow church members complain about how we had a Black Entertainment Television (BET) but not a White Entertainment Television. The double standard was appalling! Of course, I never even considered that most television was already full of White people.

Plus, the churches my community planted were already relatively diverse compared to many others around us. They were still mostly White, but there were enough People of Color that we had a quick defense if anyone ever did accuse the church of racism. When I was a kid, my best friend at my church was Black. That wouldn't be possible if racism still existed. Everyone just needed to chill.

When my dad served as senior pastor of our large church in Dallas, he often talked about wanting a congregation of many ethnic groups. He believed that's what heaven would be like, and as such, we should try to emulate that here on earth. He also made some interesting decisions in his quest to make this happen. I recently found an old church bulletin from the late nineties in my Teen Study Bible. One of the announcements was for a "Racial Reconciliation Sunday," where members were encouraged to bring someone of a different race to church.

I don't remember this Sunday specifically, but I can only imagine the awkward interactions this must have caused.

"Hi, do you want to come to church with me this Sunday?"

"Oh, is there anything special going on?"

"Uhhh... yes. I need to bring someone whose skin color is different than mine..."

It feels like a scene from *The Office*.

And while I believe good intentions were involved, it just confirms the lack of understanding we had about racial issues.

We believed racism could be solved by singing a couple verses of "Amazing Grace" side by side with people who looked different than us. We didn't have to think about larger racial problems because racism was a heart issue. A sin issue.

When Beecher and I were dating, we got involved at a large evangelical church not far from our graduate school. Beecher started making videos for the church part-time, while I joined the worship team.

If you went to this church on any given Sunday, you'd think it was a very diverse community based on what played on-screen. One of Beecher's main tasks each week was to record video announcements that would run during the service before the sermon. Beecher was given strict instructions to use at least one Person of Color in the videos. Our church seemed very forward-thinking in this area, and we appreciated the effort. Our church was fighting racism, one video announcement at a time!

But racism isn't just about lily-white announcements. Systemic racism, as I have learned, is about keeping People of Color out of positions of power, which is something our church also did very well.

Behind the scenes of this "diverse" church were rooms of White people discussing which non-White people to put in a video or how to get non-White people in the doors. The church was large, almost 4,000 people on a weekend, with several campuses and services. The pastoral team and staff consisted of about fifteen full-time employees. When we attended, all of them were White and most of them were men.

In our four years there, Beecher and I never saw a Person of Color in a leadership role of any substance. We never heard any sermon or lesson that talked about racism as a problem that needed to be addressed today. We had Black people around, but never in the room where meaningful decisions were made. That appeared to be the job for the White men.

These White men frequently got up onstage and talked about how they donated money to orphanages in Africa and Asia or how they'd spent thousands of dollars to visit these places with their families. When they got mud on their outfits taking pictures with the orphan kids, we'd plaster it all over social media. We couldn't do that if we were racist, right?

By now you may have noticed that when I mention evangelicalism or Christian Nationalism, the word "White" is also often mentioned. If you're like me, by this point in the book, you may have a little leftover conservative voice inside of you that is begging to scream, "WHY DO YOU HAVE TO BRING RACE INTO EVERYTHING?"

Well... because race is in everything. America was founded by a very diverse population. Some chose to come here for freedom. Others were brought here in bondage. Some were already here and forced to leave their homes or die. And if you are wondering how people were placed in these different groups, it had everything to do with skin color.

Just like we can't truthfully separate America from her racist past, it's impossible to separate Christian Nationalism from its White supremacist roots. We'll get there. Stay with me. But this is why I often throw in the word "White" when discussing evangelicalism and nationalism in the United States. Black evangelical churches and culture function very differently than the White evangelical population. The Black Church did not prophesy victories for Donald Trump, rally behind him, and call for African angels to assist his campaign. (Pastor Paula White actually did this, and yes, just like her name suggests, she is, in fact, White.[1])

White supremacy and racism within Christian Nationalism (and the country at large) didn't just happen. They didn't just appear out of nowhere. They're part of a long history of calculated decisions to keep Whiteness in power. And no, despite some conservative talking points I believed for a long time, identifying Whiteness as a huge part of Christian Nationalism is not "reverse racism."

Racism throughout our nation is both systemic—meaning it happens on a large scale—and among individuals. Most people I know,

Nationalist or not, would agree that racism is wrong. The difference is in how we define it and what we think should be done to fix it.

When I was a Christian Nationalist, I knew about slavery, and yeah, that was admittedly pretty bad—WHOOPS!—but my family had never owned slaves, and anyway that was a long time ago. Things had changed since then. Racial equality was basically achieved in the sixties when a pastor named Martin Luther King Jr. asked for it nicely and all the White Christians loved and supported his cause. While we believed racism was mostly solved then, we did acknowledge there was still some *minor* work to be done. We were there for it. We wanted racism out of our churches, too.

What I never heard of in any White evangelical community I was a part of was a discussion on just how deep the racist roots go in our country *and* religion. I was told about the Puritans coming to America to worship God freely. But I never heard about how they used the Bible to justify killing Native Americans to steal their land. Many colonizers actually convinced themselves they were the Israelites entering the Promised Land. This, they believed, gave them full permission from God to wipe out the land's current inhabitants.[2]

From the moment White men stepped onto the continent, they brought with them both personal religion and the professed desire to form a godly nation. This second element granted the colonists permission to commit horrible acts to achieve their God-ordained goal. And this centering of Whiteness did not stop at the founding of the country.

I can't even imagine the cognitive dissonance that would have allowed the Founding Fathers to sign papers declaring "all men are created equal... endowed by the creator with certain unalienable rights" while also owning men and women of darker complexion.

Part of how they got over this seemingly obvious contradiction was because preachers used the Bible to justify slavery during the Civil War and beyond. Yale sociologist Philip Gorski looks at this point in history as the moment when Whiteness really became a key component of Christian Nationalism.[3] Many Southern Christians believed the Bible not only sanctioned slavery but actually gave instructions for it.[4] They would cite the story in Genesis, where Noah cursed his son Ham's bloodline. They interpreted the cursed lineage to mean African descendants, hence justifying enslavement.[5] Or they would cite Ephesians 6:5 (NIV), which encourages slaves to "obey your earthly masters with respect and fear, and with sincerity and fear, and with sincerity of heart, just as you would obey Christ."

Baptist clergyman and seminary professor Iveson L. Brooks even referred to slavery as "an institution of heaven."[6] Encouraging Confederates during the Civil War in 1862, Southern Methodist preacher J. W. Tucker said, "Your cause is the cause of God, the cause of Christ, of humanity. It is a conflict of truth with error—of Bible with northern infidelity—of pure Christianity with northern fanaticism."[7] These Biblical justifications were given without explaining the cultural differences of 1800s America and ancient Biblical times.

And when claiming "It's in the Bible!" proved to be insufficient, other theological justifications were offered for slavery. One popular idea that was perpetuated in the colonies claimed that "heathens and captives of war" could be enslaved. This meant settlers were in the clear since enslaved people were clearly not of Christian descent. They were heathens by birthright, passed through their bloodline. Thus, the concept of hereditary heathenism was born.[8]

But claiming innate heathenism had its limits. Once enslaved people began to embrace Christianity, slave owners needed to find a new logic to ease their consciences.

One story slaveholding Christians told themselves was that they were ultimately blessing enslaved Africans by saving them from their "pagan" beliefs.[9] This "blessing" was, of course, just for their souls. Freedom would come only in eternity. But that was no small thing to Presbyterian minister Robert Lewis Dabney, who believed introducing African people to Christianity was a major benefit of slavery. In 1867, Dabney wrote, "And above all, was it nothing that [Black slaves] should be brought by the relation of servitude, under the consciences and Christian zeal of a Christian people?"[10]

But that also proved problematic since freeing the oppressed is a big plot point of the gospel. White Christian slaveholders were so concerned that Biblical ideals like equality would seep into the minds of the people they owned that they carefully construed the gospel message they presented to enslaved people.[11] They wanted to keep the status quo and avoid a rebellion. There was even a "Slave Bible" that British missionaries used in the 1800s that omitted the story of Moses and the Israelites leaving Egypt for freedom. Some sermons given to enslaved people in the United States emphasized the story of Joseph's enslavement, noting that since he accepted his circumstance and kept his faith, he was rewarded in the end.[12] In his book *The Color of Compromise*, Jemar Tisby wrote that this version of Christianity "could save one's soul but not break one's chains."[13]

Now, having a White-controlled nation is not part of Christian Nationalism's posted talking points today. It's not something most would say they desire or agree with. But the correlation is hard to ignore. Historically, when White men have attempted to gain or retain power in American history, arguing that God wants them in power has served as an effective tool. The authority of the Church and racial injustice have always gone hand in hand in America.

There's a reason the Ku Klux Klan used a burning cross and an American flag as two of their main symbols. This was an organization overtly founded on Christian Nationalist ideals, using evangelical tenets to justify attacks against anyone they deemed not 100% American—or White Protestant Christians, basically. The term "100% American" became a favorite of the KKK in the 1920s. Just like Christian Nationalism of today, the KKK had a very narrow worldview, which they used to justify their use of violence and intimidation against anyone who fell outside of it.[14]

I know most Christian Nationalists today want nothing to do with the KKK. I'm not saying they're the same. I'm just saying there are enough similarities to sound alarms. Just look at the *Kloran*, the official KKK handbook. (Did you know there was such a thing? There is, and it is scary.) Before anyone could officially join the KKK, they had to decisively answer yes to a set of questions. Here are a few of the highlights:

- Do you believe in the tenets of the Christian religion?
- Do you esteem the United States of America and its institutions above any other government, civil, political and ecclesiastical, in the whole world?
- Will you, without mental reservation, take a solemn oath to defend, preserve and enforce same?
- Will you faithfully obey our constitution and laws, and conform willingly to all our usages, requirements and regulations?[15]

Hmm. Who does that sound like? Narrow view of Christianity? Check. Nationalism that raises America above all else? Check. Elevating and celebrating 100 percent pure American patriotism? Check.

Of course, there are differences. We don't typically see current Christian Nationalism openly asking people to "faithfully strive for the eternal maintenance of white supremacy," like the KKK did. But racism is still racism, whether it's overt or subtle.

And the KKK has always had close ties with Christianity, as membership was restricted to White Christians.[16] The KKK's official writings in 1920 said, "Patriotism and Christianity are preeminently the moving principles of the Knights of the Ku Klux Klan" and the "Flag, the Constitution and the Holy Bible are the keystones of Klan principles."[17]

The connection between the KKK and Christianity is even clearer when you watch the 1915 film *The Birth of a Nation*. This was in the early decades of filmmaking, and this movie proved to be the first real blockbuster, captivating audiences across the country. The scaling epic portrayed KKK members as heroes overcoming the villains of the story—Black people (most of whom were White people in blackface). In the last scene, a White Jesus is superimposed over a celebration, continuing to cement Christianity together with the KKK's mission to elevate Whiteness. The film condemns the mixing of the races as Union and Confederate soldiers unite for the "common defence of their Aryan birthright."[18]

Did Christians largely condemn this overt display of racism? No. No, they did not. President Woodrow Wilson even held a private screening of *Birth of a Nation* at the White House.[19]

Growing up in my nondenominational congregations, we didn't really talk about the KKK, and if the topic came up, the group was unequivocally condemned. Want to know who we talked about a lot, though? Abraham Lincoln. You know, the *White Republican* president who ended slavery. He was the moral savior who went to war to successfully free the slaves. Sure, Harriet Tubman and Frederick Douglass were around, too, but they were side characters to good ole Honest Abe's heroic quest.

In the narrative I believed, it was White Christians who did the heavy lifting to abolish slavery, sticking it to those ungodly slave owners. I don't know why I never clocked that the Confederacy was actually full of Christians. If this idea was ever hinted at, there was a quick rebuke of their salvation: "Well they weren't *real* Christians. Real Christians can't be racist."

As the saying goes, "History is written by the victors." And for most of American history, the story was written by White men, to favor White men. As a result, most of my problems in fully understanding racism were less about what I *was* taught and more about what I *wasn't* taught.

For instance, I wasn't taught that the Southern Baptist Convention split from the Baptist Church only because they refused to abandon their support of slavery.[20]

It was never mentioned that Bob Jones University, a conservative evangelical college, lost its tax-exempt status in a 1983 Supreme Court ruling because the school refused to allow interracial dating among students. A ban they did not overturn until the year 2000.[21]

No one ever discussed the Tulsa Massacre in 1921, where an affluent African American community, also known as Black Wall Street, was burned to the ground by White people. As many as three hundred people died. Local newspapers covered what White pastors said in sermons following the massacre, including this choice tidbit from First Presbyterian Church Reverend C. W. Kerr: "The colored people must understand they started it."[22]

I never learned how redlining kept People of Color from buying houses, which had the effect of keeping Black people from acquiring and passing down wealth. Neighborhoods that did allow Black people often saw White residents move out. This White flight wasn't limited to housing, though. Many churches also relocated to newly White neighborhoods instead of staying in areas that were becoming more diverse.[23] Author Richard Rothstein called this process a "state-sponsored system of segregation."[24] This information was conveniently left out of history class or majorly downplayed.

The list goes on: income disparities, mass incarceration because of the Thirteenth Amendment, property taxes funding public education, health care discrimination—there are too many systemic disparities to describe. All these things were left out of the dialogue in my White evangelical circles, and now, in my thirties, I am finally wrestling with the reason why.

In Christian Nationalist dogma these days, there is vocal support to get culture back to the "good ole days." Growing up, I heard countless sermons and conversations about how America was a godly, holy place that was slowly slipping into the hands of the devil. We never really discussed *when* exactly America was heaven on earth, but it was just a fully accepted fact that it used to be amazing and could be again.

To be clear, it's not just Christian Nationalism that looks back on history with rose-tinted glasses. It's actually a common psychological experience for people. "Declinism," or the idea that everything is getting worse, has been a mindset throughout history. Humans often look back on memories more favorably than how the experience actually was in the moment.[25]

It's kind of like the trip we took to Disney World a few years ago. Beecher and I often talk about how great it was to see our three-year-old's reaction to the Haunted Mansion ride or recall the joy on our five-year-old's face when Princess Rapunzel waved at her. Looking at photos of the vacation brings back a flood of warm, good memories.

But if I really think back on the trip, I remember Beecher getting incredibly frustrated with the new Genie FastPass app that glitched more than it worked. We missed *one* ride, and it took Beecher about an hour to cool down. I then recall how our older daughter ate too much ice cream and crashed in a nauseous fit in line for Buzz Lightyear's Space Ranger Spin. Or how the fireworks show was so crowded that we were unable to find each other. It was an exhausting trip. But I look back on it fondly because I don't think about it long enough to remember the more difficult aspects. And we didn't take pictures of the puking—just the smiles!

This is kind of how it works when we look back at the history of our country and see only how our nation has been "blessed" by God—Those amber waves of grain! The purple mountains majesty! Our veterans storming the beach at Normandy!— And we ignore the darker parts of our history. 'Merica!

Because when has the country ever been great for Black, Indigenous, and other People of Color?

Here's what my experience has taught me: If we acknowledge our racist history, it's harder to perpetuate American exceptionalism. It's harder to genuinely say, "Make America great again." It's harder to ignore systemic White supremacy and racism that still exists.

And if we acknowledge those hard truths, we either need to do something to fix them or consciously decide to uphold the status quo, knowing the harm that causes. White Christians can't do the latter without being the bad guy, and we rally behind being the good guys. But White Christians are in power, and they can't "fix" systemic problems without losing some of that power. So instead, they often demonize the ones calling out systemic racism. If you can believe that systemic racism isn't really a thing, then you can keep on keeping on while still being the good guy in your own mind.

Because once you take off the rose-colored glasses Christian Nationalism told you to wear, you can't unsee the deep-rooted racism of your church, your community, and your nation. And you have a choice: Be the bad guy and uphold the status quo, or fight for racial equity.

It's easy to see why Christian Nationalism desperately wants to avoid the topic of race. It's better for them if their followers can stay colorblind.

I'm optimistic that more and more people will continue to uncover the truth of White supremacy's role in the origins of Christian Nationalism. Identifying the issue is the first step in solving the vast problem of systemic racism. We have a long way to go. But if we take off our colorblind glasses, the ugly truth is easy to see. Christian Nationalism and White supremacy are as connected as a burning cross in front of that American flag.

CHAPTER 5

In God We Trump

Some people who meet me now—or come across my videos online—don't believe I was ever actually conservative or evangelical. I've been accused of faking my entire history, of pretending to be a Christian and ex-evangelical just to agitate, divide, and lead people astray.

Here are a few of the accusations I've heard:

- "Lies! You were never a conservative."
- "You were never a Republican!"
- "You are pretending to be a Christian to spread hate about them."
- "You have no clue who Jesus is."
- "I think this woman is some kind of communist. She has no idea what's in the Bible... she's never been to church."
- "You have never been conservative. The things that you are saying indicate a willingness to lie."

These arguments always make me laugh. I mean, why would anyone do that? What would be the end game? I went undercover and pretended to be super conservative since birth so that one day, in my thirties, I could play the ultimate Uno Reverse card where I make a liberal video that goes kinda viral and I piss off my community, making church ladies and Theobros regularly call me a demonic liar, which leads me to an early midlife crisis, all because I wanted to make conservatives look bad! It's like *Ocean's Eleven*, but evangelical. Call it Hillsong *Ocean's Eleven*.

But it's also funny to me because I haven't deleted my old posts. If you scroll down far enough, you can still see them. Like this one, where I endorsed Trump years before he ran for president:

"Say what you want about Trump, but he sure has Obama sweating as obvious from the Correspondence Dinner. #trump2012"

Look, I didn't even correct the spelling and make it say Correspondents' Dinner here, which is the actual name of the annual gathering, just to show how legit these posts are.

Or this one, after Obama won the 2012 election:

"If only I could be liberal and not have Christian morals or economic common sense, then I could be happy, too."

(Narrator: A decade later she did, in fact, become a happy little liberal.)

So what changed? people often ask. How did someone like me go from being a dutiful culture warrior to a "little mindless meat puppet flapping her gums" because "her demons are shaking her cage now"? (And yes, that's a real comment someone made about me.)

The short answer is easy: Donald Trump.

But the more accurate answer is longer and more nuanced and requires us to look back at how we got here in the first place. We've already established that one of the goals of Christian Nationalism is to make America a Christian nation so she will be blessed by God. But to understand why that is, and how it came to be, we need to look back at the history of how the Republican Party and Christianity came together, why this partnership was intentionally arranged, and who profited from the resulting marriage.

But first, a story:

In 2015, a lady I knew from my dad's church invited me to join a Facebook group she created for Christians to pray for America. The group description said this was a place for all Christians to unite and "set aside our differences and focus on our commonalities, our faith in the Lord Jesus Christ and His love for the United States of America!"

There was no mention of political parties or candidates and it seemed well-meaning enough. I wanted to pray for the country, too, and hadn't yet developed an aversion to Christian Nationalism, so I joined in good faith.

Turns out the differences they were willing to set aside were not political ones. I learned the hard way that the people in that group assumed everyone who joined was not only a Republican but a Trump supporter.

I was a Christian. I was still a Republican even. But I was not a Trump supporter. Needless to say, they weren't fans of me.

Throughout Trump's presidency, they never stopped praising, defending, and championing him as a hero of the faith to save America.

The prayers for the country in that group were focused on uplifting the Republican Party, Democrats be damned—quite literally. On Election Day 2020, the group leader posted a prayer that asked God to close the doors "to anyone going to [the] polls who would vote contrary to His will."

God's will, of course, was voting for Trump.

Now, before you ask, "How do you know that's what they meant, April?" let me show you. That same person also posted this:

"ANY 'Christian' who does not plan to vote for our President's re-election is missing the will of God... PERIOD!"

I was now the dreaded "Christian" in quotes.

That's like being called a MFer in evangelical.

To their credit, they never kicked me out. I just stopped engaging. It wasn't fun to be dogpiled by the 2,000-some members after a while.

But how did we get here? Trump emboldened Christian Nationalism, but he certainly didn't start it.

We can't pin the origins of Christian Nationalism on any one person or event. In the last century, countless pastors, politicians, and laypeople have contributed to make Christian Nationalism what it is today. But there is one man in particular who was the matchmaker, giving the GOP first date butterflies as she pursued her future mate, White evangelicals. That man was Billy Graham.

Now wait. Before you get mad at me for trashing Saint Billy, hear me out. I appreciate Billy Graham. He was beloved and one of the most influential people in the modern history of Christianity. And it's true that Billy Graham is generally known for condemning the combination of political aspirations and Christianity. In the 1980s, Graham distanced himself from Jerry Falwell's "Moral Majority" when he said in an interview, "It would disturb me if there was a wedding between the religious fundamentalists and the political right. The hard right has no interest in religion except to manipulate it."[1]

Listen to that liberal sheep! That certainly couldn't come from someone who was monumental in bringing evangelicals and the GOP together, right?!

But a younger Billy Graham was quite different.

To be fair, Graham's intention always seemed to be saving souls rather than gaining political power. In memorializing Graham, his own *Decision Magazine* wrote, "The reality that every soul will face judgment—and be rewarded with either eternal life with God by faith in Jesus Christ, or eternal separation from God for rejecting Him—moved Billy Graham to preach a simple Gospel message with power and passion around the world."[2]

But the famous preacher also used his driving mission of saving souls to springboard into the national and political conversation in the 1950s. Graham was monumental in Dwight Eisenhower's presidency, beginning with a letter in which Graham urged Eisenhower to run for president. Though Graham never officially endorsed Eisenhower, his actions let his will be known. During his campaign, Eisenhower carried around a Bible that Graham gave him, and the two were seen golfing together.[3] Graham even guided Eisenhower on which Bible verses to include in his inaugural address.[4]

At the height of the Cold War, the two men united in their quest to fight off "godless communism."[5] In a speech, Graham said, "I believe today that the battle is between communism and Christianity!...And I believe the only way that we're going to win that battle is for America to turn back to Christ and back to the Bible at this hour."[6]

Eisenhower shared this sentiment and invited Graham to the White

House as a spiritual adviser. Soon after, in 1953, the tradition of the National Prayer Breakfast began, and Graham urged Eisenhower to attend.[7] Then in 1954, Congress officially added the words "under God" to the Pledge of Allegiance for the first time in history.[8] In 1956, Eisenhower made "In God We Trust" the country's official motto, signing it into law and putting it on all US currency (it was already being displayed on coins).[9] Because if God was a capitalist, which American Jesus obviously was, it'd be easier to defeat communism.

When I was a Christian Nationalist, I fought to make Christianity and the American government almost synonymous. When people brought up the importance of the separation of church and state, citing the Constitution, I'd argue how the Pledge of Allegiance included the phrase "under God" and how all our money said, "In God We Trust." Why would the Founding Fathers do that if they wanted religion to be separate, huh?

Turns out they didn't. Those bits were added almost two hundred years later. But why let facts get in the way of a good argument?

Now, I can't put the whole Christian Nationalism thing on just Billy Graham. Lots of people helped make the ideology what it is today.

In the 1970s, Phyllis Schlafly rallied Christian women around godly "family values" to fight against women's rights and equality, believing women should stay home, despite not doing so herself.[10] In the 1980s, evangelical leader James Dobson of Focus on the Family started the Family Research Council, which openly advocated for "pro-family" political policies. These later included running television ads asking then-president Bill Clinton to resign in 1998.[11] Televangelist Pat Robertson blurred the lines of church and politics when he founded the Christian Broadcasting Network (my former employer) and the popular Christian talk show *The 700 Club* in the 1960s. Robertson used the power of media to endorse Republican candidates, encourage viewers to sign petitions, and create the Christian Coalition that hoped to "influence and impact the trajectory and turn [the GOP] into a pro-life, pro-family party."[12] He also ran for president in 1988, though he lost in the Republican primary to George H. W. Bush.

But if Billy Graham was the matchmaker for Evangelicals and Republicans, Jerry Falwell Sr. officiated the wedding. He took a head-on approach, arguing that being politically active was something good Christians *should* do. And of course, he made it easy by telling you exactly what party to vote for and which issues to oppose.

Falwell was a household name for me growing up. My dad attended and played basketball at Falwell's college, Lynchburg Baptist College (now known as Liberty University). Even though my family was Pentecostal and we disagreed with Falwell on some doctrinal issues, Falwell was still well-respected in our home. We had a common goal, after all: turning America back to God.

Falwell took an opposite trajectory from Graham. In a 1964 sermon, he actually preached *against* mixing religion and politics, when he said, "Preachers are not called to be politicians, but soul winners." Though that message was viewed more as a rebuke of Martin Luther King Jr., as Falwell also said, "If as much effort could be put into winning people to Jesus across the land as is being exerted in the present civil rights movement, America would be turned upside down for God." But by the 1970s, he had become one of the loudest proponents of Christian political activism.[13]

And unsurprisingly, it was pretty much all because of racism (hello again). That's right. Laws ending racial segregation in schools in the sixties and seventies got Falwell and other religious leaders so riled up, they had to act! They didn't like the government interfering with their private Christian institutions, which they seemingly preferred to keep segregated. They got especially mad when they learned they could lose their tax-exempt status if they didn't follow integration laws.[14]

Of course, Falwell didn't come out and say he was fighting against racial integration. Instead, he framed the debate in terms of religious freedom. He didn't think the government should be allowed to tell religious schools how they should be run. Remember when I mentioned in the last chapter that Bob Jones University took its fight to maintain racially discriminatory policies all the way to the Supreme Court? Yeah.

That happened. They lost the case and their tax-exempt status for not conforming.[15] Then, perhaps realizing that overtly fighting for White supremacy was a losing battle, the Religious Right soon pivoted their focus to abortion, gender roles, homosexuality, and other issues that are still at the frontlines of the culture war today.

In 1979, Falwell started the Moral Majority, a political organization that combined morality with conservative politics. Falwell was much more overt in his quest to rally Christians around Republican causes, drawing lines in the sand. His own website's mission statement said that their purpose was "to promote traditional family values and battle the liberals who would attempt to destroy these godly principles."[16] His attempts to rally Christians included statements like this one, in 1987, when he said, "God destroyed Sodom and Gomorrah primarily because of the sin of homosexuality. Today He is again bringing judgment against this wicked practice through AIDS."[17] Or when he blamed the September 11th attacks on "the pagans, and the abortionists, and the feminists, and the gays, and the lesbians" and even "the ACLU, People for the American Way" and anyone else who "tried to secularise America."[18] Or in 2006 when he said of the Democratic primary race, "I hope she's the candidate because nothing will energize my [constituency] like Hillary Clinton.... If Lucifer ran, he wouldn't."[19] There was good and there was evil, and all Christians needed to choose whom they would serve—and it clearly couldn't be the worse-than-Satan-Hillary or her devilish party.

But Falwell was a force to be reckoned with. He and his Moral Majority are widely credited with helping Ronald Reagan win the White House in 1980. Falwell himself traveled the country, speaking at conferences and churches and rallying the religious right.[20] Reagan's victory showed the country that the evangelical "Moral Majority" were an influential voting bloc. [21]

After the election, there was no denying Falwell's impact on holding evangelicalism and Republican politics together. But even with his abrasive and harmful rhetoric, he still put an emphasis on righteousness and morality—hence the "moral" in moral majority. And to his credit,

Falwell seemed to practice what he preached. He was never involved in any sex scandal like other televangelists were and was married to his wife for forty-nine years before he passed away in 2007.[22]

I didn't see the nationalism in Falwell's position because it just seemed a more aggressive version of my own beliefs: that moral character mattered. Because of this, Christian Nationalism disguised itself quietly in evangelicalism for decades, slowly and seamlessly infusing American patriotism into a requirement for following Jesus. By exclusively voting Republican, I thought we were just actively supporting the moral, godly party in American politics.

I especially remember Falwell making waves during Bill Clinton's presidency. He even marketed a VHS tape (yours for a donation of at least $43) that featured nearly two hours of wild allegations against Clinton, from sexual improprieties to murder. Falwell even played clips from the videotape on his *Old-Time Gospel Hour* cable television show. Falwell called Clinton "the most radical and controversial President in our nation's history."[23] This was obviously before Obama's tan suit scandal of the century.

This was also *before* Clinton's sex scandal with Monica Lewinsky came to light, when the calls to remove the president from office escalated.

I remember playing in our living room one night as a kid when something on the television caught my eye. My parents were watching the news, and President Bill Clinton appeared on the screen and earnestly addressed reporters in the room, saying, "I did not have sexual relations with that woman."

This was my first real introduction into politics. Despite only being ten years old with a very minimal understanding of sex, even I knew that sex outside of marriage was bad. Like, the worst thing you could ever do bad. Like, it would be better to kill someone than sleep with them bad (a sentiment that would mess me up intensely, but that's another story).

I remember asking my dad a lot of questions about Bill Clinton in the months leading up to his impeachment. My dad did his best to explain it to me in an age-appropriate way.

"April, this man was unfaithful to his wife *and* lied about it. If he could lie to his *family*, how can we ever trust him to be honest with us—the American people?" He would go on to explain how *our side* cared about right and wrong and thus wanted to remove Clinton from office. Democrats, on the other hand, didn't care about morality, and the clear proof of this was that they didn't want Clinton impeached.

It taught me a very important lesson from an early age: Character mattered to Christians and Republicans (which were basically one and the same) and that made us good. Democrats, on the other hand, were scandal-filled heathens who didn't care for righteousness and thus were bad.

I took this to heart. I was able to apply this narrative pretty smoothly through George W. Bush's presidency and during the campaigns of John McCain and Mitt Romney. The logic held. These were all decent, family men who were led by their morals and a belief in a higher power. Sure, they weren't perfect, but they were good enough for my worldview to remain unshaken.

And then Donald Trump happened.

Let's go back to the Moral Majority for a moment. If Jerry Falwell Sr. was the wedding officiant who put a ring on the GOP and evangelicals, then his son, Jerry Falwell Jr., was the dude in the corner creepily watching the two consummate the marriage. (Pool boy, anyone?)

Jerry Jr., who eventually took over for his father at Liberty University, was one of the first major evangelical leaders to endorse Donald Trump's presidential candidacy, encouraging other evangelical leaders to follow suit.[24] Jerry Jr. even had Trump speak at Liberty, the largest evangelical college in the world, where the GOP-evangelical relationship was demonstrating full-on PDA. From Jerry Jr. introducing Trump as someone who "lives a life of loving and helping others as Jesus taught" to Trump saying, "We're going to protect Christianity, I can say that, I don't have to be politically correct,"[25] these two were in it to win it. Despite Trump's infamous "Two Corinthians" flub, the Jerry Jr.–Trump union legitimized Trump in the eyes of many evangelicals and, in so doing, helped pave his way to the White House.

Initially, I didn't think much of Trump's campaign other than thinking the GOP debates would be more entertaining with him in them. Which they absolutely were. But as time went on, I was left shocked at how my fellow evangelicals embraced Trump as if he were one of us. As if he were chosen by God to literally Make America Great Again.

I thought it was a glitch in the Matrix. He was a reality TV star. He seemed so immoral. There is no way that my "pro-family" party of righteous believers would nominate a man who'd had multiple affairs, used foul language, rarely attended church, and lacked many core principles of being a Christian. I mean, in my church, if a pastor was caught looking at porn, they'd have to take a break from leadership. But now I was supposed to support a man who literally slept with a porn star and bragged about his sexual escapades? It was unthinkable.

"That's in his past, April, and we don't judge people for their lives before Jesus." This was a common refrain I heard from Christians around me, and it was a sentiment I understood. As a Christian, I knew someone's testimony was the bedrock of their faith. A testimony is a salvation story. The formula goes—a terrible sinner finds Jesus, changes their ways, and now lives a life of smooth sailing with God as their captain. Amazing Grace, right?

In evangelical culture, the worse you were in your BJ years (Before Jesus, mind you), the more the Church exalted you in your AJ years. From this angle, Trump was set up pretty perfectly. He had a very public story of immorality from his checkered past. The only problem was, I couldn't see where Trump had the "found Jesus and changed" part. And that seemed important. I mean, no one ever took the stage and gave a testimony saying, "Alcoholism, prostitutes, drugs, bankruptcy, I was at rock bottom... and I still am! All Glory to God!"

The getting saved part is quite central to salvation. Which requires repentance and "changing your ways." It's Christianity 101.

But Trump didn't seem to even try to fit that narrative. At the Family Leadership Summit in Iowa of July 2015, Trump was asked if he ever asked God for forgiveness. This is the crux of the Sinner's Prayer, the literal gateway to becoming a Christian in the evangelical world. But Trump replied to the question like this: "That's a tough question. I don't think in terms of, I have. I, I'm a religious person." Um, did no one ever tell him it's a relationship, not a religion? Red flag right there, never mind the scathing admission that he didn't think he had ever asked God for forgiveness.[26]

I thought that surprise bout of honesty would lose him evangelical points, but nothing slowed his favor with those around me. During the primaries in 2015, I was working as a producer for the *700 Club Interactive*, one of the staple programs of the Christian Broadcasting Network (CBN). I knew the organization was getting pretty cozy with Trump as he gained momentum, but by September, it was taken to ridiculous heights.

Trump was interviewed on CBN's *The Brody File* on one of Trump's golf courses. Host David Brody asked Trump who God was to him. It was an easy softball question for even the most nominal Christian, and yet this was Trump's reply:

> "I think God is the ultimate. You know, you look at this, look at this incred—here we are in the Pacific Ocean. How did I ever own this? I bought it fifteen years ago. I made one of the great deals, they say, ever, this piece of land. I have no mortgage on it, as you, I will certify and represent to you. And I was able to, you know, buy this and make a great deal. That's what I want to do for the country, make great deals. We have to, we have to bring it back...but God is the ultimate. I mean God created this. And you know, here's the Pacific Ocean right behind so, uhhhh, nobody, no thing, there's nothing like God."

What a testimony! God is the ultimate! But look at me! I own this. I made this great deal. I made this...I mean God created the ocean, so he's cool, too.

Well, CBN seemed to like it. The official article headline of the interview read, "Donald Trump Exclaims, 'God Is the Ultimate!'" and the write-up over the video said, "Watch below as Trump talks about what

God means to him. He calls God 'the ultimate' and 'there's nothing but God.'"[27]

As Trump's Christian gaffes continued, his support never wavered. If anything, he seemed to gain more favor with White evangelicals. *They will come to their senses,* I assured myself as I attempted to bury my concern.

But when Trump won the Republican nomination, I could no longer ignore it. This was the moment I started questioning the conservative evangelical circles I had always existed in. This was when I looked in the mirror and began wondering if being a Christian really meant I had to vote Republican.

I started asking questions out loud on my personal Facebook page, confused by how my moral Republican Party could let all of Trump's untoward behavior slide. I hoped my evangelical friends and family could explain it to me, because I still thought character mattered.

What surprised me more than anything was the heavy condemnation I was met with from people I cared about. Between public comments and private messages and texts, I was suddenly on the receiving end of some very passionate vitriol. Many of my fellow evangelicals were very direct: Yes, as a Christian, I did have to vote for Trump. Seeing a Republican in office was the most important thing. Some of these family friends went as far as to say my late father would be disappointed in me if I didn't vote for Trump. In their messages, I recognized the same patriotism and fervor I had once used to fight liberal atheists.

The White evangelicals around me were so loud and confident that I even started to doubt myself. *Am I the crazy one? Am I just missing something?* But as I watched Trump mock a disabled person or come up with another degrading nickname for a woman, I knew it couldn't be me. Their defenses for his behavior were not holding water:

- "He's just a baby Christian."
- "We're not electing a pastor."
- "God forgave him; we should, too."
- "We need conservative Supreme Court justices!"

There was also a growing number of "Trump prophets" leading up to the election, many of whom believed in the Seven Mountain Mandate. These were ministers that prophesied that God wanted Trump to be president to put the nation back on track to holiness. *But why would God use the unholiest presidential candidate in my lifetime to accomplish that?*

But my questions and concerns went unheeded. Trump won the 2016 presidential election with 81 percent of the White evangelical vote.[28]

How did we get here? How do we go from being the party of morality to the party of the narcissistic, billionaire playboy from the reality television show *The Apprentice*? Trump was the catalyst that forced me to start asking hard questions: Has it always been like this? Was my evangelical patriotism actually a power-at-all-cost form of Christian Nationalism the whole time?

These questions became my turning point. Over ensuing years, I have read lots of books, listened to podcasts, watched documentaries, and had many deep conversations about the history of and rise of Christian Nationalism. And what I found is, well, long and complicated. There are a lot of great resources available out there if you're interested in learning more. But Trump did much more than just change my mind on Christian Nationalism. He drastically altered my ideology altogether, and here's why:

Trump said the quiet parts of Christian Nationalism out loud.

He proclaimed that America should be first. That it's about winning no matter what. That life is about fighting and defeating those who work against you. That bullying and name-calling and oppressing groups of people are legitimate ways to act. But instead of being condemned by evangelicals, he was celebrated for it.

Even the pastor of my own church at the time jumped on the bandwagon. The Sunday before the 2016 election, my family and I were attending a church in Dalton, Georgia (the same district that Marjorie Taylor Greene represents). The pastor got up and encouraged us all to vote, saying, "Here at our church, we're not going to tell you who to vote for in the upcoming election. As long as you vote for the candidate who is pro-life, pro-Israel, pro–Second Amendment, and against gay marriage."

Interestingly, he didn't suggest we remember the Christian ideals of taking care of the poor, the sick, the orphans, and the widows when we went to the ballot box. That would have complicated his point, and he clearly wanted us all to vote for Trump.

For my twenty-eight years in the movement, a politician's strong Christian character was believed to be just as important as the bills they were going to pass. I'm not saying we did extensive background checks on a candidate's faith and personal life, but if someone showed rampant immorality, we knew not to vote for them. We wanted candidates that could lead America to a more Christian way of life, and that started in their private lives.

In my dad's book *America Say Jesus*, he spent a chapter talking about the importance of Christ changing the hearts of our presidents and electing Christian leaders of deep faith. That was a cornerstone of his desire for taking America back for Jesus. Good character mattered.

But this was where Trump disrupted Christian Nationalism at large. After Republicans lost two presidential elections in a row, the movement seemingly no longer required a certain level of morality or faith. They were so tired of losing, they were willing to overlook a video of Trump bragging about grabbing women by their genitals. This would have doomed any candidate of either party in the years before.

Billy Graham used American politics to spread his faith more widely. Jerry Falwell used faith to wield political influence. Falwell Jr. used faith to push forward a man who would do his bidding in exchange for power. Trump practically disregarded faith while offering results, and evangelicals seemed more than fine with that.

Some have openly admitted as much. Megan Basham, a Christian conservative pundit and writer for *The Daily Wire*, tweeted on November 15, 2022, "I don't especially care if a politician is sincere in his or her pro-life stance. . . . I'll take effective hypocrisy over ineffective sincerity any day of the week."[29]

Effective hypocrisy. That's what the ideology I had once pushed earnestly had become. I wanted out.

And that's when this wild ride really took off.

PART THREE

TACTICS OF CHRISTIAN NATIONALISM

As we've already established, I loved my country, so I naturally wanted it to be governed exclusively by Christians—aka evangelicals. This was just good common sense. Why wouldn't we want God's people in charge of the greatest country on earth? When I was a Christian Nationalist, this kind of logic was so obvious that it didn't really need to be articulated.

Instead, we spent much of our time focused on things that more directly affected everyday life—or things that just made people mad. And if I'm honest, getting people riled up garnered a more passionate, supportive following, while it simultaneously branded our opposition as enemies. This furthered an "us versus them" mentality that ultimately benefited Christian Nationalism.

Once I got out of Christian Nationalism, I could see it so clearly. In these next chapters, I'm going to share some of the tactics used by Christian Nationalists to both raise the profile of their ideas and gather support for them. Now, many of the tactics I am going to point out are not exclusive to Christian Nationalism. The ideology has a pattern of taking beliefs and vulnerabilities that already exist inside evangelicalism and manipulating them to further radicalize its base. Some of these tactics are focused on outsiders, while others are used on those already inside the movement.

Some of these tactics—such as boycotts—are well-known and much discussed, while other strategies may never be mentioned, perhaps even denied (like wanting to be persecuted). But I noticed them happening enough from my time inside Christian Nationalism that I wanted to discuss them here.

Please do not use these tactics at home. Or anywhere, for that matter.

CHAPTER 6

Saving Ben Stiller: Influence Through Media

Buzz buzz.

I looked at the text message that had just come through on my phone. It was from a girl in my small group. All it said was, "GOD'S NOT DEAD!"

I got that same text from a few other people, too, and I was confused. Easter, the empty tomb, and all the hours I spent volunteering at church every Resurrection Sunday? I clearly already knew God was not dead.

"Is this about that new movie?" I asked her, curiosity getting the best of me.

Buzz buzz.

"Yeah!! At the end of the movie, they encourage us to text everyone we know with that message to save souls! It's a powerful movie; you should see it!"

With that kind of endorsement, Beecher and I felt sure we were missing out on a Christian Academy Award–winning film, and as aspiring filmmakers ourselves, we felt like we had to see it. So Beecher and I went to the theater and bought two tickets for *God's Not Dead.*

I don't know if it was the cheesy acting or if it was the celebration that happened after the worst villain in the world—obviously an atheist professor—*died* at the end of the film, but I was unimpressed. Even though I was still a staunch conservative evangelical at the time, it felt weird to me that the Christian protagonist didn't help the car-crushed atheist dying in the middle of the street by using his phone to call an ambulance or offering some medical aid... No, he just prayed with him.

But don't worry, the Newsboys were standing by to celebrate the Christian student who *owned* the late idiot atheist professor in a debate about God's existence.

And sure enough, at the end of the movie, there was a message about how YOU the audience can save the day too (but not the atheist—RIP) by texting everyone you know "GOD'S NOT DEAD."

I did not text that message to anyone. Even as an evangelical, the propaganda left a bad taste in my mouth. *Jesus is good enough and we don't need to manipulate the viewer with over-the-top stereotypes to convert people.* I was officially annoyed with Christian media.

Which was hard to admit, because I knew there were two types of media in the world: good, inspiring, Christian media that would lead you along the right path, and those that would lead you straight to the devil.

I grew up knowing all about the evils of the secular mainstream media. We all knew it was dangerous, full of lies, run by liberal elites, and you couldn't trust it. Christian and/or conservative media were the only news you could trust. Media—entertainment, news, podcasts, books, movies—was all deemed good or bad, truth or fake news, Christian-y or demonic. All of it was filtered through a simple black-and-white ideology that directed followers to listen only to voices that align with their worldview.

The central goal in all this sorting, of course, is to control the narrative. Remember, Christian Nationalism requires a narrow view of the world. Too many voices or influences will expand someone's mindset, making them less focused at best or causing them to backslide at worst. If someone hears too many dissenting voices that open their mind up to too many new ideas, they may turn into a LIBERAL SHEEP WHO HAS SOLD THEIR SOUL TO SATAN!

As one of the mountains in the Seven Mountain Mandate, media is a primary focus for those trying to take back our country for Jesus. I knew the influence one could hold through media and I decided early on that I was going to use it to turn America back to God. I wasn't the first in my family to make media a focus.

By the time I was born, my grandfather had been hosting a Christian radio show for over a decade. It played throughout the Dallas–Fort Worth area. He even hosted a weekly Christian television show in the late 1970s. Before I married and changed my last name, I'd occasionally have people recognize my surname and ask if I was related to Pastor Bert. Moments like these enforced the legacy my family had established and reminded me of our calling.

My dad was even more vocal about his call to influence culture through media. Throughout his time in ministry, he was a guest on several prominent Christian TV shows and had his own daily radio show for years. When I was a kid, I would often sit outside his studio at our church, waiting for him to finish recording his episodes for the week. Sometimes, he'd let me come in and say something to the audience. On almost any given day in the 1990s in the Dallas–Fort Worth area, you could hear either my dad's or my grandfather's voice on the airwaves.

My dad wanted to be at the forefront of media because he believed it was a great way to spread the gospel. He often hired professional videographers to film his various crusades (the evangelical word for missions trips and conferences—let's not think too much about that problematic language) and would put together impressive highlight videos to show in churches around the world.

I believed that dedicating my life to influencing people through mass media was a worthy goal, one that could bring people to Jesus and help turn our country back to God. This was why I got my bachelor's degree in broadcasting and went on to get my master's degree in journalism.

I planned to take over the news for Jesus before launching into a thriving political career. (I had been inspired to go down this path when I heard Sarah Palin received a journalism degree before becoming governor of Alaska.) While I never heard terms like "Christian Nationalism" and "theocracy" mentioned as part of this strategy, we celebrated the notion of controlling the media for Jesus.

To influence the world through media, there are two paths for a young Christian Nationalist. The first is to get involved in producing overt Christian or conservative media, such as *The Jim Bakker Show*, *The 700 Club*, Newsmax, or Daystar. The plus side to this is you get to work in a safe environment with like-minded people who hype you up. The downside to this is your audience reach is limited because everyone knows you're conservative Christian from the jump. Another downside is your livelihood becomes based on you keeping the same beliefs and mindset forever—something you don't think about until you accidentally walk face-first into deconstruction.

The second path is through a covert operation that places the most faithful devotees in *secular* environments, to infiltrate and influence from within. You know, like the popular Christian phrase "Be in the world, not of it." The plus side to this is you get to be an undercover spy for Jesus and everyone at your church celebrates you and prays for your "mission field" work. Your reach also has bigger potential because you aren't wearing your faith on your sleeve and sinners don't see you coming. The downside is that you're aware of every hell-bound soul around you and are constantly calculating how you can save them without losing your job. On days you don't speak up, you pray that coworker doesn't get hit by a bus on the way home or their blood will be on your hands forever.

Totally normal pros and cons.

After successfully winning souls in public school, my initial plan was to take the covert route. I enrolled in graduate school at Regent University in Virginia Beach, Virginia. Regent was started by the late Pat Robertson, the founder of the Christian Broadcasting Network. While *The 700 Club*, the most famous of the network's shows, follows the overt Christian media strategy, Regent, in my view, did not shy away from trying to make secret Christian super spies for media infiltration.

My journalism classes often focused on conjoining my faith with whatever job I would end up getting. The motto of the school was "Christian Leadership to Change the World." We had a prominent law school next door, which aimed to build up Christian lawyers and politicians to influence the government for God.

My goal was to get a job at a secular news organization, build up some credibility, and then gently nudge the local news toward my Christian worldview. I would do this so sneakily that they wouldn't see it coming. Slowly, quietly, I would influence the news to focus on things that mattered to Christians and denounce the things we knew were wrong. I was ready to join heaven's CIA.

My first opportunity to go undercover came in 2012 when I interned for the NBC news affiliate in Dallas–Fort Worth. I was still in grad school and confident I was about to change the way the station did things. Imagine my surprise when, my very first day on the job, the news director sent me to interview two gay dads who became a source of scrutiny when they appeared in a JCPenney catalog.[1] It seemed perfect. Like God had sent me here specifically for such a time as this. It was my Esther moment, and I was ready.

I knew all about the "gay agenda" and how the mainstream media liked to show gay people in a positive light. This news organization didn't know that I had been trained as a good Christian to boldly stand against any sin, especially one that was destroying society. It was go time.

As I traveled to their house, my heart was pounding. I didn't know what sort of demonic stronghold I was about to encounter, but this news story—my very first to play on air—was my chance to portray how harmful homosexuality actually was, and I wasn't going to pull punches. I was going to tell the story accurately so the world could finally see the ugly truth behind the gay agenda.

In my notebook, sprinkled among my "regular questions," were ones like, "Don't you think it's better for a child to have a mom and a dad, though?" "How will your kids learn right from wrong?" and "Are you not also being intolerant of those with a different opinion than you?"

When we finally crossed enemy lines, aka the dads' home, I

immediately saw photos of them with their children hanging on the walls. Smiling. Happy. *These guys are good, but they can't fool me*, I thought to myself.

Then, when I started talking with the men, they were incredibly kind. They told me about how they adopted their children, about their day jobs, which didn't involve catalog modeling, and what their daily routine was like. They asked how long I'd been at the station, and when they heard I was a new intern, they were very encouraging. *Is this an act? If so, they are excellent actors.* I didn't know how to process all of it as I sat down behind the camera to ask the questions I had carefully typed out in advance.

As the interview went on, my confusion only grew. I even tested them at one point, referencing the fact that I attended church, to see if I could get a rise out of them. They just kept smiling at me like they were rooting for me, a young intern, to do well. *But I am a Christian. I just referenced that. Shouldn't you hate me now?*

Neither dad gave off evil vibes whatsoever. *Maybe God hasn't given them over to reprobate minds yet. Maybe they can still be saved.* I continued to ask questions as I wrestled with what to do with their souls. As much as I knew gayness was wrong and needed correction, I also couldn't bring myself to condemn them nor ask the "gotcha" questions I had prepared. Their kindness disarmed me.

As the interview ended and we got up to leave, I mustered out a "God bless you guys" as one final test.

"Thanks, you too," one of them said back to me.

"And good luck on your career. You did a great job," the other said.

I smiled while the conservative in me was ashamed that I was now communing with the enemy.

Am I sure they're my enemy?

Their eyes never turned black, I reasoned. There was no foaming at their mouths. Their children were well cared for. *Why is this wrong, again?*

On the ride back, it even crossed my mind that these might just be two human beings who loved their children...

No, that's what they want me to think! This must be a trick of Satan. No wonder people support gay marriage... Satan comes as an angel of light.

I tried to convince myself to keep my worldview intact, but it was a confusing day. It took a long time to untangle the questions that arose from that interview.

After that summer internship, I returned to Regent. In my second year there, we decided to throw an Oscar-watching party. Regent also had a film school (because Hollywood *really* needs saving), so throwing an Academy Awards watch party was relevant.

We asked the administration for permission to hold the event on campus, but we were informed that to hold it there, the gathering would also need to be a prayer party.

Okay. A prayer meeting/Oscar party. Well, it would be unconventional, but we'd make it work.

About twenty of us gathered in the ComArts building to watch the awards ceremony on a big TV. I was in student government and helped lead the event. We cheered, we fellowshipped (evangelical for socializing), we ate snacks. Then, during each commercial break, we stopped chatting to pray for a different famous person or for whoever had just won an award. Sometimes, we even prayed for the losers. The evening felt a bit like a game of Red Light, Green Light. We'd be laughing and having fun, only to have to stop in an instant to be reverent in prayer when another commercial played.

We prayed a lot that night. The prayer I remember the most for whatever reason was when we prayed for Ben Stiller's salvation.

"Dear Lord, please save his soul and let him know that you are the one true God," I earnestly prayed.

"Help him to make good choices and to share positive messages," my friend jumped in, popcorn prayer style.

"Lead him to make media that brings the world closer to Jesus," a third friend said.

Just think how much more powerful *Zoolander* or *Tropic Thunder* would've been if a character said the sinner's prayer at the end!

Even back then, we knew this was a bit ridiculous. The event lasted three hours, and over time the prayers got very repetitive. As much as I sometimes wanted to take a break from the superficial prayers, there were enough rule followers there—who really believed our prayers could save Hollywood—to keep us on the prayer schedule.

One time I was caught mid-bite when a commercial started. I stayed seated, not wanting to get up and lead another awkward prayer. My hopes of letting one break slide were thwarted when one student whispered, "Pst. April. It's a commercial. We're supposed to pray for the Costume Design team for *The Artist*."

I nodded and stood up.

Eating M&M's could wait. We had celebrities to save.

"Father God, thank you for costume designers . . . just . . . bless their hands, Father God, as they . . . umm . . . just . . . Father God . . . as they just . . . stitch modest wardrobes that are . . . um . . . pleasing to you. Amen." We all felt significant relief every time the commercial break ended.

This was how the media was treated in my circles. Entertainment was not there for us to enjoy; it was a tool for us to use. The only reason we were allowed to consume content that old church ladies might find offensive was because understanding pop culture kept us relevant enough to ultimately save the world for Jesus. It was research.

What my graduate school failed to mention was just how exhausting being undercover would be. It takes a large amount of cognitive dissonance to continually be treated so well by people who are supposed to be evil.

I worked in the corporate world when I first graduated. Everyone knew I was a Christian. From the stories I told to leaving early for worship nights, to never cussing, to praying for coworkers, it was not hard to tell. In one marketing meeting, the history of Christians dying in the Colosseum was randomly brought up and I joked, "Yeah, I definitely would've been eaten by a lion." Everyone nodded and laughed with me.

My coworkers in this secular, corporate world never made me feel bad for being Christian and I never faced backlash for my outspoken faith.

I had been told the world would hate me because of the Jesus in me. But here I was, in the world, existing openly as a Christian, and everyone was... kind? My mind had to do mental gymnastics to balance the Christian persecution I was taught existed in America and... my reality.

I worked there for a year and a half before I switched paths and went to work for the *700 Club Interactive* at CBN, which was filmed on the same campus as Regent. At CBN, I was able to easily work my Christianity into my career, which proved far less taxing. It was my job to find stories of faith, travel to interview subjects, and work with a team to create short features in a mini-doc style that uplifted the name of Jesus.

Soon, however, I started running into a different problem. While most of the stories I worked on were positive testimonials of God's miracles, I quickly grew frustrated by the lack of variety. Most people in the world don't receive full physical healings when they pray, but if you only watched our show, you would think God healed every Christian who ever asked.

This was hard for me to take. Only a few years earlier, I had witnessed my dad die of cancer as we prayed with overwhelming faith for God to take it away. Our family was met with some hurtful words after his passing. "God didn't heal him because of an unresolved sin in your family," someone would say, or "Your dad died because he was living outside of God's will." Or equally frustrating, "God did answer your prayer! He just healed your dad in heaven!"

I realized these sentiments were easier to handle than the idea that God just didn't answer our prayer. People felt the need to give a reason for my dad's death that didn't fault God. God simply not answering our prayer didn't fit the narrative, so we must have been doing something wrong to make God ignore us. With each new testimony we told at CBN, I realized the media I was producing was feeding into the idea. That God heals those who have faith. Period.

So at CBN, I tried to get the team to do a story on what happens to someone's faith when God *doesn't* answer the prayer. In my experience, that happened more often than not.

One testimony I pushed for was that of an openly gay Christian man who was actively blogging about his journey of celibacy, which was what he believed God was calling him to.

"He has a decent following and is a voice for so many gay Christians who have spent years begging for God to make them straight—only to still be gay. And yet they're still Christian. They're still going to church, choosing Christ over companionship. This is real!" I made my case in a meeting.

"Yeah, but that might be discouraging to those wanting deliverance," another producer said.

"It's more powerful to show complete healings—you know, those who are no longer gay at all but living a straight, godly lifestyle. It would be confusing to our audience if they think God keeps people gay," a different coworker chimed in.

Conversions like this didn't happen often, it turned out. But we did find some ex-gay stories to feature. The only problem was the frustratingly high number of "healed" people who would eventually come back out as queer years later. One of these people was named Scarlett. She was elevated as a hero of the faith when she identified as Jeffrey, an ex-gay and ex-trans person. "From Transgender to Transformed by God" was the title of the CBN testimonial story that lived online for years. After she came out again, I looked for an update to the story or an addendum of some sort, but there was none to be found.[2]

I stayed at CBN for a little over a year before we moved to Tennessee. What I began to understand over my time there is that people who only watch Christian shows on Christian networks, or conservative shows on conservative media, could spend their whole life believing that God makes all LGBTQ people straight if they just ask. Or that everyone who prays while sick is healed by God. Constantly silencing or ignoring stories that don't fit this narrative creates a false message. A harmful message.

One that leads people to believe that every outside narrative is a lie.

This is the reason why "secular" or "liberal" content is so often branded "FAKE NEWS!" If you censure every voice except your own, you become the ultimate source of truth for your followers.

In August 2023, CBS News released a poll in which they asked Trump supporters who they felt told them the truth. At the top of the list was Trump—above pastors, media figures, and even their own friends and family.[3] It's terrifying how well Trump used this tactic.

Listening to one source and refusing to hear other perspectives silos people. I have relatives who claim CNN is dishonest liberal garbage yet can't give me any actual examples to support this thesis. Or they just say, "They say bad things about Trump," with no regard for whether what was said about Trump was true.

Simplicity is appealing in a complicated time. It's easier to listen to and trust one voice than to try to discern truth from a plethora of news organizations. It's more appealing to zero in on one network or television star or podcast host you trust than to sort through the varying opinions, sift through the facts, and try to understand what's true and what's not.

Climate change is complicated and devastating to our planet. Climate change being a lie made up by elites is much easier to digest. Listening to the feedback and understanding the reasons your candidate lost—even though you prayed for, perhaps even prophesied, his victory—is harder than believing the simple lie that the election was stolen.

In fact, media played a huge role in the January 6th insurrection. "The big lie" that the election was stolen was wielded on conservative and Christian media alike. Because the message was repeated so often, some people were convinced there was widespread fraud, despite credible evidence to the contrary.

One of my friends shared an article online "proving" the election was stolen. Shocker—it didn't actually prove anything. But when I kindly sent her a link to a Snopes Fact Check that countered their argument, I was immediately informed that *I* was misled, and my friend promised to pray for my lost soul.

It is a humbling experience to have your old Christian Nationalist playbook used against you. Guess I had it coming.

I know from experience that it's almost an instinctual response. When I was in the movement, I learned to shut down all conflicting ideas, especially ones that included evidence that contradicted what I *knew* to be true. I had to beat it to the punch before it got into my head and made me ask questions. If an idea or an argument went against what I already believed, I could *not* open a Pandora's box of asking whether there might be some merit in it. Who knew where that might lead? Better to shut it down than be led astray.

But then things began to happen that I couldn't just shut down. Things I couldn't reconcile that gently chipped away at my preconceptions over time. When I met that kind gay couple, it pressed against what I'd been taught. When my dad died of cancer, it pushed against my beliefs.

For years, my ideology had been slowly cracking, but the dam didn't break for a long time. This is, in part, because I had enough Christian media available to surround myself with people who thought like me and could regularly confirm my biases. I threw myself into the overtly Christian environment at CBN because I was trying to keep my worldview from unraveling.

This is what the movement wants. No matter what their followers experience, Christian Nationalism wants to offer answers through *their* media that keep their own in line. By demonizing other sources, their approved media become the only voices their followers listen to.

This tactic worked on me for a long time. It convinced me that a couple of dads were my enemy despite their kindness toward me. The fact that I didn't naturally despise them meant that I needed to fight Satan's deception even harder.

I can't change the past or the part I played in Christian Nationalism, but I can allow new information to change my mind.

And thankfully, how I watch award shows.

CHAPTER 7

The Church B-B-Qanon; or, The Problem with Conspiracy Theories

Let's play a game. I'm going to name three conspiracy theories, but I made one of them up. Can you spot the fake?

1. Government-sanctioned chemical warfare turned people gay to keep people from having children.
2. Cruising on a boat with alcohol will manifest pirate demons.
3. Taylor Swift is a witch whose songs put literal spells on people, especially at her concerts, where she channels goddesses who mess with your menstrual cycle.

Made your guess?

The fake one is No. 2. But only slightly. In 2022, evangelist Bob Larson went viral for saying that he had encountered "lots of pirate demons" in the Caribbean and thought perhaps Johnny Depp's odd behavior was because pirate demons possessed him after playing Captain Jack Sparrow in the *Pirates of the Caribbean* movies.[1] No alcohol required.

No. 1: The gay chemical was a conspiracy lauded by *Infowars*' Alex Jones, who went on an infamous angry rant about how these same chemicals got in the water and turned "the friggin frogs gay."[2] It seems the belief in this "gay bomb" originated from a discussion the Air Force had in 1994 about developing potentially nonlethal weapons, including chemicals that would act as "strong aphrodisiacs" among service members of the same sex.[3] Though these chemicals never actually existed, the belief that chemicals in the water turn people gay still exists. This idea was even pushed as recently as 2023 by independent presidential candidate Robert F. Kennedy Jr., who referenced man-made chemicals as the reason to blame a rise in trans and gay children.[4]

No. 3: There have always been rumors that Taylor Swift (or almost any successful and famous woman, for that matter) is a witch. During Swift's immensely popular Eras Tour in 2023, there were countless blogs and videos that analyzed her concert appearances to "prove" she was performing witchcraft and thus Christians should stay away. Christian influencer and host of the *Heaven & Healing Podcast* Angelamarie Scafidi sounded the witch alarms especially loudly in her in-depth Eras analysis, which included her saying, "Have you ever had issues with your menstrual cycle or fertility?... That's because she's channeling goddess deities through her songs, through her lyrics and through her performances which are thus being cast onto you."[5]

Gives a whole new meaning to Taylor Swift's song "Bad Blood."

The internet's a funny thing. It's a place where you can learn how a pop star you've never met is giving you bad cramps this month, the history of maple syrup, or the science behind hot air balloons. You can even watch someone like me wearing an upside-down ladybug basket on her head (my makeshift MAGA hat) in a sketch video.

All the information in the world is at our fingertips, and despite that, I was somehow once convinced that I could only trust news from websites with URLs like: www.America-Freedom-Eagle-Patriot-News-Rapture-Jesus-Loves-You-Russian-Bot.info.

Every good Christian Nationalist knows that the more the capital-W World accepts the accuracy of a source, the less it can be trusted—hence the importance of controlling the media people consume, as we discussed in the last chapter. I used to be convinced that most educators, scientists, news organizations, legal experts, doctors, and politicians—unless they were Republican and outspokenly Christian—were untrustworthy. What terrible flaw was it that made me think that a doctor with ten years of advanced schooling and decades in practice was wrong? It was because they were *gasp* *secular* (aka controlled by the devil).

The first time I read a science book in public school that said the earth is older than 6,000 years, I dropped the book like a demon was about to manifest from the page.

"That's NOT what the Bible says," I piously muttered to the kid sitting next to me.

"But it's science..." she replied.

"I'll take GOD over science, thanks," I quipped. Not today, Satan.

Did I have any legitimate reason to doubt these experts and organizations? No. No, I did not. Did that stop me from doubting them? Also no.

It seems wild looking back, but while I was in Christian Nationalism, it wasn't at all strange. We were constantly on guard against the lies the world was trying to sell us. We heard it preached from the pulpit and shared in Bible studies and the media we consumed: We alone had the real answers. Anyone who tried to tell us differently was a liar. As we covered in the last chapter, if you control the information people consume, you can convince them of all sorts of things.

Controlling the media that people consume and believe is the hard part, but once you have them in the oven, it's pretty easy to turn up the heat. And that's when we start to get into conspiracy theory territory. A land of half-truths, almost-truths, and flat-out lies accepted based on trust in the source, not on whether they make any sense or are factually correct. These theories are eagerly shared and make people believe there are deep conspiracies at work against them.

I mean, think about it. Are you likely to storm the Capitol if you believe that liberals are just selfish and don't have your best interests in mind? Probably not.

But what if you believe liberals cheated in an election so they can continue to literally drink children's blood in the bottom of a pizza parlor in Washington DC? What if you earnestly believe that if Trump leaves the White House, the Bolshevik Rothschild elitist cabal will take over and destroy America and persecute Christians? Hold my grape juice, I'm going in!

To be fair, I fell for some conspiracy theories in my day, too. For instance, back in the nineties, I was convinced that MTV was trying to turn the kids in my generation gay. The accusation was that MTV was regularly showing gay people as cool, normal people and then asking teens, "How do you know you're not gay unless you try it?" I never watched MTV, so this was all hundredth-hand information. But boy, did I believe it! I recently found my old church notes from one of my dad's sermons where I wrote in all caps "BAN MTV!"

I echoed this in a journal from eleventh grade where I wrote a series of essays I titled, "When Life Gives You Lemons... Throw Them at a Liberal." In it, I lamented how MTV perpetuated the lie that a person could be born gay. Clearly, the network was spouting lies and needed to be stopped. Then I followed that up by boldly asking, "If it's possible to be born gay, how come there were no gays before the 1800s?!"[6] Checkmate, MTV!

My campaign against MTV was unfortunately not the only time I fell for this kind of thing. In 2012, a friend and I made a satiric video where we pretended to be liberal valley girls. In the sketch, we praised Obama with lines like, "That's really cool that you can be born in Kenya and become President of the United States."

You read that right. *I*, a never-Trumper liberal sheep, promoted the birther conspiracy as made popular by Donald Trump himself. The baseless theory claimed that President Obama was hiding his birth certificate because he was not born in the United States. If true, this was beneficial for us Christian Nationalists because it would disqualify Obama from the presidency. Problem solved. Donald Trump also spread another theory about Obama's birth certificate when he said on *The Laura Ingraham Show*, "Now, somebody told me—and I have no idea if this is bad for him or not, but perhaps it would be—that where it says 'religion,' it might have 'Muslim.'" Trump said he didn't necessarily believe that, but given the rise in Islamophobia in a post-9/11 world, the idea alone would rally Christians to vote against Obama.[7]

These ideas were all over the shows I watched on Fox News, which was obviously one of the only sources for truth. Fair and balanced. They had a Democrat on one of their shows, so obviously they were objective.

"Trump brings up good points. How do we know *for sure* Obama was born in Hawaii? Also, his middle name is HUSSEIN. Sounds pretty Muslim to me..." I remember saying to someone.

Thank God for personal growth.

But all it takes is a little bit of doubt for a small hint of a conspiracy to take root. Then it grows a little deeper with each new YouTube video recorded by men in basements with shoddy microphones and dubious facts.

When I was growing up, my family generally stayed away from the deeper conspiracy theories, although my brother Matt did go down an Illuminati rabbit hole for a couple days. He once showed me a video that broke down some Jay-Z and Beyoncé music videos, "proving" their connection to the secret community. Triangles, eyes, and goats seemed to be at the center of the devil-worshipping conspiracy. I had to admit the elaborate video was compelling. I mean, I wasn't convinced enough to stop listening to Beyoncé, but the thoughts floated in the back of my mind the next time I jammed to "Single Ladies."

Then my dad was diagnosed with Stage 4 nonsmoker's lung cancer. While my dad was going through chemotherapy, a family friend and pastor, who was already overseeing multiple church campuses, took over my dad's church. As part of the contract they drew up, the church agreed to pay my dad a certain amount for the rest of his life. The contract also stated that if Dad were to die, that money would go to my mom for the rest of her life.

At the time, this money was a lifeline for my family. While we were all expecting Dad to experience a full miraculous healing, it was nice to have some financial security for my mom just in case.

When my dad died in September 2011, the monthly pay started going to my mom as promised. She had worked with my dad in their ministry for decades and had no other source of income. No one expected her to become an unemployed widow at fifty-four, so we were all incredibly thankful that she had this support. Despite everything I'm about to share, we will always be grateful for this church's kindness to our family during my dad's untimely death.

Over the years we'd hear from this pastor from time to time, and slowly we noticed his topics of conversation became much... weirder. He started sending my mom obscure videos about the end times and wanted, sometimes demanded, her thoughts about them in return.

She felt obligated to comply. Some of the videos were heavy on conspiracy and had long run times. She would watch some and send enough thoughts to appease him.

One time, he mailed her a set of three DVDs so secret and private that she was instructed to "destroy" the discs after watching them, like it was some CIA top secret mission. She was encouraged to watch the five-plus hours of content *with* my brothers and me, because he needed *all* of us to know how to avoid kicking the Antichrist's 666 hornet's nest or something.

When my brothers and I did not participate, the pastor seemed to be angry with my mom for not forcing her adult children—two of whom lived on the other side of the country—to huddle in her home with her to learn about the nest of a satanic wasp.

In all the articles, websites, and videos he sent, the themes were similar: An evil globalist cabal of leaders, almost always Democrat, who worship Satan and may or may not drink children's blood, have taken over the government in order to usher in the Antichrist and the New World Order, aka the end of the world.

This pastor even sent my mom a link to an actual QAnon-branded video. "Q" was an anonymous source that made Trump out to be some sort of hero fighting the deep state.

[Quick sidebar about the deep state: It's a supposed secret group of influential people and career government employees who secretly manipulate and control national policy. The idea of the deep state was heavily pushed by Trump strategist Steve Bannon and gained traction leading up to the 2016 election.[8] There is no proof such a thing exists, but that didn't stop the idea from spreading.]

QAnon quickly became known for pushing a plethora of other conspiracies including a story about reptilian humanoids (an idea that has antisemitic roots)[9] and the belief that JFK Jr. is actually alive and destined to be Trump's future vice president,[10] or that Joe Biden is actually dead (and is currently some puppet clone).[11] Yes, those are all real conspiracy theories that real people in America believe today. I don't know how much of this the pastor actually believed, but we found his proximity to QAnon alarming.

My mom's responses managed to placate him successfully. Well, until he saw my Facebook post before the 2020 election.

My post was pretty moderate, honestly. I said that Christians should vote based on their own personal convictions and that no one should spiritually manipulate anyone into voting a certain way.

But I also broke the cardinal rule in the post—I admitted I was voting for a Demonrat, I mean Democrat (#ExChristianNationalist AutoCorrectProbs).

I ended with:

> Jesus isn't a Republican. Jesus isn't a Democrat. He isn't even American.
> He is God of all and He loves us all unconditionally.
> I want Biden to win the presidency but far more importantly,
> I want to see Christ put back in Christian.
> P.S. I know I have friends and family voting for Trump
> & you should know that I love you no matter what.

The post received 100 or so comments, which was significant for my personal Facebook page. One of those comments was from the daughter of that pastor. She wrote, in a sincere way, that she didn't understand how a Christian could vote for Biden because "Biden and his team HATE God & anything to do with Christianity."

Uh-oh. I was immediately worried. I sensed I may have just caused a problem for my mom—both her relationship with the pastor and her financial well-being.

Sure enough, the next day, the pastor asked my mom for my phone number because he wanted to tell me how Trump wasn't racist and had done many great things "for the black people." (This pastor is White, for the record. As if you couldn't tell.) I didn't have the energy to feign interest over Trump's godly mission to defeat cabal globalists, so my mom wriggled out of giving him my number.

Then on Election Day 2020, the pastor texted my mom and got straight to the point: "Hi Linda, who did you vote for?" My mom gave a long, kind answer explaining that after praying about it, she didn't vote for either presidential candidate. She did inform him that she voted for conservatives in her local elections, though. The pastor then asked my mom to call him, and when she asked why, he said, "I want to discuss your financial support."

A lawyer advised her not to talk about finances over the phone and to get any sort of fiscal discussion in writing, since a legally binding contract was already in place. In this case, it seemed like this pastor intended to cut her finances over who she voted for—a seemingly clear violation of the separation of church and state.

She asked if he could just email her. He then replied, "Linda, we have been supporting you finally [*sic*] for several years now. It's very disappointing that you can't give me an appointment time to talk on the phone. So it's best that we end the support at the end of November. Love you too." Ten points for Christian love!

My mom didn't take him to court, or anything else she was legally within her rights to do. In follow-up messages, my mom asked if they could just pay a fraction of what was promised to her until she became eligible for Medicare, also mentioning her lawyer and the signed contract.

The church agreed to pay the smaller amount until she turned sixty-five. My mom never retaliated, never put them on blast. Even though she was deeply hurt by it, she managed to make it okay.

Today, they have completely stopped paying her.

I guess my brothers should've flown to Tennessee so we could all watch that 666 Antichrist insect DVD series, after all.

Let's just quickly recap that story: A Christian pastor seemingly broke a contract to pay a widow because she didn't vote for Donald Trump. Of course, he never directly said that was the reason, but that conclusion actually makes sense, unlike anything to do with QAnon.

This family wasn't always like this. In the nineties, I was alarmed when his daughter told me she liked Bill Clinton. I never would have imagined them going further right than my family. But baseless conspiracies can radicalize even the kindest of pastors enough to choose politics over people. This pastor seemed to really believe the 2020 election was a matter of good versus evil, God versus Satan. By not voting for Trump, whom he believed was #TeamGod, my mom wasn't Christian enough. She wasn't willing to let her vote help reclaim the nation for God from godless Democrats, so I imagine the pastor felt justified in his actions.

Outlandish conspiracies are funny to laugh at until they directly harm your family.

Weird beliefs were nothing new to us. I'd heard my fair share of them growing up in evangelical circles. Satan was always the mastermind, regardless of the topic, and the theories usually pertained to the end times in some way.

A volcano erupts overseas? The rapture was imminent. Taylor Swift's popularity keeps rising? She sold her soul to Satan. Queer people keep existing? MTV turned them gay! You know, typical stuff.

But it felt like conspiracy theories reached an all-time high when the pandemic hit. Many Christians around me believed getting the "jab" (the COVID vaccine) was taking the Mark of the Beast, which would seal your eternal fate to hell.

Even mainstream evangelical figures like Bethel Church Pastor Bill

Johnson (a proponent of the Seven Mountain Mandate) teased the Mark of the Beast theory in a sermon when he said, "With the mark of the beast you can't buy or sell or do business. And without a vaccine, they want you to not be able to buy or sell or do business. Now I'm not opposing vaccines," Johnson continued, "I'm just saying this is an interesting dress rehearsal for a bigger issue in the future."[12]

There were also several wild explanations among the QAnon crowd for the vaccine, many of which I saw spread by Christians I knew: It was a government tracking device, it was a form of population control that would kill everyone who received it between twelve and eighteen months after getting it. (It's been longer than that for me and I'm still kicking over here—take that, Q!)

Some Christian Nationalists started comparing the government's push for citizens to get the COVID vaccine to yellow stars in the Holocaust.[13] *Do they hear themselves?* I'd think, continually flabbergasted by the vaccine response.

One Trump supporter told me the COVID vaccine altered my DNA, that I had betrayed my faith and was "no longer God's property." I apparently was now the "property of the vaccine creator clearly and legally stated in the patents." Who knew the God of the universe followed United States patent laws!?

One of my favorite theories said that the vaccine was magnetic and people could test this by sticking keys to their arms. It was the pandemic. We were bored, so Beecher and I made a little game out of it, trying to cross our living room with metal objects pressed to our arms. Beecher was usually the most magnetic, which meant the key stayed in place for 1.2 seconds instead of none. "*Ha!* You're Magneto!" I said. We laughed to avoid crying.

Of course, these COVID conspiracies had deadly effects. Leading into the 2021 New Year, our small city was experiencing one of our worst spikes yet. Our hospitals were overrun by COVID patients and Tennessee Republican Governor Bill Lee issued an executive order to limit indoor gatherings to ten people. While worship services were excluded from the law, churches were still encouraged to "utilize virtual services and follow safety protocols."[14]

Unbothered by the surge of infections, an evangelical ministry just a few miles from my house hosted a huge weekend conference where they bussed people in from out of state. Their live-streamed services proudly showed off hundreds of people crammed inside one room with no masks or social distancing in sight.[15] We had already seen COVID breakouts in local churches kill people. Yet these pastors didn't seem to care. They had tickets to sell.

This infuriated me, so I made a TikTok video about it. I called this ministry hypocritical for claiming to be pro-life while knowingly putting people in harm's way and profiting from it. A mask and social distancing didn't seem like a big ask for those trying to follow Christ and just be... decent human beings.

Enough people condemned the ministry's conference that the local news covered it. The segment included clips from my video as part of the story, and suddenly, I was on the receiving end of some of the worst vitriol I'd ever seen in my comments and messages.

One man took the time to find old pictures of my then four- and one-year-old kids on my Instagram and commented, "Kill commie babies." I made my social media private for a long time after that. Threatening my kids was a new low that genuinely terrified me.

But this reaction was the result of radical conspiracy theories. The people commenting on my page didn't see me as a concerned Christian mom. They saw me as a "fervent, maniacal zealot" (to quote one woman with "Jesus is my Savior, Trump is my President" in her Facebook bio) controlled by Satan and intent on destroying all churches.

Christian Nationalism keeps followers by pushing its narrative—often from a pulpit. But how could these churches do this if they had to shut down due to a deadly virus? Or how could they stay open without looking like they cared about tithe money and power more than the lives of people dying from COVID?

Hello, COVID conspiracies. It's easier to hold services if you make closing churches about deep state Christian persecution instead of saving lives. This just pushed people deeper into Christian Nationalism.

I've wondered a lot about why the more ludicrous theories seem to spread faster in times of crisis, and in the end, I think it's a defense mechanism. A survival tactic. When faced with immense suffering, we all look for something or someone to blame. It gives us a *reason* for why something bad is happening, which makes the experience more palatable. As evangelicals, we are especially well-trained to do this. We grow up knowing that God is in complete control and is only good. We are taught that nothing bad can come from God and everything happens for a reason. So when bad things happen, we immediately go into "find an answer" mode.

This has historically led Christians to respond rather oddly to mass tragedies. When the bubonic plague hit Europe in the mid-1300s, it is estimated that 25 million people died in five years. That's about 40 percent of all Europeans.[16] Just for context, in the three years at the height of COVID, just under 7 million people died across a much more populated world.[17]

So how did Christians respond to this plague without YouTube videos to suck them into conspiracies? Meet the Flagellants. My first introduction to them was in the classic film *Monty Python and the Holy Grail*, where groups of hunched-over cloaked people hit themselves in the back with whips. I thought this joke was just a random addition to the film but have since learned that this was based on real occurrences.

Apparently, in response to the mass tragedy of the Black Death, this sect of Christianity turned to beating themselves, hoping God would show mercy on them. If they punished themselves sufficiently, maybe God would refrain from killing them with the plague. The practice became so widespread, the Pope banned it in 1349.[18] Sounds like something the Antichrist would do. Just kidding. Old habits die hard.

It's human nature to want to grasp a semblance of control when the world is in chaos. We desperately search for reasons to explain suffering and look for scapegoats. For evangelicals during the COVID pandemic, those scapegoats became Democrats, the government, China, big pharma, and for some reason, evil globalists performing satanic rituals at New World Order meetings.

The idea that COVID is a random, unpredictable, unstoppable pandemic spread by an invisible virus is scary. The fact that you and everyone around you could get sick and die at any moment renders us helpless. Out of our control. And *that* is a debilitating feeling, no matter what you believe. You can see how, bit by bit, conspiracies might start to take hold.

It's kind of like how I thought all the teenagers coming out in the nineties were a result of MTV's lies. I refused to accept that they were... just gay. Because if they were just gay, that would open a whole can of worms. *If people weren't* turned *gay, that means they were* born *gay. And if they're born gay, then that means God made them gay. But the Bible says...*

Nope. That is a recipe for an existential crisis. Let's just blame those music videos.

So, on some level, I understand why conspiracy theories exist. That part I can track with. But I have often wondered why these theories have to get so... weird.

Like how the jelly bracelets I wore as a teen were supposedly actually sex bracelets that, based on a secret bead color code, indicated my willingness to perform sex acts on whatever stranger broke my bracelet.[19]

"Red is for a lap dance, you know," the strange woman said to me.

"Oh... okay," I said, making a mental note to avoid wearing jelly bracelets to Mardel Christian Bookstores going forward.

One benefit of the crazier theories, though, is that the more outlandish (and "secret") they are, the harder they are to debunk. It's not hard to discredit a single person or action. But a secret network of people sending coded messages through microchips implanted through vaccines and controlling everything? Now, that's hard to disprove. And the fact that you can't find any evidence that it's true? That's not because it doesn't exist. That's because the liberal sheep/lizard monsters are doing such an amazing job of staying SECRET! See how effective they are!

Another bonus is that the more complicated the theory, the less likely you are to trust anyone else. Every news organization, every government official, every person that tells you something different can be written off as part of the enemy. *They* just don't get it because *they* have been bought by the deep state!

Unfortunately, there are countless algorithms that only exacerbate this conspiracy theory problem. Web pages are designed to keep people engaged. Users are constantly fed similar content on repeat, whether the information is fact-based, propaganda, or misinformation spread by extremists.

Here's the point: Christian Nationalism uses the internet and media to advance conspiracy theories to keep followers engaged, fired up, and doubting outside voices. These theories reinforce the "us versus them" mentality that fuels momentum in the movement. Convincing followers that there is a secret satanic society of Democrats gives them a righteous calling—to fight these demonic forces and turn America back to God. It makes followers believe that voting red, keeping churches open in a pandemic, or taking money from a widow is fighting off satanic globalists and taking us one step closer to making America the Christian nation she was meant to be.

This radicalization can morph good, well-meaning people into enraged, paranoid conspiracy theorists who storm the Capitol with Jesus flags.

So the next time life gives you lemons, it *might* be a government tracking device. But it's probably just a lemon.

CHAPTER 8

Naked Christians in the Air: Manipulating End Times Eschatology

Conspiracy theories have been around forever and are not exclusive to Christian Nationalism. But there is one thing that typically sets Christian Nationalist conspiracies apart from the rest: They often allude to the Biblical end times.

Why have a normal conspiracy theory about the elites when you can mix in some vague apocalyptic Revelation end-of-days terror that deals with beasts, seals, dragons, and trumpets?

Manipulating end times eschatology to motivate followers is another tactic often employed in Christian Nationalism.

Back in my day, we stuck to fairly simple accusations, like calling someone we didn't like a Book of Revelation villain such as a "false prophet." Today, these accusations can be as elaborate as saying the Russian invasion of Ukraine is kick-starting the war of Gog and Magog as prophesied in Ezekiel 38, and while what Putin is doing is bad, "he's being compelled by God" because of the impending apocalypse. (Please note that this is something Pat Robertson actually said.)[1]

Invoking the end times is nothing new. When I was a Christian Nationalist, any time the news discussed warfare happening overseas, rapture alarms went off in my head. After all, Matthew 24:6 (NIV) says

"You will hear wars and rumors of wars, but see to it that you are not alarmed. Such things must happen, but the end is still to come." Wars = Jesus is coming back soon. Since there's been no shortage of wars, the rapture was always imminent.

Sometimes we like to play "sounds like" games. 1 Corinthians 15:52 (ESV) says, "In a moment, in the twinkling of an eye, at the last trumpet," and 1 Thessalonians 4:16 (NIV) says, "For the Lord himself will come down from heaven . . . with the trumpet call of God." Lots of evangelicals interpret this to mean a trumpet sound will initiate the end of days. I'm not kidding when I say I've heard evangelicals claim that the "trumpet" mentioned in the Bible directly referenced Trump-Pence (because it *sounds* like trum-pet). This, of course, meant God chose Trump to save America, and therefore, every Christian should vote for him.

It sounds ridiculous, but I bought into some of these theories, fully convinced that we were living in the last days and the rapture would happen at any moment. There were even bumper stickers on cars in our church parking lot that said, IN CASE OF RAPTURE THIS CAR WILL BE UNMANNED—a warning to the heathens on the highway that they were following a destined-to-disappear-at-any-moment righteous one.

For those who didn't grow up believing in the rapture, perhaps now would be a good time to explain. The rapture, based on selectively interpreted passages from the Bible (mostly Paul's first letter to the Thessalonians) is the belief that Jesus Christ will return to the sky one day and every single Christian alive will meet him in the air to go with him to heaven without having to die. This event will trigger the remaining end times events, which we interpreted from the book of Revelation. Rapture theology, sometimes called dispensational premillennialism, also believes that there will be signs of Biblical prophecy being fulfilled leading up to the rapture, so Christians can know when the end is near.

We've already discussed wars as a sign, but other signs in Matthew 24 include false teachers (liberal pastors, anyone?), natural disasters (climate change who?), increased wickedness (Disney putting queer characters in movies—hello!), Christian persecution (pandemic shutdowns weren't actually about saving lives but closing churches!), and preaching the gospel—all of which are super vague and why every generation thinks they're in the last days.

Of course, with so many people instantaneously disappearing from the earth, the rapture will lead to mass chaos that will ultimately result in a One World Government, sometimes called the New World Order. The new governing body will be led by the Antichrist, who will also morph all beliefs into one worldwide religion. This starts the Great Tribulation, a seven-year period that starts off with peace on earth but halfway through turns into wars, famine, and utter despair.

Even though my church was pre-trib (meaning we believed the rapture would occur *before* the tribulation), there were other evangelicals who thought the rapture would happen mid-trib or post-trib (this meant believing Christians would remain for part, if not all, of the tribulation). So we had to be aware of signs of the tribulation, too, just in case we were wrong (although we had great concerns about the well-being of post-tribbers—major red flag).

Being on guard about this future one-world government made us very wary of countries coming together in a meaningful way. The United Nations, for obvious reasons, was always suspect. Then again, it probably didn't help that the Left Behind series turned a former head of the UN into the Antichrist.[2] Sure, the UN purported to promote "peace, dignity, and equality on a healthy planet,"[3] but we knew what they were really up to.

I remember being mad at the UN for condemning the US-led war in Iraq. I even went on a United Nations rant in my throw-lemons-at-liberals journal, saying the UN was full of people who hated Americans and "probably rejoiced when our towers went down."

I know. Yikes. But not liking the UN is par for the course for Christian Nationalists and I was just following suit. Some of that dislike can show up in ridiculous ways.

In 2021, the UN put up a statue in New York that they called "a guardian for international peace and security," and many evangelicals went haywire over it. It looked like a cross between a jaguar and an eagle, which had many Christians believing it could be the end times beast mentioned in Daniel 7 and Revelation 13. Some even cited 1 Thessalonians 5:3 (NASB) as proof: "While they are saying, 'Peace and safety!' then sudden destruction will come upon them . . ."[4]

I cannot even begin to describe the mind warp you experience when you can't root for peace. While we all said we wanted peace, too much peace was suspicious. *Is this person calling for world peace actually the Antichrist? Is the Great Tribulation about to start?* It's all fun and games until Christian Nationalism sneaks in and convinces you to jeopardize Middle East peace talks.

Believing all this to be absolute truth does a number on your psyche—especially when you're a kid.

I remember standing in the kitchen with my brothers one day when I was young.

"Ten . . . nine . . . eight . . ." we counted down as we stared out the kitchen window of our Texas ranch-style home. It was a sunny spring morning with few clouds in the sky. Three cereal bowls with leftover milk sat on the table as our mom was getting our schoolbooks out for the day.

"Seven . . . six . . . five . . ." I was eight years old, and my twin brothers were a year-and-a-half younger than me. We were applying the childlike faith we'd heard encouraged from the pulpit.

"Four . . . three . . . two . . . one . . ." Our excitement was palpable. We closed our eyes and held our breath in anticipation. We knew that Jesus could come back at any moment and were hopeful we were about to hear that trumpet sound and see him appear in the clouds.

"Zero . . ." We opened our eyes.

Nothing happened.

"Let's do it again. We must've had our timing off," I said. We counted down from ten again. We repeated this several more times, only to be disappointed.

Jesus didn't come back that day. Nevertheless, the rapture remained an elusive but ever-present possibility. Each day we stayed eager, looking to the sky in between schoolwork and playing Super Nintendo. We knew all the signs were pointing to Christ's imminent return—hurricanes, wars, the wickedness of Super Bowl halftime shows, the chaos of the approaching Y2K. Well, that's at least what the adults at church claimed, and we had no reason to think otherwise.

We were genuinely excited for Jesus to come back. It was our "blessed hope." That was what we heard it called from the pulpit (reciting Titus 2:13). The rapture meant skipping death and going straight to live with Jesus in heaven—our forever home.

Before my brothers and I would sing in church, our dad let us take turns saying something into the microphone. One of our favorites was to ask the congregation, "Are you ready for the rapture?" This question always prompted cheers and "Amens" from the audience. Because there's nothing cuter than toddlers talking about impending doom.

When the *Left Behind: The Kids* book series came out in 1998, I couldn't read them fast enough. My parents wouldn't let me have the adult versions, so I devoured these young adult rapture novels. The story gripped me intensely because I believed each page was not really a work of fiction but a foretelling of a reality to come. As the movies later claimed, it was a true story that just hadn't happened yet.

The kids' books didn't hold back, and they included all the typical premillennial dispensationalism tropes: Christians disappearing and leaving a pile of clothes behind (because supposedly only our bodies go to heaven, meaning it would be *naked* Christians meeting Jesus in the air—a scary thought in itself if you're a purity culture baby), the Mark of the Beast, people refusing that Mark to follow Jesus, underground churches, Christian persecution, deaths by guillotine, and of course, the Antichrist himself. You know, normal childhood stuff.

We also had all the rapture films. When my parents were young, they had *A Thief in the Night* to terrify them. While I don't have specific memories of that film personally, I wasn't short of Christian apocalyptic media. My family and I watched just about every single low-budget, straight-to-VHS rapture movie that was ever released.

These films gave me vivid dreams. At eleven, I'd close my eyes and find myself secretly trying to convince people to refuse the Mark of the Beast lest they damn their soul to hell for eternity. Wearing all black clothing that hid my forehead and wrists, I'd be sent on underground missions to witness to as many people as I could until I got caught. Then I would boldly shout "Jesus can save you" as the guillotine blade crashed into me. I would wake up both relieved that it was just a dream, and a bit unnerved at how real this dream *could* be one day. *Just stay a good, Christian girl, April...*

Sometimes a small part of me wished I *could* be left behind to take part in the Christian resistance fighting back. I could only imagine the rewards those end times warriors would get in heaven!

But I knew that wouldn't happen for me. It's not like I had committed any grievous sins as a child. I mean, sometimes I slightly elbowed my brothers when they were touching me in the back seat. And I said "butthead" once. But other than that, I had no reason to fear being left behind from the rapture.

Fast-forward to my early teenage years. One afternoon, I was peacefully enjoying my turn to use the family computer and our fancy dial-up internet. I used my time to chat on AOL Instant Messenger and flirt in the WWJD website chat room (yes, that was a thing, and yes, it was as awkward as it sounds). I was deep in the throes of evangelical sexting—aka a dude was telling me how many chairs he could stack at youth group.

Suddenly, I noticed the house was quiet. I couldn't remember the last time I'd heard anyone.

Rapture.

The thought appeared as quickly as I shook it away. I was a Christian; I couldn't be left behind. Those were the rules.

But you've been flirting. What if you thought about kissing that boy right before...

"Mom? Dad?" I shouted from the den.

No response.

I turned the rolling office chair toward the hallway and yelled for my brothers, "Matt? Andrew?"

Still nothing.

A slight panic. *There has to be a logical reason…* I reassured myself as I turned on my AIM Away Message and left the room. The message, obviously, consisted of a DC Talk quote followed by "*~*{<3BRB <3}*~*."

I entered the living room and called for my family again. Silence.

Maybe they went to the store and I just didn't hear them…

I opened the door to the garage. Both cars were still there. Now my heart was racing.

I started thinking through all the potential sins I committed that day. *When was the last time I prayed the sinner's prayer? Jesus, forgive me if I forgot…*

I walked into my parents' room. My mom's purse was on the dresser and a pile of folded clothes was on the bed—a clear sign of the rapture according to those Left Behind books.

Coincidence. Mom must've done laundry…

I walked to the front door and opened it.

"MOM?!? DAD?!? TIGER?!"

Not even my dog was responding. I didn't know the theology around pets being raptured, but I didn't find his absence comforting.

I picked up the pace, on the verge of a panic attack. I walked back inside and searched every room of the house thoroughly.

I had to give myself a pep talk to fight back the tears that were forming behind my eyes.

It's okay. You can refuse the Mark of the Beast. Death by guillotine will be quick and then eternity in heaven. You can do this…

I opened the door to the backyard and went outside.

How could you be so stupid? That boy isn't even that cute, and you know lust is the same as committing adultery…

I walked onto the golf course behind our house and looked in both directions. Still no sign of my family.

"MOOOOOOMMMMM!!! DAAAAADDD! MAATTTT!!??? ANDREWWWW??" I was shouting as loud as I could.

You can use Mom and Dad's credit cards for a while before the Mark of the Beast comes into play...get military food packs and supplies...there's that one shop...you can drive without a license under these circumstances...

I picked a direction and began to walk, shouting the entire way. I could hear my heart beating as a tear rolled down my cheek.

"God. Why would you leave me? You know I love you..." I prayed aloud.

I heard a dog bark in the distance. It sounded familiar.

"Tiger?!" I shouted, a twinge of hope rising in me.

I heard the bark again. I started running toward the sound and kept calling for my trusted miniature pinscher to come to me.

I finally saw Tiger running toward me from around the curve. Relief rushed through me as I spotted my family behind him. They were on a leisurely stroll, blissfully unaware of the torment I'd endured for the last twenty minutes.

I felt like an idiot, but I played it off. I didn't tell them that I thought they had been raptured without me. That would only make my dad ask what sins were in my life that would make me think I could be left behind. I didn't have the energy. I was still recovering from my plans to be a teenage martyr and lose my head for Jesus. (Christians being decapitated after the rapture is another key part in those darn books.)

We walked back to our home, and I quietly snuck back into my room and begged God to forgive my sins...just in case.

My feelings about Jesus' return fluctuated between excitement and dread, depending on the day. I yearned for the rapture when life was hard. I remember praying for Christ to come back every day in seventh grade when my basketball coaches made our lives a living heck by making us run until we puked.

But when those teenage hormones kicked in, my prayers turned into asking God to hold off the rapture until after I could have sex. I didn't want to leave the world a virgin, but I also wasn't going to risk my soul by having premarital sex. The simple solution was just to ask Jesus to come back the night of my future wedding, right after consummating the marriage. And I said that prayer a lot...before immediately asking

God to forgive me for thinking of my own fleshly desires over his glorious return. But I still wanted sex, too. It was a confusing time.

When I was in high school, I remember looking in my Bible concordance for the word "rapture" and couldn't find it. Assuming user error, I asked my dad where in the Bible I could find the word "rapture." When he told me the word wasn't actually in there, I was confused. He explained that we get the word "rapture" from the Latin word *rapiemur*, meaning "to snatch" or be "caught up," and it is based on 1 Thessalonians 4:17 (KJ21):

> Then we who are alive and remain shall be caught up together with them in the clouds to meet the Lord in the air. And so shall we ever be with the Lord.

My dad also reminded me of all the end times prophecies in the Book of Revelation, specifically what to expect during the Great Tribulation, the rise of the Antichrist and what he will do. There are a few other verses scattered throughout the Bible that are used to push end times theology (such as Matthew 24:30–44, 1 Corinthians 15:51–53, Mark 13:32, Acts 1:7, Daniel 12:1–2, Luke 17:26–37, Philippians 3:20–21, and John 14:3).

I knew the verses and how to interpret them, but it was still hard for me to see the Left Behind narrative clearly spelled out in the Bible. But I shoved those thoughts down and continued to live as if the trumpet would sound any day. I believed the rapture was an essential part of the Christian faith and I couldn't falter.

It was only a few years ago that I actually looked up the history of the belief in the rapture and learned that it didn't become a widespread theology in Christianity until the nineteenth century. Most scholars credit the belief's origin to John Nelson Darby, an Anglo-Irish theologian, who began spreading the idea of our modern rapture belief in the 1830s.[5] Some reports say that he based the idea on a vision from a fifteen-year-old girl named Margaret MacDonald.[6]

I was shocked. The way it was talked about in church, I fully believed the pre-trib rapture was a foundational belief of Christianity, right next to the Resurrection and the Virgin Mary. But when I learned the whole idea came from an 1800s British preacher and possibly a young girl's odd dream, I finally moved on from this anxiety-inducing theology. Still, it's hard to let go. Even now, if it gets too quiet in my house, my first thought is that I've been left behind.

Despite its murky history, the rapture isn't just some obscure radical belief we're talking about here. This is pretty mainstream. A 2022 Pew Research study found that 55% of all US adults believe Jesus will return to earth one day and 63% of Protestant evangelicals believe we are currently in the end times.[7] It is a real and widely held belief that affects both our country and our international relations.

See, one of the core tenets of the premillennial rapture belief is that Israel must occupy all of God's promised land before Jesus can come back.[8] This was just one of several requirements for the return of Christ, at least as imagined by author Hal Lindsey in his 1970 book *The Late Great Planet Earth*. In this book, which sold more in the United States than any other nonfiction title in the 1970s, Lindsey argues that three things will occur before Jesus comes back: The Jews will occupy Palestine, they will take back the sacred sites of Jerusalem, and they will rebuild Solomon's temple at its original location.

These beliefs have shaped our nation's international politics, including our alliance with Israel and against Palestine. They also explain why, in 2018, Donald Trump, probably at the urging of his evangelical advisers, moved the US diplomatic embassy from Tel Aviv to Jerusalem.[9] Unsurprisingly, evangelicals loudly praised the move, seeing it as an official acknowledgment of Israel's ownership, despite Palestinians' claims to the land. Let's usher in the end times!

Pastor Robert Jeffress of First Baptist Church in Dallas prayed at the new embassy in Jerusalem, saying that Trump was the one who "stands on the right side of you, O God, when it comes to Israel."[10] There were conveniently zero prayers or mention of the fifty Palestinians who died in the violent protests and unrest this move caused in the region.[11]

All of this was taken to the next level when, in the fall of 2023, Israel declared war on Palestine after Hamas, a Palestinian terrorist organization, attacked Israel. Christian Nationalists were quick to rally behind Israel. The reason for this is twofold: Evangelicals believe God will bless those who stand with Israel based on Scripture. After all, Numbers 24:9 (GNT) says, "Whoever blesses Israel will be blessed." The second reason is the end times belief that all of Israel must be under Jewish occupation before Jesus can come back.

The Israeli attacks that killed thousands of innocent Palestinian children in Gaza didn't sway evangelical support of Israel. Texas megachurch pastor John Hagee called for American intervention in supporting Israel.[12] Tennessee Pastor Greg Locke said he hoped the war would "usher in the coming of Jesus," and said, "Israel should make the Gaza Strip a parking lot by this time next week."[13] Georgia Pastor Wayne J. Edwards wrote in a church blog, "Israel's enemies do not recognize that God has given that land to the Jews, and that the Jews must be in the land for the final end-time prophecies to be fulfilled." And despite a rising death toll of innocent lives, Edwards ended his blog with "Rejoice! The King is coming!"[14]

Real. Life. Consequences.

In other words, end times theology isn't just for scaring the crap out of children anymore. It's actually influencing international policy and major world events, leading to the slaughter of thousands of innocent lives. And it's being championed and cheered on by Christians in an effort to *accelerate the end of the world.*

This is, needless to say, dangerous. Deadly. When politicians ignore sociopolitical realities in favor of fulfilling Biblical prophecy that's embraced by only a small part of the population, there are tragic consequences for other religions and people groups. It's one thing to read the Left Behind series as a community group in church. It's another thing entirely to use the fictional horror story as a bellwether for real foreign policy decisions.

Let me be clear: Believing in the rapture does not make someone a

Christian Nationalist. But I also want to be clear that the movement uses end times eschatology to manipulate its base into cheering on harmful foreign policy in the hopes of fulfilling Biblical prophecy, fighting against world peace in favor of American independence, and remaining fearful of whatever villain they can compare to Revelation bad guys.

It's bad enough that Christian Nationalism affects American policy. But the influence it has on worldwide political events makes it even more dangerous. And we need to be paying attention to it.

And I would go into more detail, but I oddly just heard a trumpet sound, so I'm going to go check and make sure everything's oka—

Just kidding. The rapture didn't happen. But I'm calling my therapist.

CHAPTER 9

Grandma Is Watching: Eternal Fearmongering

When I wasn't concerned about being sucked up naked into the sky before I could have married sex, or—equally bad, being left behind—I had plenty of other fears to fill my mind.

Christian Nationalism doesn't have to fabricate new fears to manipulate evangelicals into its throes. There are plenty of scary ideas built into the belief system that the ideology uses for its own gain. We already discussed the end times, but there's another deeply evangelical belief that is even more terrifying: eternity.

Did you immediately think of hell? Yeah, me too. But the eternal fears go beyond just burning alive forever. I had weird fears about heaven, too.

It's all "Faith over fear!" until you're told that every moment of your life is being secretly recorded and you will have to watch it back in front of all your loved ones and Jesus in heaven one day. That sounds more like hell, honestly.

When I was around thirteen, I remember taking a shower when that intrusive, yet familiar thought popped into my head. *When I get to heaven, I'll rewatch my entire life with all my loved ones. What if my grandparents watch this exact moment? And I'm naked?*

Suddenly very aware of the R-rating I was giving my life movie, I tried to wash myself modestly. I wasn't sure if heaven's films included censor bars or not, but I wasn't taking chances. The task of *not* looking naked while *being* naked proved quite difficult. If anyone in my "cloud of witnesses" (Hebrews 12:1 ESV) was watching, I'm sure they got a good chuckle at my ridiculous attempt.

I don't know exactly where this belief originated because, for the life of me, I can't find it in the Bible. But my spouse, Beecher, who was brought up Baptist, also believed that every moment of their life would be replayed in front of everyone they knew. As a kid, Beecher would wink at corners of the rooms, assuming that was where heaven's hidden cameras were recording. While I thought my life film was rated R, Beecher's life movie would play out more like an episode of *The Office*.

I wanted to find out the origins of this strange idea, so I did the obvious thing. I made a TikTok about it. It was met with hundreds of comments from people who believed this same weird idea, too. One viewer pointed out a Chick Tract called *This Was Your Life* that was originally published in 1964. It all started coming back to me.

For reference, Chick Tracts were a brand of gospel tracts. These were small proselytizing pamphlets that you could give to people to try and save their eternal souls without really having to talk to them. Just hand and scram.

This Was Your Life tells the story of a man who dies and wakes up naked in the spiritual realm (again, clothes don't make it there for some reason), where an angel flies him away to face his Judgment Day in heaven. The man pleads with the angel, "I've lived a real good life! I was no different than anyone else!" The angel responds with "*Everything* has been recorded!"[1]

The comic then shows a large screen in what appears to be a dark theater under the stars where everyone views this person's life, both public and private moments, from birth to death. At one point the man says, "I remember doing that—but no one saw me!" It even shows him going to church before he takes his final breath and the film fades to black. Then a faceless figure appears in heaven and says, "Open the Book of Life!" The angel replies, "His name does not appear, Lord!" and then the man is cast into an eternity of "everlasting fire."

The next page has bold letters that read, "THIS CAN BE YOUR LIFE!" before a second version of the story appears where we watch the man repent of his sins before he dies and is sent to heaven instead. Nothing like a good old-fashioned hell scare in the form of a Sunday morning comic strip to convince people of 24/7 heavenly surveillance to save souls.

This strange belief also showed up in a song released by Amy Grant in 1979 called "Father's Eyes." Verse 2 references Judgment Day and how everything we've done will be shown, "good and bad, they'll all be had, to see by everyone."

Regardless of where the idea originated, it became a widespread belief somehow. This was a special kind of post-death anxiety. So many different afterlife fears to deal with: eternity in hell, missing the rapture, and the idea that everything I did would one day be displayed for Jesus *and* my grandparents to see. I had plenty of reasons to be a good girl. Call me Miss Goody Two-shoes, but I was not going to risk disappointing my Nanny and Bobo in the afterlife.

I was a good kid, and yet I was still afraid.

One of the recurring lessons we church kids learned was that lying was a sin. "Even a simple fib is a sin that makes you worthy of hell," the green worm puppet said to the crowd of kids at Sunday school. The push to be good and avoid sinning was reinforced through all sorts of Christian kid shows: a man in purple-and-gold tights called Bibleman, a giant singing songbook with a human face named Psalty and his creepy Pennywise-looking dog named Blooper, an old man named Mr. Whittaker who provided *Adventures in Odyssey*, a man with a talking doughnut who taught us that God's love could fill our doughnut-sized heart holes, talking vegetables... the list of odd spokespeople-things for righteousness goes on and on.

But even with happy songs that focused on God's love, there was still an underlying message that came through: If we sinned right before getting hit by a bus and died before asking for forgiveness, we'd probably be doomed.

To this day, I have a very specific fear of being hit by a bus. That seemed to be the death of choice in kids' church and youth camps. Sometimes they talked about dying in your sleep, but honestly, that one didn't sound so bad. At least I'd have the chance to ask for forgiveness during my bedtime prayers. But the bus thing—you couldn't predict that.

Even though we were saved by grace and had the assurance of salvation, we didn't believe in eternal security like those silly Baptists. While it was emphasized we shouldn't worry about losing our salvation on small sins, we were taught that we should try our best not to sin *just in case* unrepented sins cannonballed us into the lake of fire. "Backsliding" is a word for a reason.

Not worrying about it was easier said than done. That eternity of weeping and gnashing teeth didn't sound like something I could just be chill about.

To show you how deeply this thought process affected us as kids, I'll share this horrifying piece of information: At six years old, my brother Andrew started saying "I think" after every sentence. When we asked him why, he explained that he did it *just in case* he was accidentally lying and died before he could ask for forgiveness. "I think" was his cover phrase so he was always protected from eternal damnation.

Matt and I thought this was funny and messed with him. We asked him questions like "What's your name?" and "Are you a dog?" just to giggle about his hesitant answers. But now, looking back, I see how screwed up this was, and I understand just how troubled we all were about this ever-looming, future destination.

But it did sometimes make witnessing easier.

"You need Jesus in your heart," six-year-old me said to my slightly older neighbor friend.

"Why?" she asked.

"Because if you don't, you'll go to hell," I said matter-of-factly.

"Oh, okay." She agreed and prayed right there. It was the easiest conversion of my life.

If a little prayer is all it takes to avoid eternal damnation, then it makes complete sense to just say it. Get that assurance of salvation, girlfriend!

But if we ever did feel secure in our salvation, there was always a church play or event to put the fear of God right back into us.

One time, our church hosted the play *Heaven's Gates and Hell's Flames*, a touring production put on by Reality Outreach Ministries.

Just imagine a Christian version of the *Final Destination* movie franchise and you get pretty darn close to the narrative. It depicts people from all walks of life dying in various ways. It then veers off into stories where each person is taken to the gates of heaven to receive judgment—either heaven with Jesus or traumatically going to hell.

When our church did it, we had actors from our congregation perform. One of these actors was an older teenage girl I looked up to. She played a partying teen who died suddenly. Her body was severely bloodied (the image still lives rent-free in my head) and her screams of terror as demons maniacally dragged her to hell gave me nightmares for a long time. I couldn't look at her at church for a while without seeing the horrified look on her melting, red corn-syruped face.

I remember another scene where a family was in a car crash, and everyone went to hell except one girl. She was a Christian who had tried to convert her family to no avail. During their judgment, she bawled in horror as her family members were judged and sent to hell. She ran into Jesus' arms crying, the lights shone bright, and angels started singing in celebration as Jesus wiped away her tears. "He will wipe away every tear from their eyes," was recited from Revelation 21:4 (ESV) during the altar call. The girl danced joyfully as she entered heaven's gates.

Talk about a mood swing. Even back then this didn't sit well with me. I just couldn't imagine being that happy after my family was ripped away from me and sent to hell, even if Jesus used his tear-free happy magic.

If all of this sounds unreal, it's not. You can go see it for yourself. Horrifyingly, micro-budget productions of this play are still put on by enthusiastic church volunteers around the country.[2]

The upshot here is that whether I was preparing for the rapture, repeatedly answering the altar call for extra assurance of salvation, or worrying about my heavenly life movie revealing that time I was sixteen and snuck into an R-rated movie so I could watch my crush, Orlando Bloom, I learned that fear generally works to keep people in line. (Well, it does if your crush is not involved.)

When people are afraid, they are more easily controlled, especially when you also offer a solution that can eradicate their fear. I've seen first-hand how the dread of hell is used not only to convert people but to keep us in line.

I remember having questions growing up about certain aspects of the Bible, especially hell. Why does God send good people to hell? What if a kid isn't saved? Where do aborted babies go? Where would I go if I asked forgiveness for my future sins and then stole a cookie and then immediately died? You know, the typical musings of a child.

My Sunday school teachers, kids' pastors, and even my dad would answer my questions, citing Scripture that sometimes satisfied me, but often led to more questions.

But if I asked too many questions, I would be gently warned, "Careful. Too many questions lead to doubt. Doubt leads to sin. Sin leads to backsliding, and next thing you know, you wake up one day an atheist and go to hell."

I didn't want my curiosity to lead me down the infamous slippery slope, so I trained myself to shove down whatever didn't have an answer and cling to the statement "God works in mysterious ways." When in doubt, just believe harder.

Don't ask questions. Stay in line. Fear what we say to fear.

Using fear to motivate believers is not new, of course. Some of the greatest revivals North America has ever seen came from using the idea of hell. The Great Awakening occurred in the 1700s when a preacher named Jonathan Edwards gave a sermon titled "Sinners in the Hands of an Angry God." Most of Edwards's sermons until that point had been focused on the love and sovereignty of God.[3] Yet it wasn't until he gave a sermon comparing us to spiders being held over an open fire that his message had such a national and historical impact.[4]

In a little less doom and gloom fashion, the late Reverend Billy Graham put the fate of people's afterlife front and center. As already discussed, Graham was known for his crusades to save souls in stadiums and on televisions around the world. On the website of Graham's own *Decision Magazine* is a dedicated page called "Billy Graham's Eternal Legacy" with a subheading that reads, "Testimonies of souls saved from hell."[5]

Keeping it in the family, Billy's son Franklin Graham has used the realities of hell as a reason to rally his followers. In May 2023, Franklin spoke at the National Religious Broadcasters International Christian Media Convention and warned the audience that "every demon from hell" has been "turned loose" on society, leading to a cancel culture that wants to "destroy Christian organizations."[6] He has also said, "Hell is a very real place that will be the eternal destination of souls who reject the forgiveness and salvation that a loving God offers us through His Son, Jesus Christ."[7]

Now, if you believe in a literal hell, saving souls from it seems like a noble cause. But Franklin Graham has also been very politically active and a vocal Trump supporter. In 2016 on his *Decision America* national tour, he encouraged attendees to decide to accept Christ (eternal salvation from the bad place) and also make a decision to "vote Biblically."[8] We all know what that means, but if there was any doubt, Graham said he believed "God showed up" in 2016 after Trump won the election.[9]

Here's the point: If you believe that Satan and his demons are on the prowl to deceive people through any means—including godless Democrats—so he can imprison them in hell for all eternity, then voting becomes about more than just politics. It's not just about the soul of America but the souls of Americans.

This was the main reason my dad wanted America to turn back to God. His entire purpose in life was to tell people about Jesus so they could have eternal salvation. Yes, we wanted America to be a Christian nation, but only because it would make it easier to spread the gospel message and save more souls. It's why my dad wrote *America Say Jesus*—to inspire other Christians to say "Jesus" more often and call on government officials to do the same. He wrote, "If the devil can keep Christians from saying 'Jesus,' the unsaved world will stay lost. Souls will keep going to hell . . ."[10]

When you believe everyone who doesn't believe in Jesus is going to hell (which is a core belief for most American evangelicals), there's an urgency to speak the truth that will save them. And if literal demons from hell are infiltrating all aspects of society to shut Christians up and deceive the masses into burning forever? Well, what is more important than stopping that? That's when you get more forceful and move beyond church walls into governmental chambers.

Belief in hell is another tenet of evangelicalism that Christian Nationalism exploits for its own gain. The threat of hell is another tactic of the movement. While preachers and ministers can be very overt with this fear tactic, Christian Nationalist politicians are more pragmatic about it. They can't say things like "turn or burn" so they use less obvious language like "turn America back to God."

That teenage girl is convinced getting an abortion is just women's health care? That's a lie from Satan! We can't convince her abortion is a sin that will lead her to hell, so we better ban abortion altogether! To save babies and souls!

Satan is making countless people think they're gay and they're not listening to our warnings?! Well, we must ban gay marriage, then. Take away their choice to sin and they're more likely to get saved!

That's the logic behind it. As someone who heard and believed it for most of my life, I can tell you it was convincing. While back in my dad's day, infiltrating the government was about turning America back to God to save souls for eternity, Christian Nationalism today has taken the Republican-Evangelical union and made it almost exclusively about the here and now to take dominion over the earth. Today's Christian Nationalism has a driving goal of making the United States a Christian-run nation in *this* life, the afterlife an afterthought.

But hell still makes for a great threat, one that is often used in our national dialogue. In one charming example, Pastor Greg Locke, a known Trump prophet, said that "CNN will burn in hell with the rest of the cowards" for doing a story on him telling his congregation not to get the COVID-19 vaccine or wear a mask during the pandemic.[11]

In December 2021, Jenna Ellis, a former legal adviser to then-President Donald Trump and one of the people who pled guilty in the Georgia election interference case, tweeted: "Revelation 21. God lists COWARDS first as among those who will be cast into the lake of fire for eternity. Fear God rather than men. Do not fear the petty tyrants. I hope our Supreme Court is not full of cowards."[12] She saw the SCOTUS 2021–2022 term as a test to see "whether the Court is truly conservative."[13] Ellis brought hell up again in 2022 when she tweeted, "If you don't believe God is real or hell is a literal place, why are you so outraged that Christians believe people who haven't repented and aren't saved will spend eternity in damnation and separation from God? Because you know the Truth and want to deny consequences for sin."[14]

Sean Feucht used the threat of hell as justification for the large worship events he held during the pandemic. "I refuse to let a virus with a 99% survival rate keep me from plundering hell to populate heaven!" Feucht posted in January 2021.[15]

This way of thinking is a total disregard for Luke 15, the parable Jesus told of the lost sheep, where the shepherd leaves the ninety-nine to save the one. Thank goodness for that one sheep that Feucht wasn't his shepherd.

Hell is also used as a fallback excuse. When accused of being mean or causing harm, Christian Nationalists often use the afterlife as the justification.

In October 2022, Megan Basham, author and reporter for *The Daily Wire*, tweeted, "I make no apologies for mocking people who claim the name of Christ but have pronouns in their bio."[16] When people pushed back, she claimed the "only-gentle, only-soft Christ is a myth, perpetuated to allow wolves to come into church and lead some to Hell."[17]

I know this strategy is real because I have also used hell as a fallback excuse. I remember getting into a debate in college about politics and calling Democrats a slew of insults in the argument. My left-leaning friend said, "April, how can you say such mean things about people God wants us to love?"

"Telling the truth is love! My words are nothing compared to the torture people will get in hell. If I can wake one person up and save them, it's all worth it!"

My friend just sighed, and we moved on. I thought I was merely being righteously indignant, but as I look back now, it's clear to me that I was being something else entirely.

When people pushed back against me for saying or doing things that they found disparaging, I'd ask myself, "Wouldn't they rather have me hurt their feelings than have their flesh melt off for all of eternity?"

One time in an online discussion post with other college students in my class, I wrote, "Being soft on sin sends people to hell. I'd rather be mean and save souls than be kind and enable eternally damning sin."

In other words, the eternal ends justified the bullying means. It's hard to argue with someone who says their abrasiveness is just "tough love" meant to save people from never-ending excruciating pain.

The threat of hell is not at the forefront of today's Christian Nationalism, but it would be a mistake to overlook it. It's there quietly beneath the surface, influencing the decisions being made at the highest levels of government. It's especially scary when you look at devout Baptist Mike Johnson, who became Speaker of the House in 2023. Albert Mohler, president of Southern Baptist Theological Seminary, said "For Southern Baptists, it's like winning the lottery," about Johnson becoming Speaker.[18] Would they be this giddy if Johnson was just going to objectively pass laws and not let his staunch, Bible-believing worldview decide policy? Probably not.

Johnson has worked closely with Pastor Jim Garlow, a proponent of the Seven Mountain Mandate, whom Johnson said has "been a profound influence" on his life.[19] A few weeks before becoming Speaker, Johnson was on a web show with Garlow and lamented that America's culture was "depraved." Some of the evidence he cited for this was people not attending church and the rise of LGBTQ youth. Johnson then prayed on the show, saying, "We repent of our sins individually and collectively and we ask that you not give up on our nation, not give us the judgment that we clearly deserve."[20] He doesn't need to say hell for us to understand what ultimate judgment he's talking about.

Johnson is a believer through and through. It's eerie listening to him, honestly, because he reminds me of my dad. Even the tears Johnson dropped during his prayer on that same web show reminded me of how my dad often cried in prayer from the pulpit.[21]

Like my dad, I believe Johnson genuinely believes in a high calling to save America.

But my dad was just a preacher. Johnson is second in line to the Presidency of the United States.

Whether belief in hell is used as a threat to keep followers in line or as motivation to push politicians and preachers to save America from Satan's depravity, it's a useful tool for Christian Nationalism. The fear of going to hell kept me inside Christian Nationalism when I really should have left. It allowed me to feel good about doing un-Christlike things, like fighting to take rights away from people I deemed sinful.

Christian Nationalists can use the need for eternal salvation to shut down anyone who doubts their methods. Saving people from hell is persuasive and can convince nonpolitical Christians to stay quiet in the face of more aggressive Nationalists.

If only they knew their grandma was watching. *wink*

CHAPTER 10

Antifa Super Soldiers: Demonizing Enemies

A miracle happened in 1988.

A couple had been trying for ten years to have children to no avail. The wife had only half an ovary and doctors told her she would probably never conceive. But that year, she gave birth to a 9-pound, 13-ounce baby girl.

"Wow, a miracle baby," people exclaimed everywhere they went.

"Just imagine the great things this girl will do for God!"

And as the little girl grew, she seemed to do just that.

When she was two, she walked up onstage where her daddy was preaching and asked to sing, which began her singing career in churches all over the world.

As she grew, she started speaking up for Jesus, to anyone who would listen.

No part of her life was excluded from sharing the gospel, including dating. She even gave one non-Christian guy a Bible with his name on it as a parting breakup gift (since they obviously couldn't be unequally yoked).

She worked in Christian media and spread the gospel professionally. She married a Christian, had two Christian babies whom they had dedicated to God, and continued going to church, where she led worship.

She had everything going for her as a godly Christian woman.

Until one day, she voted for a Democrat, became a false prophet, and started being used by Satan to take thousands of souls to hell with her. Guess she was never really a Christian to begin with . . . just a really convincing actor for the first thirty years of her life.

This is my story. Kinda. All that evangelical street cred I earned was flushed down the toilet. Gone the moment I didn't vote red.

Any high-control group has tactics to keep people inside and to stop outsiders from exposing the group's weak points. I stayed in Christian Nationalism for far longer than I should have because the media I consumed was controlled, conspiracy theories were pushed as facts, end times eschatology was manipulated, and fear of eternity was weaponized.

Another tactic that's often employed by those embroiled in Christian Nationalism is demonizing enemies. Anyone who disagrees with you was obviously sent straight from the devil himself. Makes it easy.

Part of this, to be fair, is human nature. When your favorite sports team loses, it's easy to villainize the other side. They played dirty. They had the refs on their side. They're a bunch of cheaters. Anything but admit that your side just didn't play well.

Like in 2006, when my Dallas Mavericks lost to the Miami Heat in the NBA Finals. We were living in South Florida at the time, surrounded by obnoxious Heat fans who were unwilling to admit how terrible the refs were. So the day after the Heat won it all, my brothers and I wore homemade shirts to youth group that said, MAVS FANS FOR LIFE. We were jeered at all night, but I quipped back, "We know who the real champs are! Easy to win with the refs on your side!"

Tensions were high between us MFFLers and our Florida friends that night, but we all moved on the next week. No harm, no foul.

But when you're talking about people, and not sports teams, this tactic can have dire consequences.

For instance, when I was growing up, we had plenty of ways to explain what happened whenever somebody left the church:

- "She fell for Satan's trap."
- "He is backsliding away from God."

- "They just want to have sex."
- "They couldn't handle Biblical truth."
- "She has a Jezebel spirit."
- "He's under demonic influence."

The reasons posited always blamed the person who left so we never had to look inward. We were always good, and they were always bad. No problems here.

"Where has Stacey been?" my friend asked me in youth group when I was fourteen.

"Oh, I heard her family started going to a *Methodist* church," I said, rolling my eyes.

"Ew, Methodist? She did always seem lukewarm," my friend replied.

"Totally. Not everyone has what it takes to be all in for Jesus," I said confidently.

I'm sure that family leaving had nothing to do with me being a Judgy McJudgerface.

Or the time another girl in the youth group stopped coming to church. Her parents still came, though, with "unspoken" prayer requests for her. We were convinced she had joined a satanic cult because why else would she just . . . stop coming to our perfect church?

Turns out, she just wanted her Wednesday nights free. She claimed it was for dance practice. We knew that was code for witches' coven meetings.

All of which made it a shock to the system when *I* was suddenly the one being demonized. It was weird being told to repent for doing something I believed was Holy Spirit led. Let me explain.

It was the summer of 2020 in the town of Cleveland, Tennessee, where I lived at the time. A student from the local Christian college started a petition to move the Confederate statue that was situated in the center of downtown to a local museum.

Leading up to this summer, my eyes had been quietly opening to the reality of systemic racism. I'm ashamed to say that, at one point, I was firmly in the "All Lives Matter" camp. Though I had been slowly educating myself, I didn't feel comfortable speaking up.

But when I watched that cop's knee on George Floyd's neck, I could no longer be silent.[1] My privileged blinders finally fell off. It was a moment where I *knew* silence was wrong. I *knew* I had been on the wrong side. I *knew* I had to do something. I just had no idea what.

I started posting on social media, but that still didn't feel like enough. So when "Black Lives Matter" protests began in my hometown, I decided to put my words into action.

The closest thing to a protest I had ever participated in was Jesus Marches with my family growing up. These were walks put on by local churches. We marched in the streets holding Christian signs and handed out gospel tracts to people we passed. We rarely got any pushback for our Jesus Marches and often had police escorts. I had never been to a *real* protest before, so I was a bit anxious.

I asked my conservative mom to join me. To my surprise, she said yes. Our protest was aimed at petitioning the city to move a large Confederate statue to a local museum; my mom's sign said, HUMANITY > A STATUE, while I had simply written BLACK LIVES MATTER on mine.

Freshly inked signs in hand, we drove to the protest location in our small downtown.

We walked to the median in the middle of the busy street where the Confederate statue stood tall. The organizers informed us that there was a strict no-engagement policy, which meant this was a silent demonstration. We could not respond if we were addressed by counterprotesters or those driving by.

That night, we were screamed at, cussed out, flipped off, and called all sorts of names by those driving by. One elderly White woman even handed us a gospel tract out of her car window, beckoning us to repent. I suppose, in her mind, there was no way we could be Christians, though both of us had devoted our lives to ministry.

"Motherf*ckers! Get out of our town or else!" shouted a White man in a pickup truck.

By the end of that night, I was inspired to return, but I was afraid the threats had scared my reserved mom away. Once again, she surprised me when she said, "Let me know if you go back. I want to join."

And we did, coming back almost nightly for the rest of the summer.

When local conservatives (which was most people who lived in Cleveland, Tennessee) started seeing a diverse group protesting the existence of their suddenly beloved historical statue, they showed up to that same median to protest our protest. They even started a Facebook group called *Save Our Town*. For safety reasons, we started protesting across the street from the statue.

"Is it worth dying for?!" shouted a tall, large White man waving an American flag. "Which of you chicken sh*ts is going to come over here first? I can take all y'all!" he said as he stomped back and forth beside the Confederate statue, an American flag wrapped around his neck like a scarf.

When we didn't take the bait, he tried a different approach. "As long as Trump is for Jesus, I'm for Jesus," he declared. *Who said anything about Jesus?* I thought. *Or Trump?* Several other people stood by him, yelling their own takes on the situation.

Another man with a patchy gray-and-black beard, wearing a Confederate bandanna and holding a nubby tree branch he'd tied an American flag to, shouted, "Are you willing to spill my blood?!"

Their threats were met with silence, but that didn't stop them from continuing.

Sometimes the counterprotestors would blast "Yankee Doodle Dandy" or other patriotic tunes to try and drown out the MLK speeches we sometimes played over our loudspeaker. One time, a lady walked up and down the street yelling into a Chuck E. Cheese plastic toy microphone. Another time, after calling us anti-American communists, they tried to sing "God Bless America" *at* us. "Tried" being the keyword here, as many chose different starting notes and beats for the performance.

It might have been a funny scene if it weren't for the power that stood among them: current and former elected officials, pastors, and other leaders of the community. Each night, they displayed several different flags: BLUE LIVES MATTER, TRUMP 2020, MAGA, DON'T TREAD ON ME, and good old-fashioned American flags. Clearly in their eyes, the United States would be on the side of the Confederate statue—you know, the group that fought *against* the United States in the Civil War.

These community leaders who protested our demonstration refused to listen to our position: that a Confederate statue representing slave owners should be in a museum, where it could be properly contextualized, not celebrated in a place of honor. Instead, they decided to make it about *their* rights, *their* monument, and *their* town, all of which we were allegedly trying to destroy.

Another night, a local Baptist preacher shouted a sermon at us with lines like, "Do you know what color sin is—ha? Sin is resembled as black!" Another pastor with him repeatedly shouted "Amen" to the street sermon, which would go viral. The preacher later defended his words on Facebook Live, claiming that he couldn't be racist because of the Holy Spirit dwelling in him.

It was infuriating how effortlessly the counterprotesters intertwined Christianity into their cause to defend a Confederate statue. "We're the examples of good Christians over here," yelled the man who had previously bragged about his ability to fight us.

One man, who showed up most nights with his extra-long pole that featured double flags (BLUE LIVES MATTER and an American flag), tried to give us a history lesson on how Confederates were good people who "treated slaves well." He would interject little quips throughout like, "I keep hearing about this White privilege; man, where do I sign up?"

At least once an evening, we would kneel silently for eight minutes and forty-six seconds to honor George Floyd and the many beautiful Black souls who had been needlessly killed before him.

Seeing the racism in my community on full display was shocking, and I wasn't really even on the receiving end. I was simply standing beside Black and Brown people, and even so, it was dehumanizing. You know who wasn't shocked? The Black and Brown people around me.

My naivety and privilege as a White person had kept me blind to it for most of my life, but they had felt it all along. Suddenly, I could no longer deny how tangible and real racism was. I knew that what I was feeling as a White woman was only a fraction of a fraction of a fraction of what People of Color felt every day in this country. A very sobering epiphany.

One night, the counterprotesters began yelling louder than usual, spewing some alt-right conspiracies. Then, a Black woman stood up on our side and began to pray. Her words were powerful. She spoke of justice. Mercy. Love. She quoted Scripture: "If God is for us, who can be against us?" She also prayed for forgiveness of those who were against us right then.

I was in awe of her graciousness. The yells and taunts continued as she prayed, but I suddenly felt overwhelmed by that familiar, divine presence. Tears welled in my eyes. A whirlwind of emotions flooded my being. Anger. Sadness. Hope. Love. I didn't know how she was able to forgive them. I didn't know how she could have such a powerful peace in the face of such hostility. And in that moment, it felt like heaven on earth. Love filled the air and drowned out the hate. I knew with every fiber of my being I was in the presence of something holy. Something sacred. *This* was the gospel.

I assumed the people screaming at us probably believed they were doing the right thing, too. I know I did when I was part of the "All Lives Matter" crowd.

What got to me was that, despite seeing us kneeling in prayer, they seemed to refuse to believe we were also Christians. We were just the enemy and had to be painted as such. This, too, was familiar to me from my days in Christian Nationalism. The ideology uses Christian language and Scripture to justify their position and demonize whoever is against them. That summer, I found it convicting to be on the receiving end of a tactic I had once used so freely against others.

Throughout the summer, we were called communists, Marxists, and anarchists. The opposing protestors spread lies, saying that we were bussed in from out of town to spread socialism, that we were part of

Antifa, or we were getting extra class credit from our liberal college professors. An elected county commissioner went live on Facebook saying we were paid protesters being "led by a cult leader."[2]

To counter the narrative that we were just a bunch of "godless communists," I made a new sign that said, "Christ's love compels me to stand here." But it made no difference. Their minds had been made up about us. One man read my sign and yelled, "You're following a false gospel, lady! Repent!"

It was wild how members of our community labeled us so many things without any evidence for their claims. I knew I wasn't being paid by George Soros to destroy Cleveland, Tennessee, but that didn't stop the story from spreading as fact. (Hey, George, if you're reading this, I'm *still* waiting on my check.)

A former county commissioner was interviewed by the local paper and encouraged fellow citizens to "have a plan" in case we turned violent. He told the paper, "This is a communist insurrection. If you believe anything else, you are naive. These communists are your enemies. They would kill you, your wife and there's no telling what they would do to your kids."[3]

This statement surprised me. I was a Christian wife and mother of two who went to church every Sunday and had no affiliation with the Communist Party. He thought I would kill kids if given the opportunity?! All because I was silently asking for a statue to be relocated less than a mile away? Who would've thought?

Suddenly, I was doubting all the accusations I had ever heard, believed, and thrown out myself about people being communist and socialist. I believed the Clintons were communists. Obama was a socialist. Democrats were one welfare policy away from becoming full-on dictators and ushering in the New World Order. Capitalism was godly, and communism/socialism were satanic because... *Oh shoot, I don't even know why.*

That summer I realized that in all the sermons I'd heard against the evils of communism, none of them ever included a definition of the political ideology.

This is probably because the older White men who usually led the conversations on this topic didn't think it needed explaining. They grew up in the middle of the Cold War, America's period of heightened tension with the Soviet Union. This generation practiced hiding under their desks in school in case a nuclear bomb was dropped on them by a communist government on the other side of the world. Of course, they associated communism with evil! It had been ingrained in them from childhood.

But I was a child in the nineties, and I had never thought much about communism, much less advocated for it. Even stranger, I was being called a future murderer for supposedly believing in it, like we were living in *The Minority Report. I'm still changing poopy diapers. I don't have time to plot a city takeover even if I wanted to.*

Another buzzword that was frequently thrown at me that summer was "anarchist." An anarchist is a person who favors having no governmental authority whatsoever. Now, I'm a Type A rule follower. That kind of chaos honestly freaks me out. My most chaotic nights consisted of adding bean dip to my homemade nachos and bingeing a TV show with Beecher while our children slept. I would be the *worst* anarchist.

When I look back now and think about the actual aims of Christian Nationalism, it makes more sense to me why "anarchy" is a frequent horror the movement fights against. Christian Nationalists desire an authoritarian government, where everyone is controlled by strict social policies based on their Biblical worldview. They posit that the opposite of their controlling government is not freedom, but chaotic anarchy.

And in the moments when "anarchists" are not a specific enough threat, they often bring up the ever-evil, secret organization called Antifa. "Antifa" is an informal group that fights against fascist governments and policies. The moniker is literally short for anti-fascism.

What is fascism, you ask? Well, fascism is a right-wing political movement that pushes extreme nationalism, militarism, and an authoritarian government with a leader holding ultimate power. It sounds a lot like what Christian Nationalists want, honestly.

Now, most Christian Nationalists would not claim to be fascists, but it'd sure be easier to institute a powerful theocracy if the government favored extreme nationalism and gave the president singular power to force its citizens to do whatever they wanted.

The line between the two ideologies can be very blurry.

This makes Antifa a logical enemy of Christian Nationalism, and as a result, Antifa must be destroyed. But here's their biggest problem: Antifa is a decentralized movement. There is no leader. There are no official meetings. There is no budget or bank account. Anyone can claim to be Antifa at any time, anywhere in the world. When no one can be blamed, anyone can be. Christian Nationalists use this lack of centralization to accuse people they don't like of being masterminds in the group.

In the initial hours after the Capitol attack on January 6th, several Christian Nationalists I knew blamed the violence on Antifa. The group had somehow infiltrated the peaceful protestors and stormed the Capitol just to make Trump supporters look bad.

On one of the nights we were protesting in 2020, a *Save Our Town* leader went on Facebook Live and zoomed in on one of the guys standing beside me. He was wearing a mask and had long hair. She then claimed that this person was a "known auntiffa [sic] member." He was actually a soft-spoken, twenty-something student at the local Christian college whose dad was a professor at the school. Not exactly the Antifa super soldier he was made out to be.

Maybe the most random moniker they threw at us repeatedly was "Marxist." I knew of Karl Marx but wasn't even sure what being Marxist meant. Is that the same as communist? Or fascist? Or was it simply a fan of the comedian and actor Groucho Marx?

At one point that summer, I visited with some relatives who were deep in the evangelical right. I heard them complaining about Marxists and asked them what the word meant to them. Unsurprisingly, I was met with stares. No one in the room knew how to define Marxism. It was just a scary word.

It wasn't until a year after these protests that I met a real Marxist in the flesh. She lived in a bunker with AK-47s, pipe bombs, and a map of the world projected on the ceiling—

Just kidding.

This Marxist was a wife and mother of two who lived in our neighborhood and sometimes taught about the ideology at a local Christian college, among her other lessons. She was exceedingly kind and explained Marxism quite well—that it looked at history in terms of economic distinctions and theorized a world that didn't exploit the working class. It was much more in-depth and academic than I realized. I didn't become a Marxist from the conversation, but I listened as she humanized the word enough that I understood her perspective. It certainly wasn't evil.

That's one of the main lessons I learned from being called every name under the sun and insulted for months. The importance of just... listening.

Going out there with my sign, I didn't want to fight. I wanted to be heard. More importantly, I wanted the marginalized people I stood beside to be heard. But our cries fell on deaf ears, and we were villainized for taking a stand. And unfortunately, the villainizing of our group worked. The Confederate statue still stands in downtown Cleveland, Tennessee.

The lessons I learned that summer will stay with me, though. From now on, whenever someone tells me about the [insert derogatory label here] person living down the street, instead of dismissing them, I want to get to know them. So much of my learning and growth out of the Christian Nationalism mindset has happened because I sat and listened to people of different groups and mindsets.

But changing your mind can be scary and uncomfortable. It's why I chose the easier route of demonizing the unknown for so long. It's what Christian Nationalism and other high-control groups count on and how they're able to maintain power. Hearing other viewpoints made all the buzzwords lose their potency. That "godless liberal" was now just my friend in college who dressed up as a Golden Girl with me for Halloween. I didn't always agree with her, but we were more alike than we weren't.

The more people I met who carried the labels I threw, the more I realized that demonizing wasn't fair. Nor true. It's difficult to want a narrow-minded theocracy after you see the humanity in the people that the system would harm. When you look people in the eyes, know their names, learn about their lives, and find common ground, it's a lot harder to hate them.

It's easier to scream at that lanky redheaded girl and her sixty-something-year-old mother if you believe they're Antifa super soldier masterminds of Marxist anarchy trying to burn the world to the ground.

CHAPTER 11

Store Up Your Treasure Trolls in Heaven: Boycotts

If labeling enemies a scary word like "Marxist" doesn't stop the opposition, then it's time to up the ante and *demon*ize them. Literally. Mark something demonic and boycott it. Satan is on the attack and wants your kids! Tell all your friends about it and save the children!

It's not unusual for Christians to believe in demonic influence. I got an extra dose of demonic awareness because we were Pentecostal. Even though we didn't fear demons per se (because we were pros at casting those suckers out in Jesus' name), we were hyper aware of their existence. Even Jesus talked about—and even talked *to*—demons in the Bible, so it's not a far-fetched conclusion for evangelicals to look for darkness lurking in our nation today. However, Christian Nationalism can use this belief in literal demons, among other things, to fulfill another tactic used to silence enemies: boycotts.

But before you can get people to boycott Target because of an alleged demonic goat-headed statue in the kids' section, you need to lay the groundwork with some basic satanic panic.[1]

My childhood trained me well for this.

"When you wish on a Treasure Troll, who knows what might happen?" the voice on the television asked.

"I wish my violin was an electric guitar!" one girl said, smiling into the camera as multiple Treasure Trolls appeared on the screen. Each had a colorful belly jewel that matched the color of their crazy hair. I was eight years old, and I was sold.

"Mom, Dad!! Can I pleeeeeaaaase get a Treasure Troll?" I asked.

"No, April, you don't need to make a wish on a toy when you can pray to God."

"But alllllll my friends have them…" I begged. The answer was still no.

Despite the popularity of Treasure Trolls in the 1990s, I never got one. In our home, like many other evangelical households, magic of all forms was considered demonic—even if it was just pretend.

While Treasure Trolls seemed innocent enough to me, I ultimately decided that continuing to nag my parents over a potential demon doll wasn't worth it. Even though I accepted my fate, it didn't squash my desire for one or the jealousy I felt when other kids played with their own Trolls.

Then, at a friend's house one day, I saw she had a Troll. There it was in all its crazy purple-haired glory, shoved into a toy chest between a Barbie and a plastic toy pistol. The purple jewel on its belly called out to me, and I yearned to answer.

I knew I wasn't allowed to make a wish on it. I knew it *might* open a gateway to hell.

But I looked across the room at my friend, who seemed normal enough. I'm sure she had made a wish at some point, and I didn't see any open hell portals in the house.

Just rub it real quick. No one will know, I convinced myself.

I looked around the room quickly. No one was looking. So I snatched the doll and secretly rubbed the belly jewel of the troll. I closed my eyes and made a simple wish.

"I wish we could have pizza for dinner," I whispered.

I hurriedly put the doll back in the toy chest as my friend came over. My heart was pounding. I felt like I had just committed a crime. We continued playing as I anxiously awaited dinnertime.

To my disappointment, my wish did not come true. But there was a silver lining—no demons appeared. In fact, nothing really happened at all. Life continued normally. It was almost like it was *just* a toy. Weird.

I kept this information to myself. I didn't want to get in trouble for playing with a doll I technically wasn't allowed to touch. Even if I did have evidence to free the Troll doll from the demonic charges against it, I kept my mouth shut. But this experience kept me skeptical of future demonic claims.

I asked my mom recently why she had banned the Troll dolls. She said she didn't remember her reason, other than her own mother forbade her from having Troll dolls in the 1960s, also claiming they were demonic. Which, you know, didn't strike me as hard evidence. So I did some research and found other claims of these Trolls possessing demonic powers, all of them suspect. One blog post claimed that a Troll doll started dancing in the middle of a kid's bedroom while a Disney movie played music.[2] Unsurprisingly, there is no video evidence or proof for this, but stories like this persist. Another story told of a Christian school banning Troll dolls and dedicating a whole chapel service to explain why. The reasons included warnings of New Age mysticism, the occult, and satanism. Why risk exposing yourself to demonic power for a silly Troll doll?[3]

I was born in 1988, so I entered the world when *Satanic Panic* was already in full swing. The term was coined after thousands of unsubstantiated claims alleged that satanic rituals were happening across the United States in the early 1980s.[4] While the initial hysteria eventually wore off—as no fact-based evidence was ever discovered[5]—the underlying fear from the panic has continued through the decades. Whenever something new or different was introduced to evangelicals, especially if you were Pentecostal, there was always the threat of a demon lurking behind it. You could never be too careful.

Thankfully, my parents were more chill than most in our fundamentalist circles. They didn't forbid me from wearing fake tattoos because of demons, like some church parents did. No, I just wasn't allowed to wear temporary tattoos because my parents were afraid of what it might look like to others. They were ministers and had a reputation to uphold. If I wore a My Little Pony temporary tattoo to church, then the old ladies would think it'd lead me to want a real tattoo, which would lead me to a tattoo parlor, where I'd meet a guy with satanist ink who would permanently draw on my body, putting a spell on me that would make me join a witches coven, sacrificing cats, and then . . . *boom*. Straight to hell.

Preacher kid problems. Anywho.

Accusing a popular cultural product of being under demonic influence is pretty typical in evangelical circles. And if that claim alone doesn't do enough to dissuade families from buying the thing, then a boycott is called. Oftentimes, the product doesn't even need to harbor demons to get a boycott.

Sometimes a boycott is called because a brand is working as a secret vessel of the liberal left, which will cause your entire family to backslide and lose their eternal salvation. Like in June 2023, when Cracker Barrel posted a picture of a rainbow rocker and wished everyone "Happy Pride!" The company was inundated with thousands of comments lamenting the restaurant's "woke" left turn and calling for a boycott.[6]

Or when boycotts of the 2023 Macy's Thanksgiving Day Parade were called for the inclusion of not one, but *two* nonbinary performers.[7] The rapture was obviously imminent thanks to this Satanfest, and Macy's should never be shopped at again should the Lord tarry (sentiments I actually saw on Facebook).

To fight off this evil agenda, evangelicals are told never to buy anything from said company. The goal is to send a statement and hurt the pocketbooks of the big corporations that are allegedly declaring spiritual warfare on Christian households.

Growing up in this culture, the most frustrating aspect of all this was the shifting goalposts. Sometimes movies and shows were okay. But sometimes I would get attached to a TV show, only to have leaders from the top suddenly proclaim DEMONIC INFLUENCE and POOF—I could no longer watch *Power Rangers*. True story.

The moment this hit me the hardest was when I had to give up my favorite thing in my twelve-year-old life: Pokémon.

In case you live under a rock, Pokémon live in a made-up world and are basically animal-like creatures you can catch, raise, train, and fight. My brothers and I had the Pokémon games on Game Boy *and* collected the trading cards.

On any night after church, you'd find us with several friends huddled on the floor in the foyer trading cards.

"I'll give you Charmander for Haunter."

"No, but I'll take Zapdos for Haunter."

"You're crazy! Zapdos is rare *and* holographic."

Our parents were cool with it until they weren't. At some point, an elderly woman overheard us speaking of a ghost-type Pokémon and decided it was demonic. The devilish alarms began to sound.

And just like that, our "Pocket Monsters" had to go. My parents made my brothers and me load up *all* our Pokémon cards that we had worked and traded so hard for and sell them to our local GameStop.

If your heart is not feeling the magnitude of this moment yet, know that I had a First Edition Holographic Charizard, the Holy Grail of Pokémon cards. I had to sell it to a tall man in glasses for a measly $25. I knew it was a steal as he happily skipped away thinking he had pulled a fast one on me. But I had to sell them that day and didn't have the luxury of time or the ability to travel to sell it for what it was worth. I've seen some listings of the card on eBay are up to $2,500 today. Yes, I'm still salty about it.

It wasn't just our church that banned the franchise. For whatever reason, the popularity of Pokémon cards must have riled up some bigwig evangelical pastors, and they began to forbid them from pulpits across the nation. I soon learned my parents' verdict on my cards wasn't as bad as some of my friends, who had to burn or throw away theirs. At least I got some money out of it, even if I was robbed.

Interestingly, my parents still let us keep the Pokémon Game Boy games, though. Maybe because the graphics were so low-quality, even the demons couldn't work with it. Who knows? The goalposts were always moving and confusing.

I still give my mom a hard time about it. I've asked her why she made us sell our cards and she doesn't remember exactly. "Everyone around us just thought they were demonic... but I'm sorry." I appreciated hearing this from my mom, even all these years later, but I soon found out who really owes my generation an apology.

A few years ago, I sat at my computer trying to find who had instigated the great Pokémon purge that devastated middle schoolers everywhere at the turn of the century. I couldn't pinpoint who started it but one of the first things that popped up was a video from the Prophecy Club. The video features a man with a mullet giving an entire presentation on the evils of Pokémon, in which he really emphasized that the word was short for Pocket MONSTER.[8]

This man had transparent film with different images from Pokémon that he placed on an overhead projector to "prove" rampant satanism inside the children's franchise.

He claimed that Pokémon got their power "by supernatural occult ability," as if they walked among us in the real world.

He said that Mewtwo holding up three fingers in his standard pose meant "Hail Satan," ignoring the fact that Mewtwo only *has* three fingers. Something any middle schooler would have let him know if he thought to ask.

"His little satanic tail is really erect," he said about a picture of cute little mouse-like Pikachu. Slide after slide showed different images of adorable Pokémon that he managed to connect to various occult things. A picture of a normal-looking leaf was "another powerful witchcraft symbol."[9]

One of his biggest beefs with these Pocket Monsters was how they empowered kids to be the best and become Masters of Pokémon training. "You don't need Mom, you don't need Dad, you don't need grandparents, you don't need aunts and uncles, you don't need school, and you probably don't even need a church... because you're a master," he proclaimed. He warned parents of a war looming over their children "because Satan wants them really bad."

Now, I try not to hold grudges against people from my past. They did the best they could with what they knew, just like I did. I don't want to become a bitter person. However, if I ever run into this man, it's on sight. Choice words incoming.

The reality is that we may never know who actually began the Pokémon boycott. It's often very difficult to know who starts these things. Word spreads in churches and fellowship halls and no one really asks questions before following orders and ditching the newest object of evil. It's just what good evangelical fundamentalist families do.

One thing that was always banned from the very beginning was witchcraft, though. I was never allowed to dress as a witch for Halloween or pretend I had magic. We were taught that witchcraft and spells were real in our world, where covens lurked in the shadows with the intent to take down God-fearing churches. It was never clear what closing a church would do for the witches exactly, but they were in a pact with Satan and that's just what they did.

All of this meant that anything that gave even the appearance of witchcraft was forbidden. So obviously, Harry Potter was completely banned from my home. Whenever I asked my parents if I could read the books, they responded by telling me what other Christians were saying. Apparently, some evangelicals believed that the books and movies used "real spells" that held magic within them.

This made me just want to read them even more! If you want a kid not to do something, you should definitely *not* tell them that it has the power to teach you how to fly, shoot lightning out of a stick, or shape-shift.

Regardless of how enticing this was, I obeyed my parents and didn't read or watch anything Harry Potter. When friends at school asked if I read the books, I gave no hint I wasn't allowed to read them. It was embarrassing. Instead, I pretended it was my choice. "No, Harry Potter looks nerdy. I'm not into it," I'd say.

However, my cover was blown when my best friend from my Christian school had a dinner-and-a-movie sweet sixteen birthday party. Of course, the movie was the newest Harry Potter film. My friends didn't understand why I was leaving after the dinner portion. I didn't want them to think I was a bad friend, so I caved and told them the truth. Watching all of my friends walk into the theater without me was a bit humiliating, but at least I . . . no, there was no silver lining here. It sucked.

When I was a senior in college, I bought myself a Harry Potter book and read it. That was the moment I was finally infected by a demon and why I am now writing this book. If you've made it this far, you've already got one attached to you, too, and should call a Pentecostal immediately to cast it out.

I kid, I kid.

Harry Potter was not the only piece of kids' media I experienced for the first time in college. In my junior year, a friend bought Disney's *The Little Mermaid* on DVD and several of us crammed into her apartment to watch it. It was one of my favorite movies growing up and I couldn't wait to let the nostalgia of watching my fellow redheaded Ariel wash all over me.

But then a scene I didn't recognize came on. A song began that I had never heard before. Alarmed by this change, I blurted out, "I can't believe Disney would add a brand-new song!"

"What are you talking about, April?" my friend asked.

"This song was *not* in the original. Disney is ruining our childhood!"

They looked at me like I was crazy. My friend informed me that this song had, in fact, always been in the movie.

Suddenly, a memory flashed in my brain of a homemade VHS tape with handwriting on it that read THE LITTLE MERMAID. *Crap. Our version was recorded from the TV.*

Turns out, my mom had intentionally left off Ursula's iconic "Poor Unfortunate Souls" when she recorded it because it just seemed too evil. I always thought Ariel traded her voice awfully quickly in the story, but never questioned the rushed plot. The idea that my mom had edited a Disney movie never even crossed my mind!

Evangelicals at large sometimes do these things, thinking they are protecting their children from darkness. But as I have reflected on all the boycotts and demon editing I experienced growing up, I have come to see how Christian Nationalism takes boycotts a step further.

As a die-hard Republican family, we knew that every two or four years, we had a duty: campaign loudly and go to the ballot box to vote for the strongest God-loving Christian who would enact the most overt evangelical policies.

But what were we to do in between elections?

Well, we focused on controlling the business sphere of the Seven Mountain Mandate. Companies that promote agendas that go against our narrative must be stopped. After all, Christian Nationalism wants a government that enforces their beliefs, and that desire extends to all aspects of society—even the private sector. Boycotts are a perfect way to do this.

Not to mention, it helps keep followers engaged but not overworked. I mean, how easy is it *not* to do something and feel like you are fighting the good fight?

If a Christian Nationalist feels antsy and wants to participate in something when it's not election season, they can get riled up about the latest boycott and stick it to the man! This creates cohesion, community, and gives followers of the ideology a reason to communicate in slower times. And more importantly, it will hopefully discourage other companies from pushing narratives or products that go against Christian Nationalism, giving the movement more power.

In summer 2023, it was the *Barbie* movie. When the film took the world by storm with its satirical look at the patriarchy, many conservatives and Christian Nationalists tried to warn the masses of its evils. It was called woke, anti-man, and was going to indoctrinate your kids to... think women might be as capable as men? We couldn't have that. So they demonized it, some literally. One minister went viral by claiming the film would release millions of literal demons onto your children.[10] Another pastor even tried cursing the film from the pulpit.[11]

Throughout the decades, there's been no shortage of things we have boycotted. American evangelicals have tried to cancel the Teletubbies

(Jerry Falwell Sr. said the purple one was supposedly gay[12]), Procter & Gamble (their moon and stars logo was satanic[13]), Cabbage Patch Dolls (these dolls *could* be possessed by demons[14]), PetSmart (for failing to say "Christmas" in their December marketing[15]), Betty Crocker (for baking a cake for a same-sex wedding[16]), NBC (programs weren't Christian enough[17]), Starbucks (for having an immodest logo[18]and then again for the infamous holiday red cup fiasco[19]), and too many other brands to list them all.

This list doesn't even include the boycotts orchestrated by One Million Moms (OMM), an organization that boycotts just about anything that they deem goes against conservative Christian values. Their website claims that their goal is "to stop the exploitation of our children, especially by the entertainment media."[20] The group has called for boycotts or created petitions for several reasons but seem to favor targeting companies that are supportive of LGTBQ+ people or show them in a positive or normal light.

Here's a list of just *some* of the brands that OMM has gone after: Toys "R" Us,[21] Oreo Cookies,[22] Urban Outfitters,[23] Nabisco's Honey Maid and Teddy Grahams,[24] Chobani Greek Yogurt,[25] Campbell's Soup,[26] TurboTax,[27] the Hallmark Channel,[28] *Sesame Street*, Dole fruit bowls, Uber Eats, Ritz Crackers, Sabra Hummus,[29] *Scooby-Doo* cartoons,[30] Peppa Pig,[31] Zales Jewelers,[32] Carter's kids clothing,[33] Hershey's,[34] Netflix,[35] Kay Jewelers,[36] Zillow,[37] eHarmony,[38] etc. . . .

It seems ridiculous to see these mundane brands be elevated to an evil, satanic level, but it's a classic tactic of Christian Nationalism. If you believe you're on the good side, then anyone or thing who disagrees with you must be on the bad side. And they must be stopped.

Fearmongering has been used throughout history to control the masses and to obtain or keep power. Christian Nationalism wanted me and my family to be outraged, because it kept us engaged in the fight while puffing out its chest. The movement thrives if they can convince enough people that their values are under attack. Whether it's demonizing Treasure Trolls or vilifying queer people, the playbook is the same.

Boycotts are quite popular in this movement for several reasons. Christian Nationalists generally push for a theocratic government in the arena of social policies. But a theocracy gets tricky when it comes to economics. We are capitalists, after all. We can't just openly shut down businesses we disagree with because that's not a free market. This makes boycotts very appealing, because it uses the free market economic system to make our enemies pay *without* government interference. This allowed us to keep our GOP Jesus-approved capitalist membership cards. The movement orders boycotts to stop supporting brands to force businesses to behave in a way that supports Christian Nationalist ideals.

When I was in high school, we boycotted Joe's Crab Shack because the peace sign in its logo was supposedly demonic. We actually walked into the restaurant, my dad saw the sign, announced "That's the sign for the devil!" and made us leave. In hindsight, I think he confused it for a pentagram, but either way, it made for an embarrassing scene and made for a couple long years without those delicious hush puppies.

Around this same time, we tried to rile people up to boycott MTV because we thought they catered to queer people and fornicators! The channel didn't purport to be Christian and yet we were outraged that they didn't follow our beliefs.

MTV's shows—which I wasn't allowed to watch anyway—didn't affect me at all. Certainly, their business decisions and boardroom discussions had zero impact on my life. And yet because of my belief that America is a Christian Nation, any American company or person that promoted something that went against *my personal* beliefs felt like an affront to Christianity itself.

To be clear, it's one thing to avoid buying things because you feel it goes against your personal faith. "I won't buy this because it violates my beliefs." That's not Christian Nationalism.

It's another thing entirely if you try to force companies to uphold your beliefs. And if they don't, you boycott their products, join a national campaign to try and bankrupt the company, and judge everyone else who buys their products because of *your* beliefs. "No one should buy this; the company should completely go under, and all employees lose their jobs because it goes against *my* beliefs." *That* is Christian Nationalism. There's no room for other beliefs in this country. Our way or the highway.

In April 2023, I followed the Bud Light and Nike boycotts closely. These companies regularly partner with social media influencers for promotions. One of the people they worked with that spring was a trans woman named Dylan Mulvaney. The backlash against these companies for partnering with a trans person was harsh. Horrible things were said about her. Lots of conservatives posted videos of themselves destroying Bud Light cans, and some bars took the brand out of their establishments.[39, 40] Pundits urged people to boycott the companies to make them feel a negative financial impact of daring to...partner with someone whose values weren't conservative, I guess?

Seeing the size of the backlash, right-wing commentator and columnist for *The Daily Wire* Matt Walsh tweeted about the need for conservatives to get more organized with their boycotts. "By sheer numbers we have the power to inflict severe financial damage on companies that spit in our faces, but we don't. The brands know that we don't.... Here's what we should do: Pick a victim, gang up on it, and make an example of it. We can't boycott every woke company or even most of them. But we can pick one, it hardly matters which, and target it with a ruthless boycott campaign. Claim one scalp then move onto the next."[41]

No more beating around the bush. This was their tactic written out in plain language.

Having been a part of this, I can empathize with the feelings behind this response. I know hitting companies in their bottom line feels like the only way to make them listen when you're afraid. Because that's what's going on here...these boycotts are rooted in the fear of losing a culture war. They are an attempt to gain back control.

When I was a Christian Nationalist, we called ourselves "the silent majority" despite the fact that we never shut up and that we were losing numbers (we loved to ignore the popular vote results). And yet we still convinced ourselves that we had the power to shut down companies because we believed we were the majority. More than that, we thought we had the moral obligation to do so when a company created a product, a service, or an ad campaign that went against the values we held dear and wanted to see the whole nation embrace.

Nowadays, if a company does something that Nationalists deem too "left," the phrase "Go woke, go broke" is thrown around. It's often said as a threat, but at its heart, it also reveals a deep insecurity. It's a way to show outsiders a tough front, while also convincing insiders that they still have control of the culture. Sometimes it works. Bud Light lost 10.5% of its US revenue after the boycott, but because of success in other markets, the company weathered the storm fine.[42]

But boycotts usually fail. *Barbie* became the biggest film of that year, smashing all sorts of box office records.[43] Disney is still a corporate giant despite multiple boycott attempts (looking at you, Ron DeSantis). They still serve Honey Maid graham crackers in preschools around the country. MTV never went away. Pokémon is still a major franchise.

Plus, I'm happy to say that I am now collecting Pokémon cards again with my own kids. And no satanic panic mullet man is going to make me make them sell their cards.

CHAPTER 12

Condom Girl: Persecution Complex

POP QUIZ—FINISH THAT VERSE.

1. John 13:35 (NIV): "By this everyone will know that you are my disciples if you":
   A. "Vote Republican."
   B. "Display the most flags."
   C. "Love one another."
   D. "Condemn other people's sin."
   E. "Fight for your rights."

Obviously, the correct answer is C: "Love one another."

Though, if I'm being honest, sometimes that message gets lost in translation.

Exhibit A:

"Hey, Dad, what's a bigot?" I asked when I was fourteen.

"Why do you ask?" My dad said, looking up from watching the latest Gaither Vocal Band video.

"Someone called me one today in political science class. We were talking about gay marriage, and I just said the truth—that homosexuality is an abomination, and we shouldn't celebrate sin."

My dad grabbed the TV remote and pressed the pause button. "Well, people use that word negatively against those who are prejudiced toward certain groups of people. There are bad people who deserve to be called bigots. But when that word is used against us, it's usually because we're standing for Biblical truth and people like their sin too much."

Ah. I'm only being called names because I'm standing up for God... just like the early church fathers...

This was how I framed any pushback I received when I was a Christian Nationalist. I was suffering for Jesus. A victim of the larger culture wars. I was fighting to make our nation better and more favored by God, and if people didn't understand that, well, they would thank me someday. Or maybe they wouldn't, but either way, they would eventually realize I was right.

For the record, that wasn't the only time I was called a bigot. Just the first. It happened more as I got older and feistier. But if it ever got me down, I just whipped out my membership card in the persecution club. Whenever I got a negative response, it was just because I spoke up for Biblical truth. Jesus even said this would happen in John 15:20 (NIV): "If they persecuted me, they will persecute you also."

It shouldn't be surprising that persecution is something Christians strive for. It's a consistent theme throughout the New Testament. Jesus talks of it again in Luke 6:22 (NIV): "Blessed are you when people hate you, when they exclude you and insult you and reject your name as evil, because of the Son of Man." Being hated by the world was a foundational piece of the faith I grew up in.

I can't overstate this enough: Being persecuted was a *good* thing in my circles. It meant I was doing great things for God. If I wasn't hated, it was probably because I was lukewarm, and God would spit me out of his mouth (Revelation 3:16 NIV). I needed to be either hot or cold to... uhh, stay in his mouth? Cringey metaphor aside, being a good Christian required me to go all in.

I *wanted* to be persecuted. I know that sounds strange, but there was nothing that rallied a church like perceived Christian persecution.

Christian Nationalism uses the persecution narrative to create camaraderie among members of the base and get them to act. Claiming persecution also makes you a victim, which works well as a way to avoid accountability. This tactic worked on me like a charm.

I didn't get many chances to stand up for my faith early on. My day-to-day life as a homeschooled preacher's kid didn't afford me many opportunities to square off against a hostile culture. My brothers were already saved, and my teacher (my mom) loved when I talked about Jesus. I wasn't really in the lion's den.

That all changed when I was twelve years old. My father took the senior pastor position at our church, which meant my family would stop traveling and settle down. I was home long enough to attend public school for the first time. I could finally stand up for Jesus in a *secular* environment.

I was ecstatic. My dad had told me stories of his school days: how he smuggled in Christian music when he was the student DJ for a local rock 'n' roll radio station or when he shared the gospel message at a school rally. He told these stories regularly from the pulpit and often had the audience doubled over laughing at the extreme lengths to which he took his faith and the backlash he sometimes received. He was the coolest, and I couldn't wait to emulate him at my own school.

And I was extra ready because the 1999 shooting at Columbine High School had just happened the year before. The martyrdom story of Cassie Bernall was a favorite topic at Sunday school. You may remember the story of Cassie Bernall, who allegedly answered "yes" when the gunman asked if she believed in God. She was promptly shot to death, presumably for her beliefs. Bernall's parents wrote a book in her memory called *She Said Yes* hailing her a martyr for God based on what they believed was true.[1] The story inspired several Christian artists to write songs about the event. Michael W. Smith even won Song of the Year at the Dove Awards for his song "This Is Your Time," based on Cassie's story.[2] Despite later evidence that the story was most likely false, revealing that Bernall was *not* asked if she believed in God, it didn't stop Christian youth across the country from fantasizing about their own potential martyrdom at school.[3]

And I was one of them.

In bolder moments, I convinced myself that I *would* say, "Yes, I believe in God," if a gunman asked me because of course I was willing to sacrifice my life for God. *Temporary pain for eternal reward*, I'd think to myself.

Other times, I felt ashamed because I wasn't sure if, at the moment, staring down the barrel of a gun, I could willingly give my life. That's a lot of pressure for a child.

The words of Jesus in Matthew 10:33 (NKJV) flooded my mind as I walked into middle school on that first day: "Whoever denies Me before men, him I will also deny before My Father who is in heaven." No matter the cost, I was prepared to be bold at my new public school.

My preparation included spending an embarrassing amount of time cutting large letters out of a bright neon yellow poster board that said, "Jesus Saves Souls." I packed some Scotch tape in my backpack and the first thing I did when I got to school was tape it on the outside of my school locker. *Bring it on, atheists!* I looked around, anticipating the godless liberals to show up with their hate-filled monologues.

Nobody seemed to notice.

Actually, that's not completely true. My new friend Ashley said she liked my sign, which just made the situation more confusing. Not only did I not receive backlash, but I couldn't find any kids to witness to because it seemed like most of my classmates were already Christian. This was supposed to be a hedonistic public school! What was going on?

Soon, I got another chance to stand up for my faith. My English teacher gave us a prompt for our new writing assignment: What would you do to make public schools safer?

This is my chance. I took everything that the church and Christian media taught me and wrote the most fervent paper on the importance of putting God back in school.

I turned it in expecting to be reprimanded when my teacher graded it. I assumed he was an atheist in hiding, primed to mock my belief in "sky daddy." I was ready to take him on and proudly report back to my dad.

The moment arrived.

"I graded your essays and will hand them back to you now before I discuss them," the teacher said as he began passing out our papers. He walked right past my desk without giving me mine. *What does this mean? Did I get a zero?*

He finished handing them out and walked to the front. I still hadn't received mine. *Am I in trouble?*

"April, will you come to the front of the class, please?"

My heart started pounding. *It's finally happening. I'm about to be persecuted.*

As I walked up in front of all my peers, my teacher addressed the entire class.

"I saved April's paper for the end because hers is a great example..."

I was trying to keep my hands from shaking as I stood in front of the class, quietly anticipating the humiliation to come.

"...of how to properly write this assignment! She got the highest grade in the class. Her essay was so well laid out that I want her to read it out loud for all of us to hear and learn from. Here's your paper, April."

I stared at him for a moment. *Is this a trick?* As I moved toward his outstretched hand, I tried to read his face. He was smiling, which just further confused me. When I reached for my paper, he leaned over and whispered to me, "You did an amazing job. Everyone should hear this." He genuinely looked proud, which squashed my suspicions that this was a setup.

Still a bit shocked, I thanked him and turned toward the other students, essay in hand. *Okay, April, now you get to witness to the whole class.*

I proceeded to read my paper in front of that seventh-grade English class with all the passion and fire I'd seen from the Pentecostal pulpit. "THE REAL PROBLEM IN SCHOOLS TODAY IS SIN AND THE ONLY ANSWER IS PUTTING PRAYER AND GOD BACK IN THE CLASSROOM."

I finished the essay. A couple students clapped, some smiled, but most of them just stared at me. Where was the persecution?

However, things took a turn in the hallways after class.

Word of my essay/sermon spread quickly around the school. I heard murmurs and hints of nicknames being thrown around about me, but I couldn't quite make out what they were saying. *Maybe they were calling me Jesus kid? Bible Betty? Mary Martyr?* I was ready to wear whatever nickname with a badge of persecuted honor.

Or so I thought.

The nickname I got for my passionate speech was none other than "Condom Girl."

Yep.

It seems no preteen cared much about the gospel portion of my paper. Instead, they honed in on one little phrase I had included.

You see, there was a Christian musical artist at the time who was quite big among us evangelical homeschoolers. His name was Carman, and he had a series of very entertaining, overproduced music videos on VHS that my brothers and I watched on repeat.

In his song "America Again," he sings about putting God back in our country and includes the line, "If you want to see kids live right, stop handing out condoms and start handing out the word of God in schools!"

Somehow in the brain dump of writing, this sentence made it into my paper without proper citation (sorry, Carman), so it got attributed to me (sorry, me). So my little seventh-grade thin-as-a-toothpick self stood up and eagerly called for stopping the spread of sexual protection in schools in favor of Bibles. Middle schoolers are not known for their maturity, so you can imagine the fun they had with this.

The worst part was that I didn't even know what a condom was. Carman had just expressed it so passionately in his song that it seemed important to include in my paper.

Friends who weren't in the class started coming up to me and whispering, "Did you really say 'condoms' in class?" It was *big* news at this small-town Texas middle school.

I wasn't sure this counted as persecution, but I tried to convince myself of it anyway. *This is just the cross I have to bear for being a Christian.*

My freshman year of high school, I had the opportunity to attend a large public school in Florida, where my family had just moved. My boldness for God continued: praying at lunch, witnessing to my friends, joining Christian groups like Youth Alive and Fellowship of Christian Athletes, and attending See You at the Pole (you pray around the flagpole at school). I wasn't popular per se, but I was liked well enough. Life was pretty good and relatively easy.

This became a problem when our youth leaders started reading passages from *Foxe's Book of Martyrs* at my church small group. This is a book centered on the many people who were brutally killed for standing up for their Christian faith. I was at a loss. I didn't know how to be *more* faithful than I already was, yet I didn't receive any hint of the persecution this book discussed.

The cognitive dissonance was strong in my teenage brain. I'd never experienced persecution yet still believed American Christians were badly persecuted every day.

Part of this belief stemmed from what we knew of actual Christian persecution happening overseas. During one mission trip to Ethiopia, we had nightly church services and set up medical tents for locals to receive free health care. My mom, brothers, and I sang before my dad preached in front of the large open fields.

One day, the local church asked my dad to evangelize at the marketplace. One of the church members offered to interpret for my dad if he would preach. Never one to turn down an opportunity to save souls, my dad agreed. They drove my dad to the market and gave him a bullhorn. He climbed on top of the truck and started telling the market about Jesus. About twenty minutes in, people around started picking up rocks. Seeing the potential violence, the church members in the truck shouted, "Get down!" Before he could respond, my dad felt a blow to the back of his head.

They rushed my dad inside the vehicle as more stones began flying. A doctor looked at my dad's head when he got back and said that the rock just happened to hit the perfect spot. If it had been slightly off in any one direction, it could have seriously injured or even killed him.

My dad became a hero to that local church. He experienced the ultimate honor in our evangelical circles, to be physically hurt for Jesus. Several people said my dad was glowing afterward, like the Holy Spirit was all over him.

I didn't see that glow for myself, but it was a story my dad would tell many times in the years to come. We joked that Dad got "stoned"—the drug connotation being the funny part.

Jokes aside, this experience cemented our belief that Christians were persecuted and despised everywhere. We frequently referred to this story any time we needed proof.

But there's a big difference between experiencing actual physical persecution for preaching the gospel and what happens in America. In Ethiopia, my dad was preaching and had rocks thrown at him. But he was also a White man in a foreign land. Even though we didn't realize this at the time, we were basically colonizing another people with our own whitewashed religion. It makes sense that some locals would be angered by that. But my dad didn't respond by picking up rocks and throwing them back while screaming about his rights. He laid down his weapon—in his case a megaphone—and left peacefully.

However, in a country whose presidents have all claimed some form of Christianity themselves, this sort of persecution can be hard to come by. This requires Christians to get creative.

Target is allowing trans people to use the bathroom they identify with? Christian persecution. A business is being sued for refusing to provide service for a gay couple? Christian persecution. Not being given a city permit to gather a crowd of people for a worship service during a global pandemic? Christian persecution. People leaving the church and exposing the abuse they endured? Christian persecution. The government removing a tax-exempt status because a Christian university refused to allow interracial dating? Christian persecution. Queer people don't want to eat the Lord's chicken anymore? Christian persecution.

Unfortunately, I used to play this game, too. I personally joined the persecution cries and fought the good fight in 2012. After Chick-fil-A CEO Dan T. Cathy told a Christian news site that his company supported the "Biblical definition of the family unit," I rallied behind the Christian fast-food chain with my fellow conservatives.[4] Those pesky liberals were calling for a boycott, which was not cool in my book. Only *we* were allowed to boycott. The audacity.

Feeling righteously indignant, I joined in the battle to un-boycott their boycott. Chick-fil-A had already been a staple in my life, with its instrumental worship background music constantly playing on the speakers, its smiling employees, and an evangelical Sabbath-enforced work schedule (the Sunday Sabbath, not the Saturday one). Their persecution became mine, and Chick-fil-A became the only place I ate. For days, we stuffed our faces with that sacred fried chicken and baptized our palettes with their holy sweet tea. I say "we," because I obviously convinced my brothers and friends to join me.

During this time, I posted on my Facebook page, "I support Chick-fil-A and all the Christian values they stand for!" In the comments, a debate started brewing. I replied, "Many companies have pro-gay marriage and other liberal agendas and people don't have a problem." (I was conveniently ignoring the fact that plenty of people, including myself, actually *did* have a problem with that.) I continued, "But if you side with the moral side, with someone that actually still believes in right and wrong, people scream bigotry. We're choosing to side with Christian values... and most of all, Jesus. I am following the true way and refuse to waver from that."

Y'all, I really wrote that. And posted it online. Over chicken.

This act of turning any pushback into an attack on "Christian values" is a primary tactic of Christian Nationalism. You can't be held responsible for hurtful things you say and do if you can turn accountability into persecution.

In 2008, Judge Roy Moore demonstrated this perfectly. That year, he spoke at my dad's church in Texas. This was before the sexual assault allegations from then underage girls, which he has consistently denied, came to light in 2017 when he ran for Senate. When he came to our church, he was just known as the judge who refused to remove the

5,280-pound monument of the Ten Commandments that he erected inside the Alabama Judicial Building.[5] He had the monument installed because he believed the Ten Commandments were "the moral foundation of our law" and that "in order to establish justice, we must invoke 'the favor and guidance of Almighty God.'"[6] As for that pesky clause in the Constitution about the government not establishing a religion? That didn't apply here because this was *the Bible.* He was sued, and he still refused to remove the block of granite and was eventually removed from the bench.

We believed this to be blatant Christian persecution. Moore was a hero of the faith. When he walked through the doors of our church, it was like meeting a celebrity. I volunteered to work his merch table so I could stand beside this man of God.

After Moore gave countless autographs to our church members, we all went outside to take pictures with him in front of *the* Ten Commandments monument, which by then had been removed from the Alabama statehouse and was situated on an open-air trailer. He had brought the very stone that caused all the controversy. It was like being near the Holy Grail of persecution. Like if we touched it, we could all get just an ounce of oppression.

Judge Roy Moore made persecution look nice, though. He got a book deal. He also got speaking engagements and celebrity status. Who wouldn't want to be persecuted like that?

We didn't listen to the arguments against displaying the Ten Commandments on a government building, about how supporting that statue privileged one set of beliefs, about the fears that those from different belief systems might not get a fair trial. Frankly, we didn't consider other beliefs. Ours was right, and we thought our rights were being taken away when they took away that statue. This was a Christian nation, after all—or at least we were trying hard to make it one.

Christian Nationalists regularly use the persecution narrative to elevate their ideology while taking rights away from those who believe differently. Morality police are there to enforce one set of beliefs while denigrating another. This can be tricky in a country that espouses liberty and justice for *all.*

In America, we can't just openly rip up the Bill of Rights. Instead, we have to say that *our* rights as Christians are at stake if gay people are allowed to marry. We fought against the legalization of gay marriage because it was against *our* belief system. And when we lost that battle, we talked about the assault on *our* Biblical marriages and *our* children's eyes. If we couldn't prevent people from behaving in ways that weren't in line with our beliefs, *we* were the victims.

When the government asked churches not to meet in person to stop the spread of a deadly disease in a global pandemic? Blatant persecution!

Taking health care choices away from individuals and their doctors? My body my choice! (Obviously only talking about vaccine mandates... if you mean it the other way, you clearly have no morals.)

Protecting trans people from harassment? That's taking away our right to speak Biblical truth!

All the examples I've just cited are about pretty divisive topics. That's not an accident. I believe many of the policies that are pushed by Christian Nationalists today are being enacted *because* they are extremely divisive, not despite it. The more pushback and hate a bill receives, the more it's celebrated because of the persecution it generates. That proves it's representing Christian values. And what bills receive more blowback than when you threaten to take away people's rights?

Persecution also creates sympathy and loyalty. Just think for a moment how many impeachments, trials, and indictments Donald Trump has gone through. Do these turn followers away? Hardly. Every punishment he faces is viewed as persecution, which makes him a martyr. With each new indictment brought against him, the closer he gets to being Jesus incarnate. And I'm not really exaggerating. I've seen lots of posts openly equating Trump to Jesus. Umpteen photos of Trump side by side with the Son of God get reshared by Christians every time he faces the consequences of his moral failings.

Trump even shared one of these images to his Truth Social account following a court appearance in October 2023. It was an image of Jesus sitting beside Trump at the defendant's table with a caption that read, "This is the most accurate court sketch of all time. Because nobody could have made it this far alone."[7]

When Trump was arraigned during Holy Week in 2023, the comparisons of Trump to Christ were everywhere. Even Representative Marjorie Taylor Greene compared Trump's charges to the arrest of Jesus.[8] You know, because Jesus was arrested for challenging religious leaders with radical love, and Donald Trump was arrested for falsifying hush money payments to a porn star and keeping classified nuclear documents in his shower. Totally the same thing.

But I get why Christian Nationalist leaders want to leverage the idea of persecution. They use it—court it, even—because it riles up the base effectively. It also has the side benefit of giving leaders a get-out-of-jail-free card whenever their own transgressions come to light while keeping those inside from facing the realities of bad things done by their beloved leaders. Constantly claiming "witch hunt" allows for no scandal to be substantial and no hero to fall from grace.

But the main benefit of claiming persecution is that it allows Christian Nationalists to take controversial stands and push legislation that advances their own agendas without regard for anyone else. They can insist that their values become the values everyone in the nation must live by, whether others believe them or not. And when people disagree—often, those whose rights are actually being impinged upon—the persecution card is played.

It all seems so obvious now from the outside looking in. The movement I supported for so long is *not* oppressed, but instead frequently plays the role of the oppressor. Christian Nationalism casts its followers as victims in order to harness the power of collective outrage in an effort to center its own agenda and enforce its own preferred morality on others.

It's devious, it's insidious, and it's unfortunately kind of genius. It's also enormously effective. Way more effective than my campaign to replace condoms with Bibles in public schools.

PART FOUR

FRONTLINES OF CHRISTIAN NATIONALISM

Every movement has various frontline causes that rally the masses. In American politics, these are often called "wedge issues" that keep the public engaged and fired up. They are often sensationalized and the conversations around them can lack nuance—making a clear right versus wrong situation. Christian Nationalism is no different, and the movement has exploited these issues in varying ways. Some of the frontline topics are the same as when I was in the movement, while others are new or repackaged in recent years.

For instance, my preferred president never had a mug shot or criminal charges that I needed to defend constantly. That's new.

Other than that, I fought on many of the same frontlines as Christian Nationalism today—guns, abortion, education, and LGBTQ issues. I was a pro at wielding my own verbal weapons against those who dared fight for the other side.

This section will dive into these main issues of Christian Nationalism and explore how the movement uses various tactics around them to advance their own agenda, tenets, and quest for power.

CHAPTER 13

Holy Mosh Pits: Guns, Violence, and Other Christian Things

One day after school, I was alone in my bathroom at home. I looked in the mirror, rounded my lips, and grunted, "JESUS LOVES YOU!!!"

My eighteen-year-old voice cracked. *My voice needs to be deeper.*

I tried again, lowering my chin and reaching into my lowest guttural range. With all my might, I screamed, "JESUS LOVES YOU!!!!"

That was better.

I had recently joined my youth group's worship band. We performed at our church's Wednesday night teen service, but we weren't your grandma's youth group worship band. We were a SCREAMO worship band. It was like a normal band, but at least one of the members could scream-grunt the lyrics. We performed typical worship songs from Hillsong like everybody else, but we also sang *original* songs that included intense screamo parts.

Our fearless leader wrote many of the songs we sang. He was a Black man in his thirties. He wore stud earrings—so cool—and was the head worship pastor of the large Florida church. But on Wednesday nights, he was *our* hardcore worship leader. He bounced around that youth group stage with boundless energy. This was his time to let loose in a way that he couldn't on Sunday mornings, around the old people in choir robes.

During certain worship sets, we would intentionally carve out room in front of the stage for a mosh pit. This gave the audience room to throw air punches and use their bodies like human bumper cars. The focus of this rage dancing was not really rhythm or looking good; it was about letting out as much energy as possible, flailing limbs with abandon. And yes, if you were brave enough to venture into this section, you probably left with some bruises. I can testify to that personally.

If it seems strange to you to find a mosh pit in the middle of a youth group worship set, I should probably point out that there was a lot of repression going on in that room. We were supposed to push down all our feelings that weren't approved by our parents and Jesus and put on a happy face to win people to Christ. There was a lot of angst buried not too deep there. These mosh pits were the one place we could let out our aggression in a parent- and Jesus-approved way. And if the sessions led to a few injuries sometimes, well, a little pain was a small price to pay to let a bunch of good evangelical kids let off some steam.

Violence, aggression, anger—these were emotions we weren't supposed to feel, especially if you were a girl. If someone mistreated us, we were supposed to turn the other cheek, not retaliate. Show them the love of Jesus. Sunday school teachers regularly taught us that Christians should be peaceful because violence was wrong. One of the Ten Commandments was "Thou shalt not kill," and we believed killing was sinful. Christ had told his followers to lay down their weapons. Sure, he flipped a couple of tables that one time, but he wanted us to be nonviolent. We needed to be full of love, peace, self-control, kindness, and all the other fruits of the spirit. Since I was a preacher's daughter, it was especially important that my life reflect these good qualities. Lots of people were watching me.

Holy mosh pits helped but could alleviate only so much. This led to suppressing my more aggressive feelings, especially once my teenage angst arrived. Good Christians don't get angry.

But there were exceptions.

We could be angry at the devil. Violence against Satan was A-OK.

My family spent a summer ministering in Singapore when I was seventeen. One night, we rented out a huge convention center for a special play my dad had come up with. Local churches partnered with us and had homemade costumes ready for this special "one night only" event where we turned the stage into a giant boxing ring.

In my dad's corner of the ring were several actors wearing long white dresses splashed with something shimmery, which made them sparkle. These were angels. On the other side was Satan, played by my brother Matt. He wore a black skeleton bodysuit with a black cape and had spiked his freshly red-chalked hair. His face was painted white, with dark eyebrows and large painted-on white teeth over the entire lower half of his face. He looked like Heath Ledger as the Joker if that costume department had a shoestring budget. My other brother, Andrew, was backing him up as the demon of greed. You knew this because he had the word GREED written on his all-black outfit. I began the production by walking through the ring holding a huge sign that said, "Round 1."

The event was a visual representation of spiritual warfare—a literal fight between my dad and the devil. Punches. Kicks. Wrestling.

Sometimes the demons would run into the ring and attack my dad because they obviously didn't play fair. Satan would play mind games with my dad saying things like, "You can't win . . . you're so weak when you don't read the Bible!" My dad lost that round.

Then Jesus appeared, wearing a hippie flower-power wig and a flamboyant purple-and-white dress. Hippie Jesus approached my dad and encouraged him with lines like "Just believe in me. You can do it with me!" That's when the fight turned. My dad worked with Jesus to eventually *Mortal Kombat* KO Satan right to the ground. The crowd of thousands went wild!

Beyond fights against the devil, when I was growing up, military language was used frequently in sermons and lessons. Christian kids were told they were on the "frontlines" in public schools, fighting to stop Satan from stealing kids' hearts and minds. Men battled for their souls every day not to watch porn. Women were charged to raise the next generation of warriors for Christ. One youth camp speaker brought out a real sword to illustrate how we must fight off the sinister sin of flirting. Not kidding.

As kids, my brothers and I often sang a song called "I'm in the Lord's Army," with lyrics like: "I may never march in the infantry, ride in the cavalry." The song included other military activities that us kids may never do, but we were still "in the Lord's army"—a phrase repeated throughout the song while we marched in place.

This is why it probably shouldn't have been surprising when everyone in my evangelical circles seemed to support that invasion of Iraq in 2003. Jesus was the Prince of Peace and violence was never the answer, but this was different. There were weapons of mass destruction and it was our job to destroy them! We were on Team America.

We just knew that Jesus was on America's side, too. God had already supernaturally blessed our country to kill lots of bad guys in pretty much every war we ever fought in, so clearly God was okay with us killing for the greater good.

The few times I heard about the muddy morality of the Vietnam War or about how the United States dropped nuclear bombs on civilians in Japan, I struggled to understand. *The innocent children*... I would think before quickly shoving it down with *God's ways are above our own*. I was a teenager; there must be something I just didn't understand yet. God understood, and so did all the Christian leaders around me. America was always right, and I just needed to squash my sissy, pacifist thoughts.

Outside of war, I learned it was also okay to use violence if you were defending yourself. I was a Texan, after all. Owning a gun was our "God-given right." And since anything from God was good, then guns were also good. The Second Amendment was sacred. The holy-inspired Constitution featured the right to bear arms.

I don't remember a time when my family didn't own guns. We would go out to the country and shoot skeet and tin cans for fun. I remember feeling so proud when I shot my first 12-gauge shotgun at ten years old and didn't fall over from the kickback. I stood my ground, and my dad gave me a high five.

I also shot my first (and only) duck when I was ten years old (it was a big year for me). I named him Fred. As I held his lifeless body, I whispered,

"I'm sorry," to him before quickly shoving down the rising guilt. The local pastor we went with took pictures of my dad and me, smiling among a dozen dead ducks. Several church members heard about it and lauded me for my shooting abilities. Animals didn't have souls, so no one cared about the ducks. And I pretended not to care either.

When I was thirteen, my family and I spent a summer in South Africa. On a day off from ministry, we went with some locals on a wildebeest hunt. We hiked up a mountain and tiptoed beside cliff edges, looking for what was said to be a record-breaking beast, both in size and age.

After several hours, we spotted him a few hundred yards away. My dad was handed the rifle, as everyone wanted the American evangelist to make the shot. He did, and the kickback was so strong, the scope of the rifle hit him between his eyes, causing blood to rush down his face. He would have a scar there for the rest of his life. But the wildebeest fell, and we gave the meat to a local village. Then my dad had the animal stuffed by a taxidermist and sent to our home in Texas.

My dad displayed that thing in our home proudly. He loved that stuffed wildebeest. My brothers and I did, too. The wildebeest made appearances in several goofy photoshoots over the years and even played the Balrog (the giant fire monster underneath the mountain) in our homemade *Lord of the Rings* movie.

But to be honest, I always had internal conflicts over shooting animals. I love animals. I even wanted to be a veterinarian at one point. But I was always assured killing animals was okay. Animals were made for us to eat. Jesus didn't die for them. Humans had dominion over them like Genesis 1 says.

After all, I ate animals. How was it different to shoot them myself? Hunting for food was how I justified owning guns, initially. I could buy that. Shooting animals was necessary, at least if you wanted to eat meat. I didn't want anyone to take away my right to shoot my own dinner. Therefore, I was against anyone taking away my right to *any* kind of gun. Sure, I had no use for assault weapons personally, but it was a slippery slope. If you banned AR-15s, they'd come for all guns next.

The topic of gun control seemed to flare up whenever there was a mass shooting (which, admittedly, occurred more and more as the years passed). Whenever someone used a military-grade weapon to slaughter innocent people in a movie theater or a grocery store, I worried about liberals coming to take away my hunting rifle. Whenever I heard another headline, I dove right into defending my right to own guns.

Interestingly, though, my arguments about prying my guns out of my cold dead hands didn't usually have much to do with hunting. I wouldn't give up my guns because I knew that enemies of God wanted to de-arm us Christians so they could eventually take away our right to worship. It would start with gun control, but then it would turn into government control of everything! Guns, we believed, were necessary to ensure our Christian nation.

I believed this firmly and stridently until December 14, 2012. That was the day a lone gunman took a semi-automatic rifle into Sandy Hook Elementary School.[1] As each slain child's picture appeared on the news, I was gut-punched with sorrow. Even though I was loudly and stridently against gun control of any kind, as I watched those little faces flash up on the screen, I started to wonder if there were cases when maybe it might not be the worst thing in the world to not let everyone have access to military-style assault rifles.

Was it possible that *some* gun control might be a good idea? Maybe limiting access to deadly weapons might not be such a terrible thing?

As I saw the gun control debate take off in the weeks after the school massacre, I noticed a consistent lack of empathy from fellow evangelicals. Instead of talking about the problem of readily available military-style weapons, they were blaming Democrats for politicizing a tragedy. This was straight out of my playbook, but it felt different this time.

These were *children* brutally killed in their classrooms. I thought we were supposed to be the party who protected the little ones. But in those dark December days, I found I could no longer just point fingers at liberals. I wanted to fix the problem. No one on my side was talking about solutions, so I decided to actually listen to what people on the other side were saying.

I was surprised that most Democrats did *not* want to ban all guns like I had been led to believe. Some did, but most weren't arguing for that at all. Most of them supported the Second Amendment. They just wanted universal background checks and to ban semi-automatic assault rifles, or *at least* make them harder to get. They believed it should not be easy to get a weapon designed exclusively to kill lots of people.

That made sense to me.

Panic.

Am I a liberal? No, I'm sure Republicans would agree with this. It's so sensible.

But it was counterintuitive. I had been led to believe that *any* gun control was a means to an end—the end being the government banning all guns, letting communism take over, and outlawing Christianity.

But for the first time in my little Nationalist life, I wasn't convinced of this argument.

At church the Sunday after the tragedy, I overheard a fellow church member say, "You know, some people are saying Sandy Hook was an inside job. That the government faked the whole thing in order to ban guns so we won't be able to fight back. I'm not saying it's true... I'm just saying we don't know everything."

Do we always sound like this? I thought to myself, unsure why I was suddenly hearing things so differently.

My growing misgivings about guns were tested a few months later. I was about to graduate with my master's in journalism and needed a job. As part of an extensive interview with a grassroots conservative media organization, I was asked to film a news story about guns. They sent me to a couple local restaurants that, at the height of the renewed gun control debate, decided to offer a 15% discount to any customer who openly carried a gun inside.

I talked to gun-carrying patrons and restaurant owners, getting close-up shots of their guns—some were borderline crotch shots, which was more than a little uncomfortable. Everyone I talked to was thrilled to be part of the story, believing they were standing up for something good—the right to publicly carry a deadly weapon into a local café.

The two-minute feature turned out so well that the organization offered me a job. They claimed I could be the "future Rachel Maddow of conservatives." I could have beat Tomi Lahren to the throne.

But when I prayed about it, taking it didn't feel like the right thing to do. Despite not having any other job offers at the time, I turned it down.

I think growing up in the "peaceful" religion of evangelical fundamentalism, which was also pro-gun, pro-war, and pro-violence against anything we deemed evil, was finally getting to me.

All of this helps explain why I was not surprised as I watched the violence unfold on January 6th. Insurrectionists waving Jesus flags while joining a mob that bludgeoned police officers and chanted "Hang Mike Pence!" was the perfect embodiment of the cognitive dissonance I grew up with.

The only thing new about the rage happening under the banner of Christianity was where it was aimed. Trump found a way to harness something that had been there for years and wield it for his own political gain.

When he and so many right-wing talking heads touted the lie that the election was stolen, it echoed throughout congregations eager to take up arms for a righteous cause. Repressed anger builds over time until it can no longer be contained. Christian Nationalists finally had a place to release it. I believe that was one of the initial draws of Trump in that crowded Republican primary field of 2016.

He said the things you weren't supposed to say, to the delight of many evangelicals who were tired of playing nice. He emboldened the violence and hate that had remained quietly under the surface in churches across the country. Christian Nationalists wanted a bulldog. They wanted a figurehead who could fully channel the anger they couldn't really express in their own Christian lives.

I think this is one of the draws of Christian Nationalism. The Jesus that they preach about is not the gentle lamb depicted in the Bible. They prefer the Jesus who flipped over tables in righteous anger. The focus is *not* on Jesus willingly sacrificing himself, but on how Jesus *could* have smoked the Romans who crucified him if he wanted to. The only reason he didn't was because he had to die for our sins that one time. But now that part is over, and when Jesus comes back, he will return as a roaring lion looking for payback.

The Christian Nationalism version of Jesus doesn't want you to wait on his return either. He wants you to take up the fight today. It gives people an opportunity to be both Christian *and* violent if need be.

Guns are a frontline issue for Christian Nationalists for several reasons. For one thing, this issue allows them to feign persecution—"They want to take your guns away so they can ultimately throw Christians in jail!" It also allows them to keep the focus on the end times: "The Antichrist is rising, and we need to be prepared to fight in the final war!"

While Trump emboldened the cruel side of Christian Nationalism in recent years, this desire for violence has been brewing inside the ideology for a long time. From the obsession with guns to the praise of war, I saw it all. Believed it all. It's just that there seem to be more practical outlets today for individuals who want to let their violent inhibitions out.

One of the more infamous outlets is called the Oath Keepers. They are a militant extremist group founded in 2009 "to defend the Constitution against all enemies, foreign and domestic."[2] Practically, the group operates by showing up to public gatherings in full tactical gear, oftentimes inciting confrontations. Their ire might be aimed against demonstrators at Black Lives Matter rallies or even the police officers protecting the Capitol on January 6th.

The group's founder, Stewart Rhodes, is currently serving eighteen years behind bars for seditious conspiracy in the January 6th insurrection.[3] A few weeks prior to the insurrection, Rhodes spoke at a large Christian prayer rally in DC called the Jericho March, where he said if Trump did not invoke the Insurrection Act, groups like his Oath Keepers would resort to a "much more desperate, much more bloody war."[4]

For most of the Oath Keepers' existence, they used a familiar strategy to justify their aggressive methods. They framed much of their work as keeping tyranny at bay by stopping leftist groups from implementing even the smallest amount of gun regulation.[5]

It's much easier to justify violence if you can paint the other side as *more* violent. My dad did this with me when he explained America's War on Terror. We had to invade Iraq to stop them from attacking us and other countries, he said, which even then sounded a little shaky. This logic is also what I've heard pastors cite as justification for owning guns. The classic "the only thing that stops a bad guy with a gun is a good guy with a gun" argument. When I was in the movement, we didn't want to stop *all* violence. Just violence done by "bad guys."

The tragic elementary school shooting in Uvalde, Texas, in 2022 gave Christian Nationalists ample opportunity to fight on the frontlines for guns again. In an interview with Newsmax, Texas Republican Brian Babin said, "The United States of America has always had guns. It's our history. We were built on the Judeo-Christian foundation and with guns."[6]

Self-proclaimed Christian Nationalist Marjorie Taylor Greene tweeted, "We don't need more gun control. We need to return to God."[7] This is a one-two punch: Keep Guns. Add God. Rhetoric like this fuels the argument for a Christian nation. It deflects from a problem we created (gun violence) and gives a solution that empowers the cause (Christian Nationalism).

Many evangelicals want to have a godly nation, but few are eager to kill others for it. There are plenty of conservative Christians who were mortified by the violence of January 6th and value the teachings of Jesus over earthly power. But the spiritual warfare language of evangelicalism is manipulated by nationalism, emphasizing the warfare part over the spiritual one. If there's a literal war coming, it's easier to make a case for why guns are necessary.

At a Christian conference in 2022, Congresswoman Lauren Boebert even "joked" that Jesus "didn't have enough [AR-15s] to keep his government from killing him."[8] Underneath the joke is a violent belief, though.

William Wolfe, a former Trump administration official and unashamed Christian Nationalist, said the quiet part out loud at a Jesus and Politics Conference in October 2023. He warned the time was close when

Christians would need to "heed the call to arms." Condemning cowardly Christians, he read an excerpt from a 1758 sermon by Virginia preacher Samuel Davies during the French and Indian War. He quoted Davies, saying that when Christians "are in danger by the loss of our religion," then "even the God of Peace proclaims by His providence, 'To arms!' . . . and the art of war becomes a part of our religion."[9]

Video of his remarks was shared by Right Wing Watch and began spreading. While Wolfe initially doubled down and thanked the organization for sharing the clip, he later claimed he only meant taking up arms in self-defense, not calling for "proactive measures." Which is all fine and dandy until you realize that Christian Nationalists are already on the defensive. Wolfe even said that the video of his words was a "hit job" and called Right Wing Watch an "anti-Christian organization" that wants to "criminalize Christianity."[10]

Did you see how Wolfe used two Christian Nationalist tactics in one? Demonizing enemies and claiming persecution. Classics.

The thing is, as fun as it is to shoot stuff, a love for guns can make it hard to follow Jesus, who famously told his disciples to lay down their swords. Trust me, I tried to square these two opposite realities for a long time. It requires either cognitive dissonance or outright dismissal of Christ's teaching. Some Nationalists, it seems, have chosen to do the latter.

In August 2023, Russell Moore, a former top official in the Southern Baptist Convention and the editor in chief of *Christianity Today*, sounded the alarm about this very thing. In an interview with NPR, Moore said that Christianity in the United States was in crisis.

Moore said some churchgoers were complaining about sermons that included "liberal talking points" such as "turn the other cheek." When pastors defended their positions by explaining the quotes belonged to Jesus himself, the congregants responded with, "Yeah, but that doesn't work anymore. That's weak."[11]

You read that right. Classic Jesus is for sissies.

Since there is no shortage of war talk in American evangelicalism, it's likely that guns will continue to be a frontline issue. As more and more Christian Nationalists abandon their choir robes for holy mosh pits, it seems likely that more and more innocent bystanders will continue to be bruised along the way.

CHAPTER 14

Rubber Fetus for Jesus: Abortion

When I was twelve, I climbed into a plain white church van with a dozen other youth group kids. This was my first outing with the cool teenagers, and I was determined to fit in with them. No more kids' church puppet shows for me!

It was October, and we were attending a local church's Hell House. Imagine a typical haunted house, but instead of zombies or ghosts, you're terrorized by demons. Biblical demons. You walk through a warehouse and a mini drama is performed in each room you pass. Someone commits a sin in each scene—whether it's drugs, sex, or being ashamed of God in the face of a school shooter—then that sin results in a death somehow, after which Biblical demons appear and drag that person to hell. Good Christian fun.

Unlike a typical haunted house, we didn't have the luxury of telling ourselves, "It's not real." Nope. All along the route we walked, there were little reminders that THIS COULD BE YOU!

The purpose of a Hell House, after all, was to convince you that it *is* all real. Or at least it *will* be if you don't repent. When you reach the end of the Hell House, a pastor shows up and tells you everything you just saw will be real one day but don't worry! There's a get-out-of-hell-free prayer! "Just repeat these words after me and POOF! You're saved."

After standing in line for an hour outside the large warehouse-like building on this sold-out fall night, our youth group finally made it inside. We were led into a dimly lit, stuffy room. Eerie music played in the background. Distant screaming echoed from beyond the doors. Anxiety rumbled in the pit of my belly.

The hallway doors opened, and smoke escaped from behind them, filling the room we were in.

"Good news! It's y'all's turn," said the overly chipper church volunteer. He wore glasses and a JESUS LOVES THE HELL OUT OF YOU T-shirt.

I giggled nervously as we made our way into the dark room. The door shut behind us, and a spotlight lit up what looked like a hospital bed.

The first thing I saw was blood. So much blood. A blood-drenched white sheet covered up a very sick-looking girl. She looked to be about fifteen years old. There was also a doctor, a nurse, and two demons lurking in the background.

"We've convinced another silly girl that 'my body, my choice' is actually about women's rights!" one of the demons sneered.

The girl screamed. Alarms started going off in the room.

"We have a problem with the ABORTION..." the doctor said emphatically, pulling out of the girl a grotesque baby doll that gave the demon-possessed *Annabelle* a run for her money. Forget being able to fit inside an amniotic sack—this thing was the size of a six-month-old baby. No wonder there was a problem!

"Can't wait to welcome this girl to her new home in hell," the other demon said.

The doctor tried to revive the unconscious girl, but with each chest compression, blood sprayed out. It was like she had a sprinkler inside her stomach.

I held my own belly, empathetically feeling the pain. *Well, I am never having sex...* I thought to myself. This was incredibly well-scripted religious trauma.

"What a sucker! If only she'd honored her purity pledge, maybe she would have made her high school graduation! BWAHAHA," the demons laughed.

Lights shut off. A scream pierced the room. The heart monitor stopped beeping and held out one long note.

The lights came back on. The doctor and nurse were frozen in place. The only movement was from the demons, who were now dragging the screaming girl to hell.

"Jesus, I'm sorry! I shouldn't have slept with the football player!" The girl's voice faded into the background as they walked out of the room, ending the scene for Room 1.

That was my introduction to abortion.

It was by far the most graphic thing I had ever seen in my twelve years of life. Yes, these were church volunteers acting. Yes, it was probably cheesy, but I was mortified (not to mention horrified). My parents made me leave the room for graphic parts in PG movies, and now I was seeing a full-on R-rated demonic death sequence.

This scene cemented my anti-abortion stance for years. I was proudly pro-life. (This is excellent branding, by the way—who could say they were "anti-life"?) The bloody Hell House scene haunted my thoughts any time the issue came up. As I went through my teenage years, this sensationalized view of abortion remained all I had ever been taught. Abortion meant dismemberment. Decapitation. Demonic influence. Medically viable babies, murdered in the final days of pregnancy.

My views were clear and unambiguous. How could anyone kill their baby after carrying them for nine months? *Democrats want women to kill their babies*, I'd think in disgust. Everyone around me shared the same sentiment, so I never heard a different viewpoint.

Abortion was one of those things we didn't even need to talk about. If you were a Christian, you were pro-life. Period. It was a litmus test of sorts. Real Christians agreed on this. *All* life was sacred, and abortion was taking life away from the most innocent of beings: babies. We believed life began at conception. Each life had a divine purpose, formed in the womb by the Creator. It was not our job to play God.

So it didn't seem strange when, during my junior year of college, I went to an outdoor summer festival with some friends and one booth featured a pro-life ministry that handed each of us a small, rubbery fetus.

The earnest woman in capri pants told us, "Even if you abort early, *this* is what you're killing."

Honestly, it looked more alien than human. It was a creepy little thing, made of a material that attracted every dust mite and rogue hair to it. I wasn't sure handing out these eerie rubber fetuses for Jesus would have the intended effect. *Jesus Fetus. That could be a band name.*

Because we had a digital camera and too much time on our hands, my friends and I decided to use our new rubber fetuses as props for a photoshoot. We posed with our fetuses while eating pancakes at IHOP, frolicking in a field, and driving in the car. At the end of our rubber fetus photoshoot, one of my friends turned to us and asked, "What would y'all do if you found out you were pregnant right now?"

"I'd tell my parents, 'Wow, the Holy Spirit did it again! What a miracle!' " I said, giggling at my own joke. My friends laughed, too.

"Okay, but what would you really do?" she asked us again. Silence filled the air. I let myself imagine the situation. A positive pregnancy test. Unmarried. Still in college, and with parents who would be so disappointed. My dad was still pastoring a church. I knew how Christians treated unwed pregnant girls. I heard what they said about them behind their backs. My heart sank at the idea of that vitriol being directed at me.

Would I rather live with the secret shame of having an abortion than the public shaming of having a baby? I could handle it. I'd ask God for forgiveness. No one would have to know... but could I kill a baby?

I looked at the rubber fetus in my hand. Human-esque but not quite. *Could I end this... thing?*

"What about you, April?" The words interrupted my thoughts. I realized my friends had already answered.

"I don't know, but I honestly think my dad would rather hear I killed someone than hear I was pregnant. With what the church would think, I'd embarrass my entire family."

It was a sad but truthful sentiment.

"Yeah, my parents would freak, too," one friend said. "Why is the church so pro-life, but when a girl gets pregnant, they just shame her and kick her out? Like, she actually kept the baby, and did the thing they wanted her to do."

We talked in depth about it for a long while. It was the first nuanced conversation I'd ever had about abortion.

"Well, at least this won't matter for us since we're not having sex until marriage," I said toward the end of the discussion.

We all agreed. Then it was out of sight, out of mind. Abortion was murder and no Christian should support it. Even hinting at the nuance got you branded a "baby killer" so it was best to just stick to a black-and-white approach.

Abortion is a frontline issue for Christian Nationalism, and it has been for decades. The narrative is tightly controlled in conservative media, so much so that I never once heard a differing perspective on abortion. It was always murder. I never saw or read anything that would lead me to question that. When all you hear is "Democrats are baby murderers" and "Republicans protect children," choosing a side is simple.

Abortion was also presented as a form of persecution—not against Christians per se, but against innocent babies. And we loved a good persecution narrative! When presented with only that perspective, who would want to be on the side that "kills babies"?

There is a reason this has become such a frontline issue. Many Christians feel so strongly about abortion that the issue is extremely good at motivating evangelicals to turn out for elections.

One of the main arguments I heard about voting for Trump in 2016 was that we needed him because of the Supreme Court. We needed Trump to appoint pro-life justices so we could overturn *Roe v. Wade*. "Think of the babies, April!"

I could not vote for Trump, but abortion was why I voted third party in 2016. I was convinced that voting for a Democrat would put the blood of every aborted baby on my hands. I knew Trump was dangerous. I vehemently did not want him in office. But this single issue forced my hand into throwing away my vote in the two-party system. This frontline issue was a huge factor in Trump's election.

The irony is that many of the people who tried to convince me to save the babies also voted for a man who pressured his mistress to get an abortion and admitted his ex-wife mutually agreed to have two abortions while they were together. And if you think I am talking about Trump right now, you are mistaken.

For over a decade, the Fourth District of Tennessee has been represented by Scott DesJarlais in the United States House of Representatives. If you Google his name, you will quickly find a plethora of articles about his scandalous history, including a medical fine for sleeping with patients, abuse allegations from his ex-wife (which he has denied), and how he seems more than fine with women having abortions in his personal life.[1, 2, 3]

Despite all of this, pro-life Tennesseans continually vote for DesJarlais—a man who openly defies the very values they claim to espouse.

In 2020, DesJarlais was challenged by a pro-life Democrat named Chris Hale. That year, I attended a town hall where Hale spoke on abortion and passionately talked about how his faith made him value all life. He had a clear plan to lower abortion rates in the state that included greater health care spending, comprehensive sex education, and deregulating birth control.[4]

I was hopeful. What conservative would choose the candidate who had, in their minds, "murdered babies" over a pro-life candidate who hadn't? My naivety led me to believe that the conservatives around me really did care about reducing abortion rates and voting for actual pro-life candidates. I thought for sure Hale would win.

But DesJarlais won in a landslide, receiving 66.7 percent of the vote.[5]

After the results came in, I was faced with an uncomfortable realization. *It's not about saving babies.*

This was the first time I saw the abortion issue for what it was: an effective call to action to get us to vote Republican. It didn't matter if a challenging Democrat was also pro-life; the narrative that Democrats were baby murderers was too deeply ingrained to be refuted.

In the wake of the Supreme Court overturning *Roe v. Wade*, abortion continues to be a driving issue of Christian Nationalism. Even though polls consistently show that most Americans, including Republicans, want abortion to be legal, we continue to see a push for heavily restricted access, if not total abortion bans.[6]

In the days following the Supreme Court's *Dobbs* decision in 2022, we saw the horrors of not including exceptions in abortion bans across the states. After being raped, a ten-year-old girl was not allowed to receive an abortion at six-and-a-half weeks gestation due to Ohio's "fetal heartbeat law." The young girl was forced to travel to Indiana to have the procedure done.[7]

But for Christian Nationalists, the abortion issue is not just about winning elections (though that's part of it). Abortion is also used as a litmus test for God's blessing on the nation. After 9/11, I remember listening to Jerry Falwell Sr. partly blame the terrorist attacks on abortionists.[8] Though he later apologized for the comment, he was just expressing a sentiment that others had long believed. We believed God's favor on America was waning because of our moral failings—and abortion was at the top of that list. In the '80s, Falwell even wrote, "If we expect God to honor and bless our nation, we must take a stand against abortion."[9]

For many years, I earnestly believed that to get back to righteousness as the Christian nation we were supposed to be, we had to end abortion. That's what moves this issue out of religious territory and into Christian Nationalist territory—the belief that the fate of our nation is dependent on our stance on abortion. If we end abortion, God will bless our nation richly, and those who stand in the way—baby murderers—are actively working to diminish our nation in the eyes of the Lord.

This sincere belief is what allows Christian Nationalists to make laws for everyone else. They believe abortion is wrong, and so they make laws to ensure no one has access to abortions. It's not a matter of personal choice but of national responsibility. Your abortion, in other words, keeps God's blessings from me, so we have to ban it.

In February 2024, Alabama Supreme Court Chief Justice Tom Parker, who has espoused support for the Seven Mountain Mandate, agreed with his court's decision to consider frozen embryos children. In a concurring opinion, he wrote that Alabama's decision was a "theologically based view of the sanctity of life" and that "life cannot be wrongfully destroyed without incurring the wrath of a holy God."[10]

Better not trip a breaker at an IVF facility lest you be charged with mass murder for... unfreezing children? This extremism has been a long time coming.

I saw how radicalized my fellow evangelicals were becoming in the years following 2016. Vehemently disagreeing with them on Trump, I wondered if there were other things they had taught me that were wrong, or at least misguided. Since abortion was what had kept me from voting against Trump, I decided to research that issue first. And I had plenty of time during the quarantine in 2020.

Imagine my surprise when I investigated the history of the pro-life movement and learned it was actually a Republican-nominated Supreme Court that made the decision to legalize abortion through *Roe v. Wade* in 1973. At the time, polling showed that most evangelicals were either indifferent on the issue or supported access to abortion.[11]

In addition, two years before the *Roe v. Wade* ruling, the Southern Baptist Convention passed a resolution that encouraged SBC members "to work for legislation that will allow the possibility of abortion under such conditions as rape, incest, clear evidence of severe fetal deformity, and carefully ascertained evidence of the likelihood of damage to the emotional, mental, and physical health of the mother."[12]

Can you imagine the SBC releasing a statement like that today? They would be accused of being part of the woke, liberal mob trying to destroy this nation.

W. A. Criswell, a former president of the Southern Baptist Convention, pastored First Baptist Church in Texas at the time (now pastored by famed Trump enthusiast Robert Jeffress). He was so pleased with the SCOTUS decision that he said, "I have always felt that it was only after a child was born and had a life separate from its mother that it became an individual person, and it has always, therefore, seemed to me that what is best for the mother and for the future should be allowed."[13]

Now that we are in a post-*Roe* world, Christian Nationalism has moved beyond just saving babies to punishing women. Part of this strategy includes turning constituents into pro-life vigilantes, where they can report people who are "aiding or abetting a post-heartbeat abortion." Texas implemented this bounty hunter–type law that allows citizens to sue for $10,000 if they discover an abortion was performed past six weeks. This targets a woman's support system, hoping to intimidate doctors, family, and friends of pregnant women.[14]

If that's not bad enough, let's talk for a moment about the giddiness some Christian Nationalists have displayed at criminalizing abortion. At the 2022 annual Road to Majority Policy Conference, Chelsey Youman, a national legislation adviser to an anti-abortion organization called Human Coalition Action, was thrilled about criminalizing legal, out-of-state abortions and allowing regular citizens to report on women who get them. "It creates a wrongful death cause of action, so we're excited about that," she said. In discussing plans to also target abortion pills, she said, "Our next big bill is going to make the Heartbeat Act look tame, you guys; they're going to freak out!"[15]

The strategy also demonizes anyone who merely votes for a pro-choice candidate. Many pastors believe that church members who vote for pro-choice candidates should be placed under church discipline. After Senate Democrats tried and failed to codify abortion rights in May 2022,[16] Texas pastor Tom Buck said to his 50,000+ X followers that "we are rapidly reaching the point that voting for a Democrat should be a matter of church discipline."[17]

William Wolfe, former Deputy Assistant Secretary of Defense for President Trump and proponent of Christian Nationalism, said in a now-deleted post that Christians "who support pro-abortion politicians should be completely cancelled. They should be viewed with *greater* repulsion than professing Christians who support 'white supremacy.' "[18]

Publicly saying it's better to be a White supremacist than to vote blue is quite the take. But it's not an isolated one.

During the 2020 Black Lives Matter protests I attended, we were repeatedly asked, "How many of you have had abortions lately?!?!"

"HA HA HA! Bet you want three abortion clinics on every damn corner, don't ya?" yelled another.

Never mind that the issue we were supporting—moving a Confederate monument to a museum—had literally nothing to do with abortion. Despite their assumptions, none of us had abortion punch cards. Some of us were even Republican! But because we were standing for racial justice, they just assumed we were Democrats and thus baby murderers.

The confusion about abortion and race within conservative circles isn't new, though. Remember when I told you how I investigated the history of the pro-life movement? Here's something else I learned. The original issue that united the Religious Right and made them a political force was not abortion at all. No, they united to fight racial integration in schools. White conservative Christians didn't like the government forcing them to accept non-White people in their private Christian schools.[19]

Wait a minute. *The Religious Right was originally created to fight against racial equality in society? And we were generally indifferent on abortion?*

This was a lot for me to take in. I was on the verge of having an existential crisis in 2020. So much of my passionate beliefs were centered around this cause and based on a historical understanding that turned out to be... wrong?

As I looked further into the issue, I came across several different facts that pushed the subject of abortion into a more complicated space for me:

- Countries with more restrictive abortion laws have higher abortion rates.[20] (In the year following the overturning of *Roe v. Wade*, the abortion rate increased nationwide.[21])

- The most effective way to reduce abortion is by making birth control free and easily accessible and teaching comprehensive sex education, things I had consistently fought against.[22]
- A D&C (dilation and curettage) is the same procedure whether it's assisting a woman having a miscarriage or performing an abortion. Banning abortion puts women who miscarry at risk of being denied a D&C or in legal trouble if they cannot prove the miscarriage was accidental.[23]
- Only 1.3% of all abortions happen after 21 weeks (the notorious "late-term abortions") and those are almost entirely because of "lethal fetal anomalies or threats to the health of the mother." Exactly zero women carry a baby for 9 months and then choose to just get rid of a healthy baby willy-nilly.[24]

During the pandemic, I continued to read stories from women who shared their personal, heart-wrenching experiences around abortion. They were not the murderers I was told they were. Some didn't want to be trapped with their abuser. Others had no financial means to raise a child. Some were teenagers. Many of them already had children and, upon learning of grave fetal abnormalities and a high risk of dying themselves, made the difficult decision to choose their own life. I put myself in that position—my life or the one in my womb. Could I knowingly leave my two daughters without a mother to save a third child? I didn't know what I would choose, but I knew I would like that choice to be mine and Beecher's.

The more I learned, the more nuanced the issue became. Sure, I could've researched it myself at any point prior to this, but I had no reason to doubt my Christian leaders. You don't know what you don't know, and it's not exactly fun to learn things that undo a lifetime of beliefs. It's called an existential *crisis* for a reason.

But since I was a Christian, there was one important question I still needed to tackle.

What does the Bible say about abortion?

I knew "Thou shall not kill" in the Ten Commandments, but that clearly seemed to address Cain and Abel–type murder. I knew "Before I formed you in the womb, I knew you," but that didn't actually address abortion. I mean, lots of Christian Nationalists staked one's salvation on their abortion stance, so surely there was something concrete about it in the Bible that I just missed.

The Gospels? Nope.

Paul's letters? Nada.

The Old Testament? Not really . . . wait a minute.

Exodus 21:22–23 (GNT) states a law that insinuates the pregnant woman's life is more valuable than that of the baby in her womb. The law states that if a person accidentally causes a woman to miscarry, then the punishment is a fine. But if the woman dies, then the punishment is death.

Now to be fair, I saw some translations say that the Scripture meant a fine for premature birth and death for a miscarriage, but then I realized that ancient Judaism had always interpreted it to mean imposing the death penalty only if the mother dies.[25] The Hebrew Bible was Jewish text long before it ever belonged to an American evangelical, so I think I would defer to the rabbis.

Either way, it was ambiguous. Certainly not a clear condemnation of an issue that supposedly sent people to hell.

So much for "the Bible is clear."

I felt like I was discovering something new because, well, it was new to me. I needed to talk about it. *Other people need to know we've been misled!*

I tried to engage others and share what I was learning, asking questions out loud. I very quickly learned that very few Christians want to have a genuine conversation about this issue. Nuance is a dogma killer. It's a tactic we see repeatedly. Demonize the doubters, sensationalize the issue, make it about saving children. Who wouldn't vote Republican when you believe the other side is literally *murdering* babies?!

It's far less motivating when you realize that abortion is merely a symptom of a problem. The problem is unwanted pregnancies, lack of health care and childcare, and a shortage of sex ed and access to sexual protection. Solve the problem and the symptom typically goes away.

But Christian Nationalists are slapping Band-Aids on gushing wounds and anyone who suggests going to a doctor for stitches is placed under church discipline. Not very pro-life if you ask me, but what do I know? I was just a Band-Aid-slapping, abortion-is-murder, pro-life die-hard for thirty years.

And like Chris Hale, I still consider myself pro-life. But pro-all life—the mothers, children even after they're born, immigrants, the man on death row, people killed by gunfire. All life is sacred, not just the unborn.

It was a harsh reality when I realized my anti-abortion, pro-life position was really just pro-birth. Now that I've left Christian Nationalism, I feel like I'm actually pro-life... even though I'm now regularly called a baby murderer. Life comes at you fast.

CHAPTER 15

Drowning Dinosaurs: Education

In the last chapter, we looked at how Christian Nationalism embraces, promotes, and weaponizes pro-life narratives to rally its base and motivate voters to elect members of the Republican Party into government office. They use language about protecting innocent lives to create a groundswell of support for their positions of power and use that power to legislate morality, as they understand it, for all. But abortion is not the only issue that Christian Nationalism frames as being about protecting the innocent.

Education is another frontline issue that, on the surface, appears to be about something very good—protecting children's innocence by carefully monitoring what's taught in schools—but it's actually another area where Christian Nationalism manipulates its constituents to protect its own.

I understand that may sound jaded. Let me explain. To do so, let me tell you a little story about dinosaurs.

My academic history is a bit abnormal. Aside from the short time in middle school when I tried to be persecuted for my faith and the one year spent at public high school, I was either homeschooled or attended Christian schools. I learned the same basic things kids learned in public schools, but from a Christian perspective. So I learned math, reading, writing, history, and even science. I even learned about evolution—but only because the government required it be included in the curriculum. I know this because every time a Christian teacher brought up evolution, they explained how they were forced to tell us about Darwin and his silly idea. "We know this isn't true, but..." was how the lessons typically began.

Usually, the conversation lasted about one class period, and the word "theory" was heavily emphasized. "Theory" was defined as just some guy's possible explanation for something that may or may not be true. I left those classes with a greater understanding of their definition of the word "theory" than I did about anything regarding evolution.

The government-mandated evolution lesson was typically followed by several class periods in which we studied Young Earth Creationism. This was where I learned that the earth is 6,000 years old, that God created it in exactly seven days (six plus one for resting), and that God made every creature exactly as it appears to us today with no changes at all. The teacher usually said that even though Young Earth Creation is technically also a theory, it could be trusted because it was based on the totally true and literal creation story in Genesis. Since the Bible is inerrant because it came directly from God and God is perfect and we shouldn't question God... Well, you get the picture.

But Young Earth Creationism had one huge problem that left curious kids with lots of questions: dinosaurs.

There's evidence that dinosaurs existed on earth, so why doesn't the Bible mention them? Why didn't Noah take them on the ark? Where did they go?

The answer we were usually given was that the Bible couldn't possibly mention everything in existence and dinosaurs drowned in the Great Flood because Noah couldn't fit a T. rex on his boat.

But how does one explain fossils that are radioactively dated to be 68 million years old and somehow ended up on a planet we were told was only 6,000 years old? It didn't compute.

One theory that tackles this question is called Old Earth Creationism. It states that when God created everything in six literal days, he decided to create an aged earth instead of a shiny new one. You know, make it look vintage. Like buying distressed jeans. God made the earth with dead dinosaur bones already inside. If any student had the gall to ask why God would do that, we were given the classic "God works in mysterious ways" line.

Another theory I heard was that Satan himself planted dinosaur fossils to trick liberals into believing in science over faith. Since getting people to believe in evolution was one of the devil's most impressive feats, this one checked out.

I think the wildest idea I heard thrown around was from a lecture video featuring Ken Ham.

Now, Ken Ham is an Australian Christian apologist who is pretty famously known as the creation guy. He debated Bill Nye the Science Guy about the beginning of the world. He started the group Answers in Genesis, whose purpose is to debunk evolution and prove Young Earth Creationism as truth. He also started the Creation Museum and is responsible for the giant Ark Encounter (a supposed replica of Noah's Ark) in Kentucky.

Just to give a quick idea of what is taught there, Answers in Genesis shared a video on YouTube from the sloth exhibit at the Ark Encounter. Standing beside a real sloth, a guy with a microphone says: "Sloths by definition are slow. That's how they are made to operate. And it shouldn't surprise us they move slowly. And in today's lessons, we see something that should not surprise us as well: That is, Christians are persecuted. Sloths move slow while Christians are persecuted. That kind of happens because of who we are."[1]

Talk about whiplash.

But back to the point. In this lecture video, I remember Ken Ham talking about something called the Water Vapor Canopy Theory while standing in front of a diagram illustrating a water bubble enveloping the entire earth. This theory posits that the "waters above" mentioned in Genesis 1 were a literal ring of water floating above the planet. Whether it was a vapor, water, or ice canopy didn't matter. All that mattered was that one fateful day, all the liquid dropped down at once, causing the earth's very first rain and consequently, the great flood.[2] This sounded...

unlikely. But who was I to question my teachers, some of whom had gone to college?

Luckily, Noah and his ark full of animals were ready. His obedience to God saved all of creation from death. While the water bubble part of this explanation was called a theory, the Noah part was presented as fact because the Bible told us so.

Now to be fair, Ham didn't say he believed the water vapor thing in this video, but he seemed to place it in the same category of plausibility as evolution. Because they were both THEORIES.

In other lessons, we were properly equipped to fight science. Not with facts, obviously, but with the knowledge that scientists were controlled by Satan. *That's* why they didn't support Young Earth Creationism—because they were brainwashed servants of the devil.

This educational upbringing ingrained in me a natural distrust of all things relating to science. My teachers covered the basic material, but the learning itself wasn't the most important thing. In just about every subject, we had Bible lessons thrown in. Morality and Biblical knowledge were emphasized more than actual education.

For example, my high school geometry teacher used angles and shapes to teach abstinence. She told us a personal story of when she was in high school, and a boy tried to get her to go horizontal with him on a couch. She obliged for mere moments and almost ruined her purity. I can still picture her hand motions and sincere tone when she pleaded with us to "never go a hundred and eighty degrees horizontal, always stay vertical" when spending time with the opposite sex.

Looking back on my schooling now, I can acknowledge that the Bible was the foundation of my education—more so than the scientific method, the Socratic method, or any other method. Learning was important, sure, but not as important as salvation. Life is but a vapor, after all, but eternity is forever.

But not every teacher was completely on board with this. There were a few professors at these Christian institutions who pushed me to think outside of my safe worldview. At my Assemblies of God college, a sociology professor completely rocked my world when he said it was okay to ask questions. In fact, he said it wasn't just okay, but necessary. He emphasized critical thinking and taught us what types of things to ask and what sort of sources to trust. He especially rattled my cage when he said you can't trust everything your pastor says, telling me that one's interpretation of Scripture is most likely biased and based on their own experiences.

Um, I'm sorry. Scripture doesn't need interpreting. It's all written out clear as can be.

My dad had been my pastor for most of my life, and at first, I took this lesson as a personal attack against him. I was taught not to touch God's anointed, based on 1 Chronicles 16:22. Any pastor or minister was considered God's anointed, and we were to tread lightly when questioning someone's spiritual authority. Was my professor at this so-called Christian university telling me to go against that? To consider the possibility that our pastors might get it wrong sometimes?

Yes, he was. And as much as I disliked him initially, he got to me. He told me to read the Bible for myself and draw my own conclusions. Up until this point, my youth pastors, Sunday school leaders, and Christian teachers had told me *what* to think. But now I had someone teaching me *how* to think for myself.

Soon after, a Bible professor suggested that it was possible to believe in evolution *and* the Bible simultaneously. She said that the creation story in Genesis may not have been intended to be taken literally, after all. I nearly passed out when she told us she personally believed in the Big Bang Theory. *Well, hot dang... what kind of Christian college is this?*

Hearing this heresy from someone who was a Christian, from someone who was on *my* side, caused me to stop and reflect on the earth's origins for the first time. I started to read theories that didn't start with the assumption that the Bible was a science textbook. Suddenly, I was no longer studying for a test. I was questioning. Deciding what I believed, like I finally had a choice in the matter.

This questioning is one reason so many evangelical conservatives are souring on higher education today, as more and more claim that universities are just indoctrination camps hurting the country.[3] Pundits rail against liberal Marxist professors brainwashing the youth at public colleges and elite private institutions. I only ever went to very conservative Christian colleges, and my mind was still changed on many things. So perhaps it's not "indoctrination," after all, and just... learning?

But I digress.

While college expanded my views in many areas, there was one perspective I wasn't ready to reexamine. I could not consider America to be anything but a good, moral country that had been blessed by God to be the greatest nation on earth.

Since our founding, our country was about God, for God, and governed with God's guidance. We wanted to freely worship God! What a noble cause. Of course we weren't perfect, but God supernaturally made our troops win all the wars. Because we were good. If we *weren't* good, then I would have to ask a much bigger question about God... and I was still reeling over evolution. No thanks.

One time, a fellow student argued that America wasn't always the good guy.

"Our country committed mass genocide against native Americans. We stole their homes and killed them. In what world does that make us good?" she asked in political science class.

"That *is* bad. But there are always a few bad apples. That doesn't mean the tree is rotten, though," I deflected.

I couldn't refute her facts, but I couldn't believe what she was saying. Unable to reconcile what she said with my own ingrained beliefs, I tucked my doubts away for another day.

Everything in my world was filtered through a patriotic lens. In my circles, patriotism was close to godliness. Looking back now, I can see that it was probably at least partly due to the fact that the majority of my higher education occurred in the shadow of September 11, 2001.

I was in eighth grade when my mom woke me up that morning after the first plane hit the World Trade Center building. "April, you need to wake up. Our country is under attack." I thought I was dreaming, not only because what she said was so shocking, but also because she was wearing one of those green clay facial masks and looked like an alien.

I groggily got out of bed to join her in the living room to watch the news. We witnessed the second plane hit the second World Trade Center building live on television. Then I watched in terror as both buildings collapsed. It's one of those moments that I'll never forget.

September 11th awoke a political fire within me. Up until that point, I knew Republicans were the good guys and George W. Bush was a godly man, and that was about it. But after watching both World Trade Center Towers fall, I felt the urgency to fight. Justice had to be done, no matter how many wars needed to be won. Our country had to do something. *I* had to do something.

That next year, I attended a large public high school in Florida. I was very vocal and passionate in sharing my conservative Christian views, and the culture surprisingly seemed to embrace it.

The War in Iraq was *the* hot political topic. Weapons of mass destruction seemed to be on everyone's mind as our country geared up to continue the war on terrorism. In those days, my dad spent a lot of time explaining what he believed about the war.

"There's a time for war in defense of innocent life. These terrorists want to see America and our allies destroyed. They see the West as Christian and want us killed. This war is not only justice but self-defense from future attacks. We're trying to save more people," my dad would explain.

Then we would watch Fox News hosts for hours, which further solidified our positions.

Iraq had weapons of mass destruction. They intended to use them against America. And even though Al-Qaeda, the group responsible for 9/11, was in Afghanistan, they were all in cahoots and Saddam Hussein was the biggest threat now. America was good and needed as a form of global police. We were protectors of the earth!

During this time, my dad wrote a small pamphlet he titled, "The Truth About Terrorism." In it, he claimed that one of the goals of Islam was to eradicate Christians. Convert or perish. Even if many Muslim people were peaceful, the religion was not. My dad didn't make this stuff up. He was repeating views he'd heard on Fox News and conservative Christian talk radio. We viewed peaceful Muslims the same way we did lukewarm Christians—not true followers of the faith. He ended the tract with the sinner's prayer and handed them out as he witnessed to people.

I took all of these talking points I heard from my dad and conservative media and regurgitated them in my political science class at school. I regularly claimed we were in a Holy War, and those around me seemed to agree.

Except for one girl. In discussing the war, she raised her hand.

"America is committing war crimes against innocent people in Iraq. We shouldn't be above the law. And this isn't the first time we've killed innocent people. Look at our bloody history."

She said bloody in the literal sense, not the British sense.

The audacity. A hit dog hollers, and I was hit.

"Innocent people die in every war, but we have to rid them of their evil leaders for the greater good, saving more lives in the long run," I piped back.

She got to me, though. Deep down I wondered if she was right. Were we killing innocent people in Iraq? What were war crimes anyway? I couldn't reconcile my belief that America was good and blessed by God with the idea that we were killing innocent lives in our quest for justice. It threatened to unravel my Christian Nationalist worldview, so instead of considering her points, I argued with her.

As I look back, it's clear how much of our rhetoric during this time led to widespread Islamophobia in evangelicalism and America at large. In the years after 9/11, hate crimes against peaceful Muslims rose drastically. And unfortunately, much of it continues today.

We all know now that the truth of the war was more complicated than what was presented back then. There were no weapons of mass destruction found in Iraq. Over 185,000 Iraqi civilians were killed.[4] When we did leave Afghanistan, after a twenty-year occupation, the

Taliban quickly took it back over.[5] The United States spent $8 trillion on two decades of wars since 9/11 that caused 900,000 deaths and delivered murky results at best.[6]

And the invasion of Iraq is just one of many parts of our nation's history that reveal us as *not* the good guy.

I was pro-life. How could I reconcile so much death?

America's dark side was always there. If I had been looking, I could have easily found it in our history. Stealing land and slaughtering her owners. Slavery. Jim Crow laws. Vietnam. State-sanctioned slavery via mass incarceration. Japanese internment camps. Murders of innocent Black people by police. War crimes. The list goes on. But I hadn't been looking and actively worked to make sure I didn't have to face such things.

The problem is that to return our country back into a Christian nation—which is the explicit goal of Christian Nationalism—we must believe in American exceptionalism. Anything that shows the United States in a bad light is a threat to Christian Nationalism. How can we get back to the "good ole days" if the ole days were actually bad?

Showing our history in anything but a clear and positive manner is another kind of threat. The ideology offers followers peace and stability by preaching fundamentalist viewpoints. Right versus wrong. It keeps everything simple.

I think that is one of the attractive draws of Christian Nationalism. While historically we are living in one of the greatest times to be alive, it doesn't come without new complications. Every day, we are constantly bombarded with bad news, updated technology, the latest apps, unsettling AI, devastating climate change, unseen political upheaval, fatal worldwide viruses, wars, and every- and anything else. News about all these terrible things is available at any given moment on our smartphones. It's enough to make anyone uneasy. And in the face of this chaos, Christian Nationalism offers solutions.

Racism? Doesn't exist. Science that supports gender as a spectrum? Made-up liberal hogwash. Abortion? Murder. War? Necessary to fight bad guys. Who has the answers? Jesus. Who do we follow? Trump—or whoever else we deem worthy. Just listen and do what we tell you and life's gonna be just fine.

But with all the world at our fingertips, keeping that narrative can be difficult. There's a reason education is also one of the spheres of the Seven Mountain Mandate. The idea is that by successfully taking over the education system, Christians can conform the minds of the youth, which will lead to a better, Christian culture in the future.

A ministry called Generals International explained that the American education system used to "unapologetically" incorporate "the Bible, prayer to the God of the Bible and Biblical values in every aspect of school life," which resulted in "the most powerful and prosperous nation the earth has ever seen." But today, America is not that because of "liberal ideologies, atheistic teaching and postmodern principles" in our schools. The Education Mountain is key in Christian dominionism and our educational system must be reintroduced to "Biblical truth and Bible-centric values" to bring about national godly change.[7]

Control what people learn, and you can control what they believe. This is why education is another frontline issue of Christian Nationalism.

Christian Nationalism is now trying to put this simplistic worldview back into public education. We see this in the war against Critical Race Theory. Any history that shows America in a bad light is quickly given a "CRT" label and dismissed as some evil woke agenda. The age-old "demonizing" tactic.

CRT has become a catch-all phrase, co-opted by right-wing talking heads, to describe anything that talks about or teaches about historical racism, current systemic racism, diversity and inclusion endeavors, race-related policies, and other discussions around race in America.

Since January 2021, forty-four states took steps or introduced bills that restricted Critical Race Theory and discussions around race and sex in general.[8] Florida Governor Ron DeSantis banned the AP course on African American studies and Diversity, Equity, and Inclusion initiatives in public institutions.[9,10] It was so important that on her first day in office, Arkansas Governor Sarah Huckabee Sanders signed an executive order that banned "indoctrination and critical race theory" in Arkansas schools.[11]

But it's not just conservative Christian politicians dismissing CRT and other topics of race. A quick Google search will bring up countless articles and posts from Christian pastors and media critiquing CRT from their Biblical perspective. Ken Ham even wrote in a rebuttal, "CRT says only the oppressors are guilty. The Bible, however, says we are all sinners."[12] Another Christian wrote an opinion piece in *The Tennessean* that posited that CRT and rehashing sins of the past only causes division because, at the end of the day, "Only Jesus can change the heart of a racist."[13]

You'd think CRT was teaching people to worship Satan with the vitriol it receives from the Christian right. So I looked up the definition to find out what it really is. Critical Race Theory is a decades-old academic tool that looks at society through a racial lens, acknowledges that racism doesn't solely exist in individual bias, but continues through systemic means.

Ah. There it is. Systemic.

If there's a systemic problem, then we can't blame individual sin. If there's a systemic problem, then it started a long time ago. Which means we've been complicit in harm.

Nope. CRT has got to go. We're colorblind over here, remember?

But it's not just CRT that's been caught in the crosshairs on the frontlines of education. There have been a series of bills in conservative states to ban books from public schools that may muddy the clear waters of Christian Nationalism.

PEN America released a report that showed more than 1,600 books were banned across over 5,000 schools nationwide in the 2021–2022 school year. Most of these books were related to the LGBTQ+ community or, again, pointed out the existence of racism. To put a fine point on it: The subjects of these books challenge the straight White evangelical worldview, and that is the only perspective Christian Nationalists want students to hear about. These bans affected nearly 4 million students in thirty-two states, and a majority were in response to pressure from conservative groups.[14]

These book bans are surprisingly not seen as a form of government overreach but are framed as "protecting kids." Tiffany Justice, cofounder of Moms for Liberty, talked about her push to ban books this way: "There are moms who love their kids, who don't want pornography in school, and then there are people who do want pornography in school."[15] Fun fact: Bridget Ziegler, another founder of *Moms for Liberty*, who has fought to ban books featuring LGBTQ characters and advocated for traditional, heterosexual family values, was asked to resign from her Florida school board position after she and her husband got caught in a totally straight three-way sex scandal with another woman.[16] Rules for thee but not for me.

In November 2023, a twenty-year-old book-banning advocate went to a Texas school board meeting and claimed a kids' book that depicted one, single kiss led her to become addicted to porn, then depressed and suicidal at age thirteen.[17]

It reminds me of the time my mom, my brother Matt, and I were fishing on a pier in Galveston, Texas. My mom caught a little whiting fish and accidentally sliced her finger on its fin. A man sitting next to us piped up in a thick, country accent and said, "Y'know, a buddy of mine cut his hand on one of them fish, too... week later he was dead." He was serious. I think a few other things probably happened in that week between the fish cut and death. But back to the single-kiss-caused-porn-addiction lady: It later came out that she may have been a plant from a right-wing publishing company that sells "Pro-God, Pro-America" books.[18] Which honestly is easier to believe than the story she was telling.

In April 2023, a bill was proposed in Texas to display the Ten Commandments in every single classroom in the state's public schools. Critics of the bill sounded the alarms of blurring the lines of the separation of church and state. Proponents of the bill used the classic "Christian nation" argument. (Remember the Roy Moore debate? It was like that, only this time it was about putting a symbol of the Christian faith in every Texas public school classroom.) Mary Elizabeth Castle represented conservative group Texas Values and spoke in favor of the bill, saying that the Ten Commandments are "actually a foundation for our laws in our society."[19]

Why teach a class as complicated as government or civics when you could just point to ten laws written on a tablet 3,000 years ago? Simple!

Another Texas bill proposed the same week would allow public school districts "to employ chaplains to perform the duties of school counselors."[20] In other words, pastors who use the Bible as their instructing text would take the place of trained professionals who are required to have years of schooling to learn multiple psychological concepts. These are moves aimed at incorporating Christian faith into public schools.

I grew up under the same educational system that Christian Nationalism wants to implement for everyone, and in the end, I realized it wasn't working and I left. I didn't change my mind because of a book I read in the library that acknowledged racism is real, or because the Ten Commandments weren't posted large enough in the cafeteria. I came to think differently and question what I had been taught because the life I experienced and the knowledge I learned pushed me beyond what Christian Nationalism taught me.

I mean, I went to conservative Christian schools and still left my Nationalist beliefs behind. There was no atheist professor brainwashing me. I just lived my life, expanded my knowledge of the world, and came to see that things just didn't add up.

You know what I wanted to do when CRT was being banned? Learn about CRT.

And that sent me down a journey to learn about a lot more ugliness in our history.

And yes, it was messy and hard and made me face some very difficult truths.

But it was truth. And it set me free from dogmatic chains.

Limiting what students learn and denying parts of our history are not the answer if we want to progress as a society for *all* people. Christian Nationalists believe controlling education will give them the upper hand and keep them in power. But it's often ineffective.

My most liberal friends were raised by staunchly conservative and Christian Nationalist parents.

I don't think it works because stunting our learning goes against our instincts. Questions are a part of life. There are things Nationalists don't have answers to and deflections only work for so long.

Even the Bible says in Romans 12:2 (ESV) to "be transformed by the renewal of your mind." Well, thankfully my mind has been renewed and has the latest iOS update, which rid itself of the Christian Nationalist bug.

CHAPTER 16

Uncoordinated Angels: LGBTQ, Part 1

Every June, social media is inundated with rainbows to celebrate Pride Month. And each year, there are also a slew of posts by Christians trying to "reclaim the rainbow for God." One popular meme has a rainbow with a cross overlaid on it that says, "June is Christianity Month—Reclaim the Rainbow." The goal is to overwhelm society with so many Christian rainbows that people forget about the queer one. LGBTQ people, like a thief in the night, stole the rainbow symbol from God himself and declared it their own. So the rainbow must be reclaimed.

Quick refresher, the rainbow in Genesis appears after God wiped out every human on earth except Noah and his family. The rainbow is supposed to represent God's promise never to commit mass genocide against humans again. So yeah. That version is clearly more family-friendly than a bunch of happy gay people.

Pride Month, on the other hand, is sinister. If you put the two words together it's obvious: PriDEMONth. Satan is hiding in plain sight!

Out of all the frontline issues, nothing seems to rev up Christian Nationalists like the existence of queer people.

When I was a Christian Nationalist, we were focused on fighting against gay marriage. It wasn't federally legal yet, and it was our job to keep it that way. Our nation's blessing from God depended on it!

I first heard the word "gay" in my preschool Sunday school class. A little boy named Kyle looked at me and asked, "Do you like Nikki?"

"Yes," I replied. She was my best friend.

"OH!! You're GAAAAYYYY!" Kyle laughed. "You like girls!"

Confused as to why they were laughing, I said, "Of course I like girls!"

"Noooo. Gay means you *like* like girls!" Kyle explained.

The teacher stopped the conversation, but I knew exactly what trick I was going to play on my brothers when I got home.

"Hey, Matt, do you like Johnny?" I asked my brother later.

"Yeah?" Matt replied, also confused.

"HAHA! You're gay!! Matt's gay!"

My dad happened to overhear.

"April!! *Never* joke about or call your brothers that. Gay is a very bad thing to call someone. Say you're sorry right now," my dad demanded.

"I'm sorry," I replied, baffled by my dad's fury. I didn't understand why the word was bad, but I accepted that it was.

When I was eight years old, our family went out to eat at a restaurant. Our waiter talked more femininely than most men I had seen. After he greeted us and left to get our drinks, my dad said, "We need to leave. Let's go, kids." My mom protested, but my dad explained he didn't think he could enjoy his food.

I asked why we were leaving, and my dad said, "The man is a homosexual." I didn't understand why we couldn't eat there. I looked back at the waiter, and the pained look on his face as he watched us leave hurt my heart. All I saw was a fellow human being. Theology hadn't taught me to hate him. Not yet.

To be fair, we sometimes left restaurants for other reasons, too. Remember Joe's Crab Shack? My dad made us leave the joint when he saw "the devil's sign" on the wall. In reality, it was just the peace symbol, but my dad thought it was satanic. But we were living in the motor home at the time, so my dad was extra stressed.

As I aged, the empathy I felt as a child was squashed as homosexuality continued to be demonized from the pulpit and by the conservative news I consumed. I learned to exhibit the same fury against homosexuals.

Now, I didn't show this rage to actual gay people. We didn't know any of them (that we knew of anyway). I just joined the choir of groans if a TV show featured a gay person. "Liberals shoving this garbage down our throats!" I'd pipe in after seeing one gay character out of hundreds of straight ones.

But most of my angst was directed at Christians who were too nice to gay people.

One time, I got into a heated debate in college on the official class discussion boards about same-sex marriage. A girl brought up the site gaychristian.net to show that some gay people were even *gasp* Christian! At the time, I could not let such heresy go unchecked and replied that "gay Christian is an oxymoron. The Bible clearly says homosexuality is an abomination."

Yep, I was *that* person. I was more April Annoy than April Ajoy.

In my circles, there were only two possible explanations for why gay people existed. The first was that they were possessed by demons. At a certain age, this reasoning stopped working for me. Of all the gay people I had interacted with, none had red eyes or spoke in multiple voices. None of them flinched when I said "Jesus," the telltale sign of a demonic presence.

The next possible explanation was that they were making a conscious choice to disobey God. I never understood why people would choose to have a sexuality that would alienate them from their families and the community around them, but when I brought this up in Sunday school, I was offered a convoluted explanation on the difference between demonic *possession* and *oppression*. Possession was when the demon went *inside* the body and controlled the person. Oppression was demonic influence on the *outside* of the body, convincing them to choose sin—which is just a complicated combination of the demon and choice theories. So demons again.

This idea was further enforced in my head by Christian author Frank Peretti's novels such as *This Present Darkness* (1986) and the sequel

Piercing the Darkness (1989). In these books, Peretti gave names and personalities to both angels and demons who lived just beyond our human realm. Angels were assigned to various Christians based on the strength of their spiritual life. Basically, if characters prayed and read the Bible a lot, they got a super buff angel. If a character smoked and had recently gotten a hickey from a make-out sesh, their angel would be lazy and uncoordinated. Demons, on the other hand, were always powerful and scary. They were able to sneak in and influence Christians (demonic *oppression*) who weren't praying enough.

Even though these books were fiction, I knew spiritual warfare was real. I believed these books *probably* gave us a decent look at the real spiritual realm. This messed up my teenage brain.

Is this thought a whisper from a demon? Is my angel off duty right now? When was the last time I prayed and read my Bible? Maybe I won't buy that NSYNC poster...

This thinking led me to believe that gay people desiring to be with a member of the same sex was like me wanting a secular CD my parents forbade. I fought against my desires all the time, so why couldn't gay people do the same? Being a good person was about squashing our human, sin nature, not about being happy.

But in 2015, I found myself at odds with that belief.

Ding. Buzz. Beep. All the phones around me went off simultaneously. A big story had to be breaking.

I was working at the Christian Broadcasting Network at the time, sitting in my cubicle, editing a testimony piece that would later air on *The 700 Club*. I had left my corporate job the previous year and took a pay cut to be a TV producer at CBN. But this was Kingdom work with the biggest reward to come in heaven, so it would all be worth it.

"Lord! NO!!" I heard the first wail of despair a few cubicles over.

"Jesus, come quick!" another coworker lamented.

What on earth... I took my headphones off and minimized my editing software to see what was going on.

"Take us, Lord Jesus!!" another voice moaned.

Are we under attack? I wondered, confused by the sudden outburst of hopelessness. I'm pretty sure I heard someone crying.

"The evil gay agenda is taking over!!" someone near my cubicle said.

Oh my gosh...

I opened CNN on my browser to find my suspicions confirmed.

"Supreme Court rules in favor of same-sex marriage nationwide," the headline read. I was expecting the ruling to happen soon but was *not* expecting this reaction from my colleagues.

I doubt it's what Matthew 13:42 (NIV) means when it says, "There will be weeping and gnashing of teeth," but that could have easily described that summer day in the CBN cubicles.

I shouldn't have been surprised. My coworkers were simply reacting with the same despair I would have felt not too long ago. This was what we had been fighting and praying against. This was the liberal gay agenda replacing God's truth at the highest levels. This was the opposite of what Christian Nationalism had been working toward for so long. With the nation officially endorsing such a grave sin, God was sure to lift protections off America, which would inevitably lead to our nation losing global superpower status.

But that day, the despair eluded me for some reason. Beecher and I had just celebrated our first anniversary. Even if I theologically disagreed with gay marriage, I wasn't sure why I was supposed to deprive gay people of the right to marry as well.

I pulled up the live news coverage from Washington DC as hundreds of ecstatic gay men and women celebrated on TV. Unadulterated joy shone on their faces. I felt... happy for them? *What on earth is wrong with me?*

It was like that moment with the gay waiter—my heart disagreed with the Christians around me. Even though I technically held the same theology, something sacred was gently pulling me toward a new perspective.

I believe God was preparing me for what was to come.

Just a few weeks later, my twenty-six-year-old brother Andrew flew across the country to visit us. As he and I sat at the kitchen table one afternoon, he said, "April... there's something I need to tell you..."

I sat up straight and looked Andrew in the eye, completely unaware that my life was about to change.

"I've never..." Tears began to well up in his eyes. "I've never been attracted to women...only the same sex..." He began sobbing.

Now I began crying. I walked to the other side of the table where Andrew sat and threw my arms around him.

"It's okay," was all I could say, over and over again. We both cried as all the homophobic things I had ever said in front of him flashed in my mind.

I was the first person he had ever told. He had known since middle school. He'd cried himself to sleep countless nights, begging God to make him straight. God never did.

This was no longer a political discussion. It wasn't a theological debate dissecting words written 2,000 years ago. This was my brother.

As we embraced each other in tears, those familiar thoughts popped into my brain.

You can't enable this. It's still a sin. What if it leads to hell...you don't want your own brother's blood on your hands.

"Well...we know what the Bible says," I heard myself say out of obligation. I felt gross saying it at such an emotional moment but also relieved that I was bold enough to speak it.

After that, I couldn't just let go of the ingrained religious belief, but politically I dropped my weapons and officially supported gay marriage. It was like a light bulb went off and I realized my personal beliefs shouldn't be enforced on others who think differently. I could support a person's legal rights, even if they didn't align with my religious beliefs. "If you don't like gay marriage, then don't get gay married" finally started to make sense.

I may have laid down my sword, but the LGBTQ battle is still one of the frontline battles of Christian Nationalism. And while gay marriage isn't the main focus these days, it's not in the clear.

In the 2022 decision to overturn *Roe v. Wade*, Supreme Court Justice Clarence Thomas suggested the court should reconsider its ruling on gay marriage as well.[1] Several GOP lawmakers tried to assure people this wouldn't happen, but didn't everyone say the same thing about *Roe v. Wade*? If the Supreme Court took away gay marriage, what would happen to my happily married gay friends? Could one niche group force its religious beliefs to become the law of the land?

It could, I knew. I had fought to make it so for most of my life.

In 2020, Pastor Ralph Drollinger, who led a weekly Bible study for members of Trump's cabinet, claimed the coronavirus pandemic could partially be blamed on those who have "a proclivity toward lesbianism and homosexuality."[2]

This rhetoric seems ridiculous, but evangelicals demonized homosexuality like this constantly when I was growing up. Remember, just two days after September 11, 2001, the late Jerry Falwell Sr. went on *The 700 Club* and said that "the gays and the lesbians who are actively trying to make that an alternative lifestyle" were partially to blame for the attack on the World Trade Center in New York City.[3] He later apologized after receiving backlash.

After Hurricane Katrina devastated New Orleans, megachurch pastor John Hagee said in an NPR interview, "New Orleans had a level of sin that was offensive to God... there was to be a homosexual parade there on the Monday that Katrina came... I believe that the Hurricane Katrina was, in fact, the judgment of God against the city of New Orleans."[4]

These outlandish claims can have disastrous consequences. According to a 2020 national survey conducted by the Trevor Project, 1 in 3 LGBTQ youth reported they had been "physically threatened or harmed in their lifetime due to their sexual orientation or gender identity." The study also revealed that queer youth who had unsupportive family were more than twice as likely to attempt suicide.[5]

High suicide rates among queer youth were not a subject I heard about in evangelical culture. If they were ever mentioned, such suicides were blamed on demons, not the Christian parents who abandoned their kids or forced them to attend conversion therapy.

Everywhere you turn, it's clear that Christian Nationalism sees LGBTQ people as a clear opponent. The movement would have you believe it's because of what the Bible says. But this falls flat when you read the text and see how the Bible condemns lots of things including eating shellfish and wearing mixed fabrics. And yet evangelicals can be found dining in seafood restaurants while wearing cotton-polyester blends.

I think it comes down to queer people not conforming to the patriarchy (we'll dive more into that in the next chapter). Not to mention, when a person comes out as queer in evangelical circles, they will most likely lose family, friends, and their comfortable place in society. It's unfortunately a very common result of living authentically inside Christian Nationalistic families. When someone marches in a Pride Parade, they are demonstrating their willingness to be ostracized and moved to a seat of less privilege to find fulfillment. They have given up power for inner peace, the opposite of Christian Nationalism.

The inability to conform is supposed to lead to pain and isolation, not joy and community.

It's so clear to me now that my previous fight against gay marriage wasn't actually about gay people. It was about how they threatened my worldview. My brother coming out forced me to confront that. It's hard to stay in a black-and-white belief system after you've seen glimpses of color. I'll forever be grateful that Andrew showed me the rainbow.

CHAPTER 17

Walking Dead Demons: LGBTQ, Part 2

While my fight on the LGBTQ frontline issue was focused on gay marriage, today's Christian Nationalism is more focused on the "T" in LGBTQ. That stands for trans, by the way. And today's fight is just as harmful.

Churches across America have added blurbs on their website that say, "God made them MALE and FEMALE and he doesn't make mistakes!"

A relative of mine hosted a children's "Rainbow Parade" last June that featured a song with lyrics that thanked God for only making two genders with lines like: "Girls are girls. Boys are boys. Na-na-na-naturally."

Intersex people are Na-na-na-naturally not going to be mentioned in this special song.

This only-two-kinds-of-genitals push comes in response to a culture growing more accepting of transgender identities, and queerness in general. Beyond their theological belief around LGBTQ issues, I believe Christian Nationalism fights against this inclusion because it goes directly against traditional gender roles that uphold the patriarchal system the movement needs to survive.

These gender roles affect more than just trans people. As a cisgender woman, even I had a hard time fitting into my prescribed gender roles. I had opinions but was often told to stay in my quiet, submissive lane.

In my debate class in college, I was tasked with arguing against the use of steroids in professional sports. My opponent was an overconfident guy in the class...

"Chicks dig the long ball," he chimed as he ended his opening argument. "Long ball" is baseball slang for a home run.

I stood up to give my rebuttal. "It's true that chicks may dig the long ball...but chicks will not dig the *shriveled* balls that come from using steroids!"

Mic drop. The class broke out in laughter.

It was moments like these that earned me the "Most likely to win every argument with their spouse" award at the end of the semester.

Thinking the superlative was funny, I shared it on Facebook.

The very first comment I received came from a Christian single guy from my old youth group. He was not amused.

This aspiring pastor wrote, "A woman of God doesn't argue with her spouse" before quoting 1 Peter 3:1 (NKJV), "Wives, likewise, be submissive to your own husbands, that even if some do not obey the word, they, without a word, may be won by the conduct of their wives." He ended his comment with "I would like to emphasize the without a word part."

This is a Christianese way of saying, "Shut up, woman."

I did not, in fact, shut up. But I had to fight for my voice regularly in these evangelical circles.

Even though the church taught about male leadership and female submission, my dad instilled a different message in me.

When I was five years old, I remember running to my dad to tell him that I had figured it out. "The boys preach, and the girls sing! Just like you preach and Mom sings!" I exclaimed.

My dad gave an endearing laugh and kneeled to look me in the eyes.

"Oh no, sweetie. Girls can preach, too, just like boys can sing. Girls can do anything boys can do. Don't let anyone tell you you can't do something because you're a girl. You can be whatever you want to be."

While I'm still in the process of sorting out the nuance of my dad's legacy, I am forever grateful he always supported me. Without his empowerment, I doubt I would've had the confidence to speak freely on social media or muster up the courage to write this book.

Unfortunately, the feminism he embraced for me was not typical of the Church at large. I knew I *could* preach because of what my dad said, but I rarely saw women preaching.

All these factors pushed me to view femininity as a weakness, which is a sentiment we still see in Christian Nationalism today. At ten years old, I decided I'd had enough. I traded in my dresses for boys' jeans. And not just any boys' jeans—I found the widest, most unflattering ones available called JNCOs (those super-wide-leg denim parachutes for pants). My skinny legs didn't even touch the fabric.

The "tomboy" look suited me for middle school, but as I entered high school, I had the troubling desire to look pretty. I say "troubling" because I hated the part of me that liked wearing makeup. The part that liked colorful, flowery journals, that wanted to be beautiful and wanted a husband and kids one day.

That was what was expected of me, and I wanted to defy expectations. I lived with this internal conflict for a long time. This contradiction became even more prominent when Beecher and I got married.

Right off the bat, we realized some of our gender roles were flipped. Beecher's ideal night involved cooking a nice dinner, followed by romantic cuddles on the couch. My ideal night involved playing *Halo* on Xbox while eating nachos between games.

We knew we didn't fit the mold, and we tried to "fix" us.

Though Beecher was a great cook, I initially made most of our dinners, as a good Christian wife should do. I melted plastic lids in the oven and oversalted the green beans the one time I remembered to make a vegetable. Beecher gave me an encouraging smile, chewing on overcooked chicken.

Attempting to be the spiritual head of the household that the church constantly told husbands to be, Beecher tried to lead Bible studies and prayer times with me. This only ever irked me.

"You don't need to lead me. My relationship with God is between me and him," I said.

"Of course it is! I'm just trying to do what the pastor said at the marriage conference. *You* asked me to do this!" Beecher replied.

"Well, I changed my mind."

We tried so hard to have that traditional Christian marriage. And we were miserable.

Husband-wife gender roles were further enforced at church events. Beecher went to the men's events that had bacon-wrapped everything. They played basketball, smashed cars, and sold raffle tickets for guns, grills, or camping trips. Most of the conversations consisted of small talk doused with bravado. The event speaker almost always mentioned pornography—the one sin that was socially acceptable for men to struggle with. Beecher pretended to relate. Beecher didn't struggle with porn, but was too terrified to reveal any actual desires.

I, on the other hand, had to attend women's gatherings, where we ate blueberry parfaits and learned about Esther for the 5,488,214th time. Our raffles were usually for a flowery prayer journal or a mug that said "Beloved" on it.

I desperately longed to be at a men's event, where I could feast on good food, play competitive games, and actually *do* things. Beecher would have loved to be at a nicely decorated table with women who wanted to have a deep conversation.

Even events we attended together were heavily focused on gender roles. The marriage conference speaker emphasized stereotypical differences between men and women. We laughed along with everyone else, but each marriage conference left us feeling weirder and more isolated in our struggles.

Cut to a decade later, we now know one reason we never fit into traditional roles is because of my spouse's gender identity. Beecher had been open with me about their gender "struggle" since we were dating, but we didn't know what gender dysphoria was at the time.

Beecher is now proudly out as nonbinary, uses "they/them" pronouns, and expresses themselves in whatever clothing they feel fits them. It was a long journey to get here—enough to fill the pages of its own book. From bouts of depression, thoughts of self-harm, demon exorcisms, twelve step groups, Christian counselors, losing employment, being cut off from church, and many, many long days and nights of emotional conversations, the trek to get here was difficult.

Beecher's gender identity required us to break out of those uncomfortable boxes that we might have attempted to remain in otherwise.

Today, our marriage has never been better. To the relief of our entire family, Beecher does most of the cooking now. They enjoy experimenting with made-up recipes and I enjoy eating the delicious results. I do my part by doing the dishes. We no longer feel pressure to fulfill roles based on our gender. We just live. True partners helping each other, living as God made us to be.

But we don't fit nicely into the patriarchal system from whence we came. Beecher's expression of authenticity, and my support of them, fractured some relationships with friends and family. We had relatives inform us that they didn't want their grandchildren around Beecher and canceled visits with us. Others expressed a desire to "protect" their kids from Beecher's "feminine side."

There wasn't really a place for people who bucked gender roles, so people had to find ways to explain Beecher's existence in a dualistic way. We heard several odd and amusing reasons people gave for *why* Beecher was nonbinary. Some family members claimed that I turned Beecher nonbinary just to get them to vote Democrat. (Yes, that's right. The diehard conservative girl that Beecher married enacted a ten-year plan to get Beecher to vote for the party she'd spent most of her life fighting against. Talk about pulling the long con!)

But our favorite theory is that Beecher is nonbinary because they watched *The Walking Dead*. Apparently when visiting a relative's house in college, Beecher insisted on watching the top-rated cable television show in the world. It was this act—watching Hershel amputate his leg as the undead raided the prison—that allowed demons to enter Beecher's body. Suddenly—*poof*—they sometimes wanted to wear a dress. AMC should have included a disclaimer: WARNING—ZOMBIE DEMONS MAY CAUSE YOU TO BE FABULOUS! We still laugh about this one.

Unfortunately, we also understood the reaction. We'd responded similarly to things we didn't understand once upon a time. It's easier to make up an excuse, even a ridiculous one, for what you don't understand instead of facing a truth that challenges your worldview. Girls wear pink, boys wear blue. End of story.

Christian Nationalism did not invent the patriarchy, but it clings to that system to hold on to its own power. Historian Kristin Du Mez shows how the late Reverend Billy Graham further enforced the marriage between American Christianity and patriarchal gender roles in the 1950s in her book *Jesus and John Wayne*. Believing that "a nation is only as strong as her homes," Graham preached that men should be the provider as "God's representative" in the nuclear family. Graham likewise encouraged housewives to love their husbands "at any cost" while making sure they stayed modest, youthful, and attractive.[1]

The idea that America's blessing from God starts at home is a sentiment that was further pushed by Phyllis Schlafly in the 1960s and '70s. Schlafly encouraged women to stay home while equating gender equality with communism.[2]

In my lifetime, the leading voice on this topic was Dr. James Dobson and his ministry, Focus on the Family. As a well-known conservative evangelical author, Dobson regularly pushes the idea that America's future depends on Biblical gender roles and "God's design of the family."[3]

In a 2022 newsletter, Dobson wrote that he believed families in America were "under siege," putting a lot of the blame on gay marriage and transgender acceptance. He compared what Christians are facing in "America's current crisis" to what Abraham Lincoln faced in the Civil War. The crisis was the government protecting trans people from discrimination by adding "gender identity" to Title IX. To protect the nation's children, he implored *every* Christian to "contact the U.S. Department of Education to let them know to keep their hands off of Title IX."[4]

Title IX, by the way, is a federal civil rights law that forbids educational institutions from discriminating based on sex. In 2021, the U.S. Department of Education confirmed that one's sex also included gender identity and sexual orientation.[5] Uh-oh. Dobson was fighting against trans people being allowed to use the bathroom they identified with, not to mention the horror of having to use different pronouns![6]

It's extra Christian Nationalistic because Title IX already includes religious exemptions.[7] So it seems Dobson was fighting for the right to discriminate everywhere.

I mean, it's getting pretty scary out there. One day you can discriminate against people you don't like and the next day you can't! What is the world coming to!

I believe Christian Nationalism enforces traditional gender roles because it relies on patriarchal "Biblical marriage" to maintain power. (The "one man, one woman" Biblical marriage, not the "bride-for-goats" or "polygamous" Biblical marriage.) The structure of this Biblical marriage emphasizes male headship and female submission based on Paul's writings in Ephesians 5:22–23 (ESV), which states: "Wives, submit to your own husbands, as to the Lord. For the husband is the head of the wife even as Christ is the head of the church..."

In case you aren't seeing what Paul is getting at, some nice men made a lovely illustration, often attributed to Christian minister Bill Gothard, to mansplain it (just imagine the arrows are umbrellas, with each umbrella getting smaller as you go down):

↓

Christ

↓

Husband

↓

Wife

↓

Children

This is called complementarianism—believing that men and women have specific roles that complement each other. Most complementarians would say men and women are still equal, just different.

While the application is on the nuclear family, there are some who apply it everywhere and don't want women in any leadership positions. Right-wing pastor Jason Graber condemned Marjorie Taylor Greene and her supporters. "And anybody who votes for her, you're not a real conservative. Fake conservatives. Why? Because Marjorie Taylor Greene should be at home being obedient to her husband."[8]

I can think of many reasons not to vote for Greene but being a woman with a job isn't one of them.

Graber's position isn't overtly mainstream within Christian Nationalism, but the belief is there. I've had many run-ins with it. When I speak out on social media, a Jezemale (my name for TheoBros—theologian bros) will offer a brilliant rebuttal that includes pasting a Bible verse and some form of "Shut up, you're a woman lol."

Some Christian Nationalists want to take complementarianism to the extreme by implementing household voting that would essentially undo women's suffrage. Anti-abortion activist and 2020 Republican National Convention speaker Abby Johnson openly pushed for head of household voting on social media that same year. She said that each family should get one vote and that "the husband would get the final say."[9]

Lori Anderson, also known as *The Transformed Wife*, whose ministry promotes "Biblical womanhood," claimed that the purpose of women's suffrage was "to undermine the husband's authority in the home." As she sees it, the man is the head of the household, and since the wife must submit to his authority anyway, voting shouldn't be any different.[10]

It seems bizarre from the outside but makes more sense when you understand how the movement views women. In his book *The Case for Christian Nationalism*, Stephen Wolfe says that "unconstrained feminine empathy" has led to "the most insane and damaging sociological trends." He believes "feminine virtues greatly benefit individuals and society," but are good only "when complemented with masculine leadership."[11]

Despite being a woman herself, Congresswoman Marjorie Taylor Greene has said more than once that women are the "weaker sex."[12] Talking about Eve eating the fruit in the Garden of Eden, Greene said, "The serpent saw the weaker sex and knew he could defeat her."[13]

When I was a Christian Nationalist, we weren't overt about our patriarchal beliefs. I thought I was fighting for women's equality, even if my beliefs said otherwise. Today's Christian Nationalists are more overt in their push to uphold the patriarchy. There's even a yearly event in Orlando called the Patriarch Convention that claims to have "helped hundreds of fathers strengthen and release the alpha patriarch within." Their mission is to rebuild the patriarchy "one man, one father, and one family at a time." Several of the convention speakers have been pastors.[14]

This same group also puts on a Make Women Great Again conference, where the overwhelmingly male speakers teach women how they are "drowning in feminism and starving for the patriarchy" and that submitting to "the leadership of a good, solid, alpha male patriarch is the only choice that can unleash natural femininity, maximum beauty, and ultimate happiness."[15]

But how does the patriarchy help take America back for God? Well, Christian Nationalists typically take the Bible literally and have a more fundamentalist interpretation like complementarianism. So they believe women in the home submitting to their husbands is Biblical. God is more likely to bless America if godly families are the bulk of her citizens.

There's a reason so many churches put lots of money into men's ministries and events. I've sat through countless sermons where the pastor said something like, "We're pulling out all the stops at our Courageous Brave Warrior Men's Event! If the man gets saved, the family is more likely to follow! And if more families are Christian, the nation will follow!"

The Stronger Men's Conference in Missouri made headlines for bringing out a guy in Chuck Norris cosplay who was dual-wielding prop guns while riding a giant army tank to squash some cars while fire blasted into the air between worship services. US Senator Josh Hawley was one of the speakers at this church event.[16] Yay, church and state things.

But the patriarchy keeps men in power, which is key to fundamentalist Christian Nationalism. This is rarely given as the overt reason, although that's starting to change. Men love women, after all. It's not them being sexist; they're just spitting the word of God truth! This is something that was actually said to me. A godly nation should be run by godly men. And pesky feminists wanting a voice and rights are getting in the way of men running their households, their churches, and the country.

Back to LGBTQ+ people. It's easy to see why Christian Nationalism fights so hard against them. By default, the queer community does not conform to traditional gender roles. If there are no clear wife and husband roles, how do they fit in a nuclear family and thus the nation? Gender nonconformity is a threat to the patriarchy and, by extension, Christian Nationalism.

Queer people cannot exist in a head-of-household world. If two men are married, who submits to whom? Can a trans man be the head of household? The head just completely falls off in queer relationships. A bunch of decapitated households don't fit the narrative. It's easier to demonize than try to understand. Put them in the "other" folder. Ban them.

And banning LGBTQ+ people seems to be the action of choice for Christian Nationalists.

Trans Legislation Tracker, an independent research resource, found 558 anti-trans bills across the United States in the first six months of 2023 alone. As of March 2024, the site was tracking 513 anti-trans bills. To put that into perspective, there were only nineteen anti-trans bills proposed nationally in 2019.[17]

Beyond laws, studies found transgender people are also over four times more likely than cisgender people to experience violent victimization, including rape and aggravated assault.[18]

These horrifying statistics fall on deaf ears. I know I ignored them when I was a Christian Nationalist because it was easier to dismiss an entire group of strangers that I was taught to hate. Sorry, I mean I was taught to "love the sinner, hate the sin."

In hindsight, I know I never loved the queer people I demonized. I said I did. I even thought I did in a "truth in love" sort of way. But I saw them as a problem to solve, not neighbors to love.

Between Beecher and Andrew, I was forced to face my theological stance around LGBTQ+ issues head-on. After years of praying and learning, I am now fully queer affirming and hold to an inclusive faith.

Being on this side of the frontline, the Christian Nationalist war against queer people hits differently.

Christian Nationalism's quest to retain its outdated power structure puts real people in the crosshairs. This is intentional. The ideology hopes this pressure will force people like Beecher and Andrew back in the closet, to conform to the binary system. It wants women like me to shut up and stay in the kitchen. To hide the light we were born with.

But for those willing to choose love over dogma, there is hope. Thankfully we've had conservative friends and family members reach out to learn more about Beecher's story. Those who took time to actually listen walked away with a new perspective. Even if they didn't fully understand, they saw our hearts and still wanted us in their lives.

Because it's hard to demonize people once you're close enough to see the divine in them.

And if you can't see God in the LGBTQ+ rainbow, you're not looking.

Final Thoughts

Sometimes people see me on social media talking about my journey out of Christian Nationalism and assume it was a painless, conscious choice I made. Like I realized in an instant that I was perpetuating something harmful, changed my mind over a strong cup of coffee, and was speaking out against it by lunchtime. But that is nowhere near the truth.

My change required years of deep reflection. There's a reason questioning and deconstruction are demonized and belittled from pulpits across the country. The process is debilitating, isolating, but also life changing. I spent countless hours reading the Bible and theology books, praying, and crying. I did a ridiculous amount of crying, actually.

Christian Nationalism offered certainty, and leaving that conclusiveness was terrifying. Researching topics and finding answers that could destroy meaningful relationships in my life was incredibly lonely. Asking God questions I was told to never ask was gut-wrenching. Acknowledging the harm I caused when I was in the movement was agonizing to reckon with.

Before this, there had always been a pastor or a church leader I could go to and ask the hard, spiritual questions. Unfortunately, the typical answers didn't work for me anymore, and the conversations couldn't go any further. I was just warned about the dangerous path I was on. There was no one to talk to, and I was tired of being reprimanded on top of already feeling lost within uncertainty. *Am I a terrible person for questioning my entire life?*

But I couldn't stop. That's the thing evangelical pastors don't mention about deconstruction. No one chooses to do it. It just happens. One day, you wake up and the years of little things that never made sense rise to the surface. Or your brother comes out to you, and you're faced with a reality you were told didn't exist. Or you see people you know storming the Capitol and realize you were a freaking Christian Nationalist the entire time.

The only choice I made over the last decade was to stop looking away from uncomfortable truths. I sat with facts that didn't fit my small narrative. I listened to people who were different from me. I considered thoughts that came from outside of my evangelical circles.

It was a million little decisions spread out over ten years. Each choice I made to face a hard truth head-on poked holes in my comfortable bubble. *That's* how I got to where I am today.

Along the way, Beecher and I lost relationships with friends and family, social status, and employment. While writing this book, I had a panic attack when I realized I would have to talk about my dad and his role in Christian Nationalism. I struggled to breathe as I bawled over the guilt of betraying him, the pain of missing him, the passion to right the wrongs of my past, and the deep love I still have for him. So many complicated feelings.

And yet it was still worth it.

Looking back, if I could point to one hidden, guiding force behind my voyage to leave Christian Nationalism, it would be the words of Jesus. So many times, when I encountered hard moments, I turned to the Red Letters in the Gospels. I attempted to read them objectively, without an agenda or a pastor interpreting them for me. I turned to the one place evangelicals told me had all the answers: Jesus.

They were right in this case. I got answers. It became so clear to me that there was nothing nationalistic about Jesus' teachings. He was the antithesis of the Christian Nationalism I had promoted. I had been so consumed with the culture wars of putting Christ back in schools, back in the country, and back in Christmas that I hadn't even noticed he needed to be put back in *Christianity*.

I had to take everything apart. I didn't know which parts of my beliefs were true to the faith versus what was a Christian Nationalist belief. Something in the foundation was rotten, and the only way to find it was to tear it all down and start over.

My desire is that people will read this book and leave with a clearer understanding of what Christian Nationalism is and how it has been manipulating Christianity. There are many definitions out there and varying levels of belief among followers, but Christian Nationalism is a disease threatening to destroy democracy and the Christian faith. Whether a Christian claims the Nationalist label or not, I hope my experience will shine a light on how Christian Nationalism exploits our faith for power while harming people outside our religion. That they will be able to spot the tenets and tactics used in today's frontline issues. The first step to solving a problem is acknowledging it.

I hope my experiences can show that Christian Nationalism's end goal is neither good nor Christlike. By shining a light on what the ideology is, we can lead more people out of it. Hopefully, they will see themselves in what is laid bare and go on a quest to purify their own faith from the grasp of nationalism.

I think many people inside Christian Nationalism have good hearts and believe they are fighting for something worthwhile. It doesn't erase the harm they cause, but it's a good reminder that most things are more nuanced than we think. I just hope current Christian Nationalists can set aside the quest for dominion and encounter the same Jesus that I did in the difficult moments. The Jesus who taught us to lay down our weapons, turn the other cheek, take care of the poor, and love one another above all else.

Reflecting on my time within Christian Nationalism has brought up a lot of mixed feelings. There are things I wish I had done differently, questioned sooner, and stood against while inside. I know nothing will undo the damage I once caused, and there's no excuse for it. I have repented for the part I played. My repentance is a huge reason why I even started speaking out against Christian Nationalism. To loudly condemn the dangerous things I used to praise.

I'm still learning to give myself grace for the things I said and did as a Christian Nationalist. I try to hold that same grace for those still inside. I believe people can change. If I ever lose hope, I just remember where I used to be. If I can change, anyone can.

And liberation followed that change. Leaving the dogma behind and being able to walk through life without fearing every new little thing is a priceless freedom I never had before. The greatest benefit of this entire long journey is the peace I feel now. The ability to get to know people from all walks of life without being afraid of new questions they may bring with them. Having genuine human relations with no ulterior motive, not based on fear but centered on love, has been one of the most beautiful experiences of my life.

Because John 3:16 (NIV) doesn't say, "For God so loved America." Jesus didn't tell us to just love *some* neighbors. We weren't commanded to pick up our swords and fight for our rights.

"For God so loved the *world*." May we learn to love the people of the world, too. May our nation be a place for all ethnicities, nationalities, orientations, identities, and beliefs. May we coexist in peace with all of God's beautiful creation, appreciating the glory in diversity and seeing the harm in oppression.

And may we end Christian Nationalism once and for all.

Acknowledgments

There were several moments throughout the writing of this book when I thought I'd never finish. We moved from Tennessee to Kentucky in the middle of this process, and I think a picture of my face from then belongs in a dictionary beside the word "stressed." I remember feeling anxiety any time I drove by a bookstore, like it was purposely taunting me. But I'm here!

There's not enough room to thank everyone who deserves it. So here's a quick list to acknowledge those who have had a profound impact on me or this book.

To Beecher: My rock. My person. The one who told me "It'll be okay" when I was drowning in boxes and rewrites. For reading my early, terrible drafts and helping me craft a plan to make it un-terrible. "I'm so glad I married a writer" was a sentence I said countless times throughout this process. But mostly, thank you, Beecher, for your love. For trusting me with your authentic self. I love you with my whole heart.

To my daughters, Rae & Lil B: I love watching you play basketball, soccer, dance, and do gymnastics. I love your giggles that light up even my darkest day. You two have my heart.

To Mom: Your strength and kindness never cease to amaze me. Thank you for your willingness to go down this journey with me. For loving me through it all. For choosing the harder path of learning new ideas for the sake of those you love. You are a rock star, and I'm so proud to call you my mother and best friend.

To Daddy: I love and miss you terribly. Thank you for teaching me how to be brave and for fiercely loving and empowering your little girl.

Even if it looks a little different than we envisioned, I still feel like I'm following in your footsteps. I know you can't read this in heaven, but I also believe you can.

To my brothers: We have had quite the adventures together. World travels, homemade music videos, cramming on that bench on *The Jim Bakker Show*. Y'all were there with me through it all and are two of my closest friends. Matt—I love that we can have deep theological discussions that still find space for *Seinfeld* quotes. Andrew—I thank you for trusting me enough to come out to me. For gently nudging me toward a more inclusive faith, while also including surprisingly relevant *Seinfeld* quotes along the way.

To Pop & Lolli: Thank you for being amazing in-laws and grandparents to our kids. For all the late-night talks, board games, and laughs. We will forever be grateful that y'all chose the harder path of walking this journey with us. Your support means the world.

MK: Thank you for telling me to write a book. For taking me under your wing and walking me through the whole publishing/writing process. For quickly giving me tips like when I just texted you asking, "How does one write acknowledgments?!" This book would not exist if it weren't for you. And I mean that literally. I will always be grateful for your friendship and how you believed in me when I didn't believe in myself.

Rachelle: my trusted agent. Thank you for being the calming voice I needed when I was freaking out. For graciously answering my millions of questions and laughing at my corny jokes. Your encouragement helped me sleep at night when I was in the thick of it all.

Beth: my amazing editor. Remember that time you told me I needed to restructure the entire book on the day I moved to a new state? Lol, me too. But you were freaking right and helped make this book so much better. Thank you for pushing me.

To the entire team at Worthy: It's been such a fun and riveting experience seeing everything that goes on behind the scenes in the publishing world. Thank you for putting *Star-Spangled Jesus* out into the universe.

And finally, thank YOU. The ones who read this book. The ones who followed me on TikTok when I was just a weird Tennessee mom wearing an upside-down ladybug basket on my head. Everyone who has ever engaged with my content (even the dude who called me April Apain because I'm "not a joy at all")—thank you! Thank you to all the people who left encouraging comments or sent messages sharing your stories with me. You made me feel less alone in my own journey and that is something I'll cherish forever.

Hopefully this book will return the favor and help others feel less alone too.

Endnotes

Introduction

1. Katelyn Polantz, "Giuliani, Who Urged Trump Supporters to Have 'Trial by Combat' Says He Wasn't Literally Calling for Insurrection," CNN, May 18, 2021, https://www.cnn.com/2021/05/18/politics/rudy-giuliani-january-6-insurrection-lawsuit/index.html.
2. Ewan Palmer, "Mo Brooks Says 'Kicking Ass' Jan. 6 Speech Was 'About Beating the RINOs,'" *Newsweek*, June 9, 2022, https://www.newsweek.com/mo-brooks-jan6-speech-msnbc-chris-hayes-trump-1714178.
3. Brian Naylor, "Read Trump's Jan. 6 Speech, A Key Part Of Impeachment Trial," NPR, February 10, 2021, HYPERLINK "https://url.us.m.mimecastprotect.com/s/732-CwpyRpSZGzk5FV9rwN?domain=npr.org" https://www.npr.org/2021/02/10/966396848/read-trumps-jan-6-speech-a-key-part-of-impeachment-trial.

4. Zoë Richards, "Jan. 6 Defendant Known as 'Zip-Tie Guy' Is Sentenced to Nearly 5 Years in Prison," *NBC News*, September 8, 2023, https://www.nbcnews.com/politics/justice-department/jan-6-defendant-known-zip-tie-guy-sentenced-nearly-5-years-prison-rcna104188.
5. Exclusions apply.
6. Andrew Whitehead and Samuel L. Perry, "The Christian Nationalism of Speaker Mike Johnson," *Time*, October 27, 2023, https://time.com/6329207/speaker-mike-johnson-christian-nationalism/.

1. America Is the Best

1. Lauren Effron, Andrew Paprella and Jeca Taudte, "The Scandals That Brought Down the Bakkers, Once Among US's Most Famous Televangelists," *ABC News*, December 20, 2019, https://abcnews.go.com/US/scandals-brought-bakkers-uss-famous-televangelists/story?id=60389342.
2. Peter Applebome, "Bakker Is Convicted on All Counts; First Felon Among TV Evangelists," *New York Times*, October 6, 1989, https://www.nytimes.com/1989/10/06/us/bakker-is-convicted-on-all-counts-first-felon-among-tv-evangelists.html.
3. Gerhard Peters and John T. Woolley, "George W. Bush, Remarks at the Simon Wiesenthal Center in Los Angeles," The American Presidency Project, March 6, 2000, https://www.presidency.ucsb.edu/documents/remarks-the-simon-wiesenthal-center-los-angeles.
4. *The Doctrine of Discovery, 1493*, The Gilder Lehrman Institute of American History, 2012, https://www.gilderlehrman.org/history-resources/spotlight-primary-source/doctrine-discovery-1493.
5. Robert P. Jones, "The Roots of Christian Nationalism Go Back Further Than You Think," *Time*, August 31, 2023, https://time.com/6309657/us-christian-nationalism-columbus-essay/.
6. Smithsonian American Art Museum, "Manifest Destiny and U.S. Westward Expansion," https://americanexperience.si.edu/wp-content/uploads/2014/08/Manifest-Destiny-and-U.S-Westward-Expansion.pdf.
7. Kaitlyn Schiess, "Politicians, You Keep Saying 'City on a Hill' but It Doesn't Mean What You Think It Means," *Christianity Today*, August 25, 2023, https://www.christianitytoday.com/ct/2023/august-web-only/gop-president-debate-republican-candidate-christian-nation.html.
8. Tara Isabella Burton, "Trump-Allied Pastor Tells Worshippers 'America Is a Christian Nation,'" *Vox*, June 25, 2018, https://www.vox.com/2018/6/25/17502170/pastor-robert-jeffress-america-christian-nation-trump-dallas-baptist.
9. Ewan Palmer, "'Let's Go Brandon' Chanted at Qanon-Linked Church Event in Texas," *Newsweek*, November 15, 2021, https://www.newsweek.com/lets-go-brandon-church-texas-qanon-1649141.
10. Alejandra Guzman-Tracy, "Video of People Chanting 'Let's Go Brandon' Inside Cornerstone Church Sparks Debate," *News4SA*, November 16, 2021, https://news4sanantonio.com/news/local/video-of-people-chanting-lets-go-brandon-inside-cornerstone-church-sparks-debate.

2. Christian = Evangelical

1. Jennifer Murtoff, "Two Natures of Christ," *Encyclopedia Britannica*, April 12, 2023, https://www.britannica.com/topic/two-natures-of-Christ.
2. The Editors of Britannica Encyclopedia, "Docetism," *Encyclopedia Britannica*, April 11, 2014, https://www.britannica.com/topic/Docetism.
3. John J. A'Becket, The Catholic Encyclopedia, "Abecedarians," *Encyclopedia Dictionary of Bible and Theology*, https://www.biblia.work/dictionaries/abecedarians/.
4. Relevant, "The Strange Christian Beliefs That Time Forgot," *Relevant Magazine*, April 7, 2022, https://relevantmagazine.com/faith/the-strange-christian-beliefs-that-time-forgot/.
5. The Editors of Britannica Encyclopedia, "Shaker—Protestant Sect," *Encyclopedia Britannica*, September 29, 2023, https://www.britannica.com/topic/Shakers.
6. Tim Hume, "'Eastern Lightning': The Banned Religious Group That Has China Worried," CNN, February 2, 2015, https://www.cnn.com/2014/06/06/world/asia/china-eastern-lightning-killing/index.html.
7. Matt Shea, "The Cult Who Kidnaps Christians and Is at War with the Chinese Government," *Vice*, July 31, 2013, https://www.vice.com/en/article/7be5ya/the-chinese-cult-who-kidnap-christians-and-paint-snakes.
8. Center for the Study of Global Christianity, "Status of Global Christianity, 2023, in the Context of 1900–2050," Gordon Conwell Theological Seminary, https://www.gordonconwell.edu/wp-content/uploads/sites/13/2023/01/Status-of-Global-Christianity-2023.pdf.
9. Jonathan Merritt, "Defining *Evangelical*," *The Atlantic*, December 7, 2015, https://www.theatlantic.com/politics/archive/2015/12/evangelical-christian/418236/.
10. Clyde Haberman, "Religion and Right-Wing Politics: How Evangelicals Reshaped Elections," *New York Times*, October 28, 2018, https://www.nytimes.com/2018/10/28/us/religion-politics-evangelicals.html.
11. PRRI Staff, "The 2020 Census of American Religion," Public Religion Research Institute, July 8, 2021, https://www.prri.org/research/2020-census-of-american-religion/.
12. Justin Nortey, "Most White Americans Who Regularly Attend Worship Services Voted for Trump in 2020," Pew Research Center, August 30, 2021, https://www.pewresearch.org/short-reads/2021/08/30/most-white-americans-who-regularly-attend-worship-services-voted-for-trump-in-2020/.
13. Yonat Shimron, "Poll: A Third of Americans Are Christian Nationalists and Most Are White Evangelicals," Religion News Service, February 8, 2023, https://religionnews.com/2023/02/08/a-third-of-americans-are-christian-nationalists-and-most-are-white-evangelicals/.
14. Andrew Whitehead and Samuel L. Perry, "The Christian Nationalism of Speaker Mike Johnson," *Time*, October 27, 2023, https://time.com/6329207/speaker-mike-johnson-christian-nationalism/.
15. Mike Hixenbaugh, "Meet the Evangelical Activist Who's Had a 'Profound Influence' on Speaker Mike Johnson," *NBC News*, October 26, 2023, https://www.nbcnews.com/news/us-news/evangelical-activist-influence-speaker-mike-johnson-rcna122313.

16. Megan Basham @megbasham, "They are making it v clear. True Christianity--the kind that looks to Scripture not culture as its moral arbiter--will now be treated as something 'extreme' that cannot be accommodated in the public square. For the church leaders and ostensibly Christian pundits who assured us pluralism was the answer--how's that working out?" *Twitter/X*, October 27, 2023, https://twitter.com/megbasham/status/1718017039594344715?t=OBRZkmP9c9e1fq2zBMG9_w&s=19.
17. Franklin Graham, "Blessed Is the Nation Whose God Is the Lord," *Decision Magazine*, October 2020, https://static.billygraham.org/sites/lp.billygraham.org/uploads/prod/2020/09/2020-Digital-Election-Guide-2.pdf.
18. Robin R. Meyers, *Saving Jesus from the Church: How to Stop Worshiping Christ and Start Following Jesus* (New York: HarperCollins, 2009), p. 14.

3. Morality Should Be Mandated

1. PRRI Staff, "The 2020 Census of American Religion," Public Religion Research Institute, July 8, 2021, https://www.prri.org/research/2020-census-of-american-religion/.
2. Jeff Diamant, "Faith on the Hill: The Religious Composition of the 118th Congress," Pew Research Center, January 3, 2023, https://www.pewresearch.org/religion/2023/01/03/faith-on-the-hill-2023/.
3. Katherine Schaeffer, "U.S. Congress Continues to Gow in Racial, Ethnic Diversity," Pew Research Center, January 9, 2023, https://www.pewresearch.org/short-reads/2023/01/09/u-s-congress-continues-to-grow-in-racial-ethnic-diversity/.
4. Got Questions Ministries, "Is the Seven Mountain Mandate Biblical? What Is the 7-M Mandate?" *Compelling Truth*, https://www.compellingtruth.org/seven-mountain-mandate.html.
5. Elle Hardy, "The 'Modern Apostles' Who Want to Reshape America Ahead of the End Times," *The Outline*, March 19, 2020, https://theoutline.com/post/8856/seven-mountain-mandate-trump-paula-white.
6. Kyle Mantyla, "'We Want Nations': Lance Wallnau Preaches Seven Mountains Dominionism," *Right Wing Watch*, March 1, 2022, https://www.rightwingwatch.org/post/we-want-nations-lance-wallnau-preaches-seven-mountains-dominionism/.
7. Dictionary.com, "theo," https://www.dictionary.com/browse/theo-; "-cracy," https://www.dictionary.com/browse/-cracy.
8. Amanda Tyler, "Opinion: Marjorie Taylor Greene's Words on Christian Nationalism Are a Wake-Up Call," CNN, July 27, 2022, https://www.cnn.com/2022/07/27/opinions/christian-nationalism-marjorie-taylor-greene-tyler/index.html.
9. Barbara Plett Usher, "Christian Nationalists—Wanting to Put God into US Government," *BBC News*, December 17, 2022, https://www.bbc.com/news/world-us-canada-63902626.
10. Michael Drummond, "'A Spiritual War': Are Christian Nationalists Threatening to Turn the US into a Religious State?," Sky News, July 29, 2023, https://news.sky.com/story/a-spiritual-war-are-christian-nationalists-threatening-to-turn-the-us-into-a-religious-state-12924092.
11. Dale Chamberlain, "Michael Flynn: Faithful Pastors Preach the Constitution Just as Much as the Bible," *ChurchLeaders*, July 13, 2022, https://churchleaders

.com/news/429290-michael-flynn-faithful-pastors-preach-the-constitution-just-as-much-as-the-bible.html.

12. Michelle R. Smith, "Former Trump Adviser Michael Flynn 'at the Center' of New Movement Based on Conspiracies and Christian Nationalism," *PBS News Hour*, September 7, 2022, https://www.pbs.org/newshour/politics/former-trump-adviser-michael-flynn-at-the-center-of-new-movement-based-on-conspiracies-and-christian-nationalism.
13. Stephen Wolfe, *The Case for Christian Nationalism*, Kindle Edition (Moscow, ID: Canon Press, 2022), p. 89.
14. Kyle Mantyla, "'Guilty as Charged': Sean Feucht Proudly Admits to Being a Christian Nationalist," *Right Wing Watch*, April 21, 2023, https://www.rightwingwatch.org/post/guilty-as-charged-sean-feucht-proudly-admits-to-being-a-christian-nationalist/.

4. Racial Reconciliation Sunday

1. Wyatte Grantham-Philips, "Pastor Paul White Calls on Angels from Africa and South America to Bring Trump Victory," *USA Today*, November 5, 2020, https://www.usatoday.com/story/news/nation/2020/11/05/paula-white-trumps-spiritual-adviser-african-south-american-angels/6173576002/.
2. Mike Cummings, "Yale Sociologist Phil Gorski on the Threat of White Christian Nationalism," *YaleNews*, March 15, 2022, https://news.yale.edu/2022/03/15/yale-sociologist-phil-gorski-threat-white-christian-nationalism.
3. Cummings, "Yale Sociologist Phil Gorski."
4. Jemar Tisby, *The Color of Compromise: The Truth About the American Church's Complicity in Racism* (Grand Rapids, MI: Zondervan, 2020), p. 80.
5. Noel Rae, "How Christian Slaveholders Used the Bible to Justify Slavery," *Time*, February 23, 2018, https://time.com/5171819/christianity-slavery-book-excerpt/.
6. "Report on Slavery and Racism in the History of the Southern Baptist Theological Seminary," Southern Baptist Theological Seminary, 2018, https://archives.sbts.edu/the-history-of-the-sbts/report-on-slavery-and-racism/.
7. Mark. A. Noll, *The Civil War as a Theological Crisis* (Chapel Hill: University of North Carolina Press, 2006), p. 19.
8. Rebecca Anne Goetz, *The Baptism of Early Modern Virginia: How Christianity Created Race* (Baltimore: John Hopkins University Press, 2012), p. 3.
9. Tisby, *The Color of Compromise*, p. 81.
10. Robert Lewis Dabney, *A Defence of Virginia (and Through Her, of the South) in Recent and Pending Contests Against the Sectional Party* (New York: E. J. Hale, 1867), p. 281.
11. Tisby, *The Color of Compromise*, p. 37.
12. Becky Little, "Why Bibles Given to Slaves Omitted Most of the Old Testament," History A&E Television, August 24, 2023, https://www.history.com/news/slave-bible-redacted-old-testament.
13. Tisby, *The Color of Compromise*, p. 37.
14. Randall J. Stephens, "The Klan, White Christianity and the Past and Present," The Religion and Culture Forum—The Marty Center of University of

Chicago Divinity School, June 2017, https://voices.uchicago.edu/religionculture/2017/06/26/the-klan-white-christianity-and-the-past-and-present-a-response-to-kelly-j-baker-by-randall-j-stephens/.

15. Knights of the Ku Klux Klan, *White Book: Kloran* (Atlanta, 1916), United Klans of America, Newsletters and Correspondence, Rare Books and Manuscripts Division, Indiana State Library, https://reimaginingmigration.org/primary-source-the-kloran/.
16. DeNeen L. Brown, "The Preacher Who Used Christianity to Revive the Ku Klux Klan," *Washington Post*, April 10, 2018, https://www.washingtonpost.com/news/retropolis/wp/2018/04/08/the-preacher-who-used-christianity-to-revive-the-ku-klux-klan/.
17. Ku Klux Klan, "Principles and Purposes of the Knights of the Ku Klux Klan," *The University of Maine—Paul W. Bean Civil War Papers*, 1920, https://digitalcommons.library.umaine.edu/cgi/viewcontent.cgi?article=1071&context=paul_bean_papers.
18. Matt Carr, "Birth of a Nation: D. W. Griffiths and Today's Far-Right Imagination." *Ceasefire*, December 14, 2012, https://ceasefiremagazine.co.uk/birth-nation-w-g-griffiths-todays-far-right-imagination/.
19. Evening Star, "Birth of a Nation in White House," *Newspapers.com*, February 18, 1915, https://www.newspapers.com/article/evening-star-birth-of-a-nation-in-white/30174748/.
20. Tom Gjelten, "Southern Baptist Seminary Confronts History of Slaveholding and 'Deep Racism,'" NPR, December 13, 2018, https://www.npr.org/2018/12/13/676333342/southern-baptist-seminary-confronts-history-of-slaveholding-and-deep-racism.
21. Evangelical Press, "Bob Jones University Drops Interracial Dating Ban," *Christianity Today*, March 1, 2000, https://www.christianitytoday.com/ct/2000/marchweb-only/53.0.html.
22. Bobby Ross Jr., "Tulsa Race Massacre Prayer Room Highlight Churches' 1921 Sins, Seeks Healing," *Oklahoma Watch*, May 30, 2021, https://oklahomawatch.org/2021/05/30/tulsa-race-massacre-prayer-room-highlights-churches-1921-sins-seeks-healing/.
23. Tisby, *The Color of Compromise*, p. 127.
24. Terry Gross, "A 'Forgotten History' of How the U.S. Government Segregated America," NPR, May 3, 2017, https://www.npr.org/2017/05/03/526655831/a-forgotten-history-of-how-the-u-s-government-segregated-america.
25. Nick Chater, "Why We Think Life Was Better in the 'Good Old Days,'" Warwick Business School the University of Warwick, January 13, 2015, https://www.wbs.ac.uk/news/why-we-think-life-was-better-in-the-good-old-days/.

5. In God We Trump

1. Marguerite Michaels, "Billy Graham: America Is Not God's Only Kingdom," *Parade Magazine*, February 1, 1970, https://www.snopes.com/fact-check/billy-graham-mixing-religion-politics/.

2. Jerry Pierce, "Three Years after His Death, Billy Graham's Ministry Still Moves Souls to the Savior," *Decision*, February 21, 2021, https://decisionmagazine.com/three-years-after-his-death-billy-grahams-ministry-still-moves-souls-to-the-savior/.
3. Staff reporters, "Billy Graham: Pastor to Presidents, for More than 50 Years," *Citizen Times*, February 21, 2018, https://www.citizen-times.com/story/news/local/2018/02/21/billy-graham-pastor-presidents-more-than-50-years/110666254/.
4. Kristin Kobes Du Mez, *Jesus and John Wayne: How White Evangelicals Corrupted a Faith and Fractured a Nation* (New York: Liveright Publishing Corporation, 2020), p. 35.
5. God in America: "Study Guide: Soul of a Nation (Episode 5)," PBS, https://www.pbs.org/godinamerica/study-guide/five.html.
6. God in America: "The Soul of a Nation," PBS, https://www.pbs.org/godinamerica/transcripts/hour-five.html.
7. Diane Winston, "The History of the National Prayer Breakfast," *Smithsonian Magazine*, February 2, 2017, https://www.smithsonianmag.com/history/national-prayer-breakfast-what-does-its-history-reveal-180962017/.
8. History.com editors, "President Eisenhower Signs 'In God We Trust' into Law," History A&E Television Networks, July 27, 2022, https://www.history.com/this-day-in-history/president-eisenhower-signs-in-god-we-trust-into-law.
9. History.com editors, "President Eisenhower Signs 'In God We Trust' into Law."
10. Chloe Foussianes, "How Phyllis Schlafly, an Anti-ERA Conservative Activist, Left an Enduring Mark on the Republican Party," *Town & Country Magazine*, April 18, 2020, https://www.townandcountrymag.com/leisure/arts-and-culture/a31944041/phyllis-schlafly-mrs-america-era-true-story/.
11. Kobes Du Mez, *Jesus and John Wayne*, p. 144.
12. Ben Finley, Peter Smith, and Deepa Bharath, "Pat Robertson United Evangelical Christians and Pushed Them into Conservative Politics," Associated Press, June 9, 2023, https://apnews.com/article/pat-robertson-evangelical-legacy-christian-broadcasting-3e42d2c44d837b1aaf61a36315dde6a1.
13. Peter Applebome, "Jerry Falwell, Leading U.S. Religious Conservative, Dies at 73," *New York Times*, May 15, 2007, https://www.nytimes.com/2007/05/15/world/americas/15iht-15obits.html.
14. Randall Balmer, "The Real Origins of the Religious Right," *Politico*, May 27, 2014, https://www.politico.com/magazine/story/2014/05/religious-right-real-origins-107133/.
15. Robert C. Cloud, The Editors of Encyclopaedia Britannica, "Bob Jones University v. United States," *Encyclopedia Britannica*, 1983, https://www.britannica.com/event/Bob-Jones-University-v-United-States.
16. Christopher Reed, "Obituary: The Rev Jerry Falwell," *The Guardian*, May 17, 2007, https://www.theguardian.com/media/2007/may/17/broadcasting.guardianobituaries.
17. Antonia Blumberg, "Fourteen Percent of Americans Believe AIDS Might Be God's Punishment: Survey," *Huffington Post*, February 28, 2014, https://www.huffpost.com/entry/aids-hiv-gods-punishment_n_4876381.

18. Reed, "Obituary: The Rev Jerry Falwell."
19. Peter Wallsten, "Falwell Says Faithful Fear Clinton More than Devil," *Los Angeles Times*, September 24, 2006, https://www.latimes.com/archives/la-xpm-2006-sep-24-na-falwell24-story.html.
20. American Experience Series, "People and Ideas: Cold War and Modern Era," PBS, https://www.pbs.org/wgbh/americanexperience/features/godinamerica-cold-war-modern/.
21. Paul Matzko, "Jerry Falwell Helps Found the Moral Majority—Timeline Event," The Association of Religion Data Archives, https://www.thearda.com/us-religion/history/timelines/entry/?etype=1&eid=46.
22. Peter Applebome, "Jerry Falwell, Moral Majority Founder, Dies at 73," *New York Times*, May 16, 2007, https://www.nytimes.com/2007/05/16/obituaries/16falwell.html.
23. Erik Eckholm, "From Right, a Rain of Anti-Clinton Salvos," *New York Times*, June 26, 1994, https://www.nytimes.com/1994/06/26/us/from-right-a-rain-of-anti-clinton-salvos.html.
24. Eugene Scott, "Jerry Falwell, Jr., Trump's Early and Effusive Evangelical Champion, Lifted a President Before His Own Fall," *Washington Post*, August 26, 2020, https://www.washingtonpost.com/politics/2020/08/26/jerry-falwell-jr-trumps-early-effusive-evangelical-champion-lifted-president-before-his-own-fall/.
25. Jessica Taylor, "Citing 'Two Corinthians,' Trump Struggles to Make the Sale to Evangelicals," January 18, 2016, NPR, https://www.npr.org/2016/01/18/463528847/citing-two-corinthians-trump-struggles-to-make-the-sale-to-evangelicals.
26. Elizabeth Barnett, "User Clip: Trump Doesn't Ask God for Forgiveness," C-SPAN Video Interview—User Clip, March 20, 2016, https://www.c-span.org/video/?c4585899/user-clip-trump-god-forgiveness.
27. David Brody, "Brody File Video Exclusive: Donald Trump Exclaims 'God Is the Ultimate!,'" *CBN News, The Brody File*, September 23, 2015, https://www1.cbn.com/thebrodyfile/archive/2015/09/23/brody-file-video-exclusive-donald-trump-exclaims-god-is-the.
28. Jessica Martínez and Gregory A. Smith, "How the Faithful Voted: A Preliminary 2016 Analysis," Pew Research Center, November 9, 2016, https://www.pewresearch.org/short-reads/2016/11/09/how-the-faithful-voted-a-preliminary-2016-analysis/.
29. Megan Basham @megbasham, "I don't especially care if a politician is sincere in his or her pro-life stance. It would be better if they were. But what I really care about is whether they pursue pro-life policies w/ vigor as promised. I'll take effective hypocrisy over ineffective sincerity any day of week," *Twitter/X*, November 15, 2022, https://twitter.com/megbasham/status/1592730905910849538.

6. Saving Ben Stiller: Influence Through Media

1. Bottom Line, "Group Objects to Gay Dads in JCPenney Catalog," *NBC News*, June 5, 2012, https://www.nbcnews.com/business/business-news/group-objects-gay-dads-jcpenney-catalog-flna814794.
2. John Riley, "Ex-Gay Jeffrey McCall Comes Out as Scarlet McCall," *Metro Weekly*, April 11, 2023, https://www.metroweekly.com/2023/04/ex-gay-jeffrey-mccall-comes-out-as-scarlet-mccall/.

3. Anthony Salvanto, Kabir Khanna, Jennifer De Pinto, and Fred Backus, "CBS News Poll Finds Trump's Big Lead Grows, as GOP Voters Dismiss Indictments," *CBS News*, August 20, 2023, https://www.cbsnews.com/news/trump-poll-indictments-2023-08-20/.

7. The ChurchB-B-QAnon: or, The Problem with Conspiracy Theories

1. Dan Alleva, " 'Satanic Panic' Pastor BOB LARSON Thinks JOHNNY DEPP Is Possessed by Pirate Demons," *Metal Injection*, May 8, 2022, https://metalinjection.net/around-the-interwebs/satanic-panic-pastor-bob-larson-thinks-johnny-depp-is-possessed-by-pirate-demons.
2. Tucker Higgins, "Alex Jones' 5 Most Disturbing and Ridiculous Conspiracy Theories," CNBC, September 14, 2018, https://www.cnbc.com/2018/09/14/alex-jones-5-most-disturbing-ridiculous-conspiracy-theories.html.
3. Dan Glaister, "Air Force Looked at Spray to Turn Enemy Gay," *The Guardian*, June 13, 2007, https://www.theguardian.com/world/2007/jun/13/usa.danglaister.
4. Abby Turner and Andrew Kaczynski, "Robert F. Kennedy, Jr. Repeatedly Suggested That Chemicals in Water Are Impacting Sexuality of Children," CNN, July 13, 2023, https://www.cnn.com/2023/07/13/politics/robert-kennedy-jr-chemicals-water-children-frogs/index.html.
5. Angelamarie Scafidi (Ucci), @Angelamariescafidi on Instagram, Reel on April 3, 2023, https://www.instagram.com/reel/CqlJhJEgwcO/.
6. Yes, I actually believed this. No, I can't cite any source for this belief other than evangelical hearsay.
7. Gregory Krieg, "14 of Trump's Most Outrageous 'Birther' Claims—Half from after 2011," CNN, September 16, 2016, https://www.cnn.com/2016/09/09/politics/donald-trump-birther/index.html.
8. Lindsey Jacobson and Gary Langer, "What You Need to Know About the 'Deep State,'" *ABC News*, April 29, 2017, https://abcnews.go.com/Politics/deep-state/story?id=47086646.
9. Lynn Stuart Parramore, "Like QAnon's Capitol Rioters, the Nashville Bomber's Lizard People Theory Is Deadly Serious," *NBC News*, January 12, 2021, https://www.nbcnews.com/think/opinion/qanon-s-capitol-rioters-nashville-bomber-s-lizard-people-theory-ncna1253819.
10. Justin Vallejo and Phil Thomas, "Why Some QAnon Believers Think JFK Jr Is Still Alive—and About to Become Vice President," *The Independent*, January 18, 2022, https://www.the-independent.com/news/world/americas/us-politics/qanon-jfk-jr-alive-trump-b1995594.html.
11. Matthew Gault and Samantha Cole, "Is Joe Biden Dead, Replaced by 10 Different Deepfake Body Doubles? An Investigation," *Vice*, July 29, 2022, https://www.vice.com/en/article/wxnn54/is-joe-biden-dead-replaced-by-10-different-deepfake-body-doubles-an-investigation.
12. Annelise Pierce, "Bethel Church's Bill Johnson Compares COVID Vaccines to 'Mark of the Beast,'" *Shasta Scout*, October 15, 2021, https://shastascout.org/bethel-churchs-bill-johnson-compares-covid-vaccines-to-mark-of-the-beast/.

13. Rachel Sharp, "Kansas Anti-Vaxxers Condemned for Comparing Vaccine Mandates to the Holocaust by Wearing Yellow Stars," *The Independent*, November 13, 2021, https://www.the-independent.com/news/world/americas/us-politics/kansas-vaccine-mandate-holocaust-republicans-b1957233.html.
14. Travis Cummings, "Cleveland Mega Church in Heat for Holding Packed and Maskless Services," *Local 3 News Chattanooga*, January 2, 2021, https://www.local3news.com/cleveland-mega-church-in-heat-for-holding-packed-and-maskless-services/article_c501e888-61f3-5d77-8363-98cfd5725efa.html.
15. Cummings, "Cleveland Mega Church in Heat."
16. Alice M. Philips and John Martin Rare Book Room, "The Black Death: The Plague, 1331–1770, Hardin Library for the Health Sciences, 2017, https://hosted.lib.uiowa.edu/histmed/plague/.
17. World Health Organization, "WHO Coronavirus (COVID-19) Dashboard," https://covid19.who.int/.
18. Leslie Toke, "Flagellants," *Catholic Encyclopedia*, Vol. 6, 1909, https://www.newadvent.org/cathen/06089c.htm.
19. Steven Ray Haberlin, "Latest Fashion Fad Raising Marion Parent's Concern," *Ocala StarBanner*, October 13, 2003, https://www.ocala.com/story/news/2003/11/13/latest-fashion-fad-raising-marion-parents-concern/31287692007/.

8. Naked Christians in the Air: Manipulating End Times Eschatology

1. Maayan Jaffe-Hoffman, "Has Biblical Gog and Magog War Begun?" *Jerusalem Post*, March 2022, https://www.jpost.com/christianworld/article-699085#google_vignette.
2. Terry Gross, "Remembering Tim LaHaye, Co-Author of the Apocalyptic 'Left Behind' Series," *Fresh Air NPR*, June 29, 2016, https://www.npr.org/2016/07/29/487863225/tim-lahaye-obit-2002.
3. United Nations Website, https://www.un.org/en/.
4. Steve Warren, "UN Sculpture Looks a Lot Like the End Times Beast Referred to in Daniel 7 and Revelation 13," CBN, December 10, 2021, https://www2.cbn.com/news/world/un-sculpture-looks-lot-end-times-beast-referred-daniel-7-and-revelation-13.
5. Jay Parini, "Even Jesus Wouldn't Buy 'the Rapture,'" CNN, July 6, 2014, https://www.cnn.com/2014/07/06/opinion/parini-rapture-real/index.html.
6. Thomas D. Ice, "Is the Pre-Trib Rapture a Satanic Deception?" *Liberty University Scholars Crossing*, Article Archives, May 2009, https://digitalcommons.liberty.edu/cgi/viewcontent.cgi?article=1051&context=pretrib_arch, p. 1.
7. Jeff Diamant, "About Four-in-Ten U.S. Adults Believe Humanity Is 'Living in the End Times,'" Pew Research Center, December 8, 2022, https://www.pewresearch.org/short-reads/2022/12/08/about-four-in-ten-u-s-adults-believe-humanity-is-living-in-the-end-times/.
8. Matthew Avery Sutton, "Jerusalem: Trump's Gift to Evangelicals," *Seattle Times*, https://www.seattletimes.com/opinion/jerusalem-trumps-gift-to-evangelicals/.
9. Diana Butler Bass, "For Many Evangelicals, Jerusalem Is About Prophecy, Not Politics," CNN, May 14, 2018, https://www.cnn.com/2017/12/08/opinions/jerusalem-israel-evangelicals-end-times-butler-bass-opinion/index.html.

10. Tara Isabella Burton, "Pastor at US Embassy Opening in Jerusalem Says Trump 'on the Right Side' of God," *Vox*, May 14, 2018, https://www.vox.com/2018/5/14/17352676/robert-jeffress-jerusalem-embassy-israel-prayer.
11. Zack Beauchamp, "Israelis Are Celebrating the US Embassy Move. Palestinians Are Dying," *Vox*, May 16, 2018, https://www.vox.com/world/2018/5/14/17352016/us-jerusalem-embassy-gaza-violence.
12. Chris Lehmann, "American Evangelicals Await the Final Battle in Gaza," *The Nation*, November 2, 2023, https://www.thenation.com/article/world/american-evangelicals-israel-gaza/.
13. Matthew Impelli, "Pro-Trump Pastor Hopes Israel War Sparks Jesus Return," *Newsweek*, October 11, 2023, https://www.newsweek.com/pro-trump-pastor-hopes-israel-war-sparks-jesus-return-1833972.
14. Talia Lavin, "These Evangelicals Are Cheering the Gaza War as the End of the World," *Rolling Stone*, November 17, 2023, https://www.rollingstone.com/politics/political-commentary/gaza-war-evangelical-leaders-cheer-end-world-1234884151/.

9. Grandma Is Watching: Eternal Fearmongering

1. Jack T. Chick, *This Was Your Life*, Reprint 2002, USA, https://chick.com/products/tract?stk=0001.
2. Upcoming Dramas, *Reality Outreach Ministries*, https://realityoutreach.org/pages/upcoming-dramas.
3. Thomas A. Schafer, "Jonathan Edwards," *Encyclopaedia Britannica*, https://www.britannica.com/biography/Jonathan-Edwards.
4. Jonathan Edwards, *Sinners in the Hands of Angry God*, W. W. Norton College History Archives, 1741, https://wwnorton.com/college/history/archive/resources/documents/ch03_03.htm.
5. *Decision Magazine* Staff, "Billy Graham's Eternal Legacy," *Decision Magazine*, February 1, 2023, https://decisionmagazine.com/billy-grahams-eternal-legacy/.
6. Deirdre Reilly, "Franklin Graham at Christian Media Convention: Every 'Demon from Hell' Has Been 'Turned Loose' in Society," *Fox News*, May 23, 2023, https://www.foxnews.com/lifestyle/franklin-graham-christian-media-convention-demon-hell-turned-loose-society.
7. Emily Jones, "HELL . . . Yes or Now? Why Franklin Graham Is Suddenly Tackling This Eternal Debate," CBN, September 23, 2018, https://www2.cbn.com/news/us/hell-yes-or-no-why-franklin-graham-suddenly-tackling-eternal-debate.
8. Eliza Griswold, "Franklin Graham's Uneasy Alliance with Donald Trump," *The New Yorker*, September 11, 2018, https://www.newyorker.com/news/dispatch/franklin-grahams-uneasy-alliance-with-donald-trump.
9. Lindsey Bever, "Franklin Graham: The Media Didn't Understand the 'God-Factor' in Trump's Win," *Washington Post*, November 10, 2016, https://www.washingtonpost.com/news/acts-of-faith/wp/2016/11/10/franklin-graham-the-media-didnt-understand-the-god-factor/.
10. David Allbritton, *America Say Jesus* (Tulsa, OK: Vision Imprints Publishing, Inc., 2005), p. 69.

11. Jesse T. Jackson, "Pastor Greg Locke Tells CNN They 'Will Burn in Hell,'" *Church Leaders*, August 5, 2021, https://churchleaders.com/news/402881-pastor-greg-locke-tells-cnn-they-will-burn-in-hell.html.
12. Jenna Ellis @JennaEllisEsq, "Revelation 21. God lists COWARDS first as among those who will be cast into the lake of fire for eternity. Fear God rather than men. Do not fear the petty tyrants. I hope our Supreme Court is not full of cowards," *Twitter/X*, December 27, 2021, https://twitter.com/JennaEllisEsq/status/1475345303628697601?t=n91ATMeJZb-IiQATFWl3Hw&s=19.
13. Jenna Ellis @JennaEllisEsq, "Here's what's upcoming at the Supreme Court for the 2021-22 term! Three very important cases will test whether the Court is truly conservative and originalist. @newsmax," *Twitter/X*, October 4, 2021, https://twitter.com/JennaEllisEsq/status/1445068539736567816.
14. Jenna Ellis @JennaEllisEsq, "If you don't believe God is real or hell is a literal place, why are you so outraged that Christians believe people who haven't repented and aren't saved will spend eternity in damnation and separation from God? Because you know the Truth and want to deny consequences for sin," *Twitter/X*, November 24, 2022, https://twitter.com/JennaEllisEsq/status/1595833010070462465?t=P7x4PpWUDnknRlH0H5IjPQ&s=19.
15. Daniel Villarreal, "Anti-Lockdown Christian Activist Holds 2,500-Person NYE Event in COVID Hotspot," *Newsweek*, January 1, 2021, https://www.newsweek.com/anti-lockdown-christian-activist-holds-2500-person-nye-event-covid-hotspot-1558470.
16. Megan Basham @megbasham, "I make no apologies for mocking people who claim the name of Christ but have pronouns in their bio," *Twitter/X*, October 8, 2022, https://twitter.com/megbasham/status/1578938917361192960.
17. Megan Basham @megbasham, "These are Jesus' words for some of his neighbors. The only-gentle, only soft Christ is a myth, perpetrated to allow wolves to come into church and lead some to Hell by preaching a Jesus who did not harshly confront the sin of those who were brazenly rewriting God's law," with screenshot of Matthew 23, *Twitter/X*, October 9, 2022, https://twitter.com/megbasham/status/1579192525075927041.
18. Ruth Graham, "'Like Winning the Lottery': Mike Johnson's Ascent Excites Conservative Christians," *New York Times*, November 5, 2023, https://www.nytimes.com/2023/11/05/us/politics/michael-johnson-house-speaker-evangelicalism.html.
19. Matthew D. Taylor, "Mike Johnson, Polite Extremist," *The Bulwark*, October 30, 2023, https://plus.thebulwark.com/p/mike-johnson-polite-extremist.
20. Tim Dickinson, "Mike Johnson: 'Depraved' America Deserves God's Wrath," *Rolling Stone*, November 15, 2023, https://www.rollingstone.com/politics/politics-features/mike-johnson-america-god-wrath-jim-garlow-1234879233/.
21. World Prayer Network, "WPN Call 279, Mike Johnson, Jody Hice—Congress Update: Concurrent Resolution and Motion to Vacate," *Well Versed*, October 4, 2023, https://wellversedworld.org/media/ps8jt9w/wpn-call-279-mike-johnson-jody-hice-congress-update-concurrent-resolution-and-motion-to-vacate.

10. *Antifa Super Soldiers: Demonizing Enemies*

1. Nicholas Bogel-Burroughs, "Prosecutors Say Derek Chauvin Knelt on George Floyd for 9 Minutes 29 Seconds, Longer than Initially Reported," *New York Times*, March 30, 2021, https://www.nytimes.com/2021/03/30/us/derek-chauvin-george-floyd-kneel-9-minutes-29-seconds.html.
2. Rondall Reynoso, "A Small Southern Town and Her Monument," *Faith on View*, September26,2020,https://www.faithonview.com/a-small-southern-town-and-her-monument.
3. Reynoso, "A Small Southern Town and Her Monument."

11. *Store Up Your Treasure Trolls in Heaven: Boycotts*

1. Philip Marcelo, "No, Target Isn't Selling Satanic Children's Clothes," Associated Press, June 2, 2023, https://apnews.com/article/fact-check-target-pride-lgbtq-satanic-998363252236.
2. Demon Buster blog, "Deliverance Manual—Trolls," *Demonbuster.com*, https://www.demonbuster.com/trolls.html.
3. J. D. Brown, "The Precendent Setting Case of Jesus vs. The Troll Dolls," *Medium*, June 29, 2020, https://medium.com/@jd911ca/the-precedent-setting-case-of-jesus-vs-the-troll-dolls-59177376c402.
4. Alan Yuhas, "It's Time to Revisit the Satanic Panic," *New York Times*, March 31, 2021, https://www.nytimes.com/2021/03/31/us/satanic-panic.html.
5. Daniel Goleman, "Proof Lacking for Ritual Abuse by Satanists," *New York Times*, October 31, 1994, https://www.nytimes.com/1994/10/31/us/proof-lacking-for-ritual-abuse-by-satanists.html.
6. Shannon Thaler, "Cracker Barrel Slammed for 'Woke' Rainbow Rocking Chair Honoring Pride Month," *New York Post*, June 9, 2023, https://nypost.com/2023/06/09/cracker-barrel-slammed-for-woke-rainbow-chair-for-pride/.
7. Stefanos Chen, "Macy's Parade Shuns Boycott Demands from Anti-L.G.B.T.Q. Group," *New York Times*, https://www.nytimes.com/2023/11/17/nyregion/thanksgiving-parade-nonbinary-lgbt-protest.html.
8. Stephen Dollins, "The Occult in Your Living Room," *The Prophecy Club*, https://www.watchprophecyclub.com/programs/the-occult-in-your-living-room.
9. Bri Na, "Pokemon EXPOSED by Ex Satanist Stephen Dollins," YouTube, April 19, 2017, video, https://www.youtube.com/watch?v=HaJd265x-Ak.
10. John Lynch, "Religious Leader Says Barbie Movie Has 'Demonic Influences' and Children Who See the Movie Will Behave Differently," *12 WBOY*, July 19, 2023, https://www.wboy.com/news/regional/religious-leader-says-barbie-movie-has-demonic-influences-and-children-who-see-the-movie-will-behave-differently/.
11. Rick Pidcock, "Why the Patriarchy Is Hyperventilating over *Barbie*," *Baptist Global News*, July 28, 2023, https://baptistnews.com/article/why-the-patriarchy-is-hyperventilating-over-barbie/.
12. Hanna Rosin, "A 'Tubby' Ache for Jerry Falwell," *Washington Post*, February 11, 1999, https://www.washingtonpost.com/wp-srv/style/tv/features/falwellteletubbies.htm.

13. Laura Blumenfeld, "Procter Gamble's Devil of a Problem," *Washington Post*, July 15, 1991, https://www.washingtonpost.com/archive/lifestyle/1991/07/15/procter-gambles-devil-of-a-problem/36f27641-e679-40f4-ac02-9d12c59a2f3b/.
14. Darian Lusk, "'Filled with Demons' Amy Duggar Reveals Toy Kids Were 'Banned' from Playing with & Accuses Controversial Family of Being like a 'Cult,'" *U.S. Sun*, January 7, 2023, https://www.the-sun.com/entertainment/7081922/amy-duggar-accuses-jim-bob-cult-family-video/.
15. Deborah Hamilton, "Why PetSmart Is in the Dog House with Some Christians," *Charisma News*, November 18, 2014, https://www.charismanews.com/us/46198-why-petsmart-is-in-the-dog-house-with-some-christians.
16. Sasha Aslanian, "Betty Crocker Bakes Cakes for State's First Same-Sex Weddings," *Minnesota Public Radio News*, July 29, 2013, https://www.mprnews.org/story/2013/07/29/betty-crocker-bakes-cakes-for-states-first-same-sex-weddings.
17. Special to the *New York Times*, "Boycott of NBC-TV and RCA Urged," *New York Times*, March 15, 1982, https://www.nytimes.com/1982/03/05/arts/boycott-of-nbc-tv-and-rca-urged.html.
18. Aislinn Simpson, "Starbucks Faces Boycott over 'Vulgar' Logo," *The Telegraph*, May 15, 2008, https://www.telegraph.co.uk/news/newstopics/howaboutthat/1960441/Starbucks-boycott-threat-over-vulgar-logo.html.
19. Alex Abad-Santos, "Starbucks's Red Cup Controversy, Explained," *Vox*, November 10, 2016, https://www.vox.com/2015/11/10/9707034/starbucks-red-cup-controversy.
20. "About Us," One Million Moms, https://onemillionmoms.com/about-us/.
21. Queer Voices, "One Million Moms Threatens Toys 'R' Us with Boycott over Archie Comics' Gay Wedding Issue," *HuffPost News*, February 28, 2012, https://www.huffpost.com/entry/one-million-moms-toys-r-us-archie-comics_n_1307689.
22. Queer Voices, "One Million Moms Condemns Oreo Cookies for Gay Pride Support," *HuffPost News*, June 29, 2012, https://www.huffpost.com/entry/one-million-moms-oreo-cookies-gay-pride_n_1638774.
23. Queer Voices, "One Million Moms Condemns Urban Outfitters' Lesbian Kiss Catalog Photo," *HuffPost News*, April 17, 2012, https://www.huffpost.com/entry/urban-outfitters-lesbian-kiss-photo-one-million-moms_n_1431134.
24. Queer Voices, "Nabisco's Gay-Inclusive Honey Maid/Teddy Grahams Commercial Slammed by One Million Moms," March 20, 2014, *HuffPost News*, March 20, 2014, https://www.huffpost.com/entry/gay-honey-maid-one-million-moms_n_5001438.
25. Curtis M. Wong, "One Million Moms Slam Chobani for 'Pushing the LGBT Agenda' with New Lesbian Ad," *HuffPost News*, June 19, 2015, https://www.huffpost.com/entry/chobani-one-million-moms_n_7623504.
26. Curtis M. Wong, "'Family Group' Is Fuming over the Campbell's Soup Ad with Gay Dads," *HuffPost News*, October 11, 2015, https://www.huffpost.com/entry/one-million-moms-campbells_n_56181dc1e4b0dbb8000e9e79.
27. Alex Bollinger, "Conservative Christians Are Trying to Cancel TurboTax over Gay Couple in Ad," *LGBTQ Nation*, January 7, 2023, https://www.lgbtqnation.com/2023/01/conservative-christians-trying-cancel-turbotax-gay-couple-ad/.

28. Madison Vanderberg, "One Million Moms Is Coming after Hallmark over LGBTQ Storylines," *Scary Mommy*, July 28, 2020, https://www.scarymommy.com/one-million-moms-hallmark-channel-lgbtq.
29. Jelisa Castrodale, "Everything 'One Million Moms' Wanted to Call the Manager About in 2020," *Vice*, December 18, 2020, https://www.vice.com/en/article/bvxdj5/everything-one-million-moms-got-mad-about-in-2020.
30. Alex Bollinger, "Conservative Christians Call for Boycott of Scooby-Doo Because Velma Is Gay," *LGBTQ Nation*, October 14, 2022, https://www.lgbtqnation.com/2022/10/conservative-christians-call-boycott-scooby-doo-velma-gay/.
31. Molly Sprayregen, "Christian Conservatives Campaign against Lesbian Polar Bear in 'Peppa Pig,'" *LGBTQ Nation*, November 19, 2022, https://www.lgbtqnation.com/2022/11/christian-conservatives-campaign-lesbian-polar-bears-peppa-pig/.
32. Graham Gremore, "One Million Moms Has Meltdown over Zales Commercial Featuring Lesbian Couple," *LGBTQ Nation*, November 25, 2016, https://www.lgbtqnation.com/2016/11/one-million-moms-meltdown-zales-commercial-featuring-lesbian-couple/.
33. David Hudson, "One Million Moms Throw Temper Tantrum over These Adorable Baby Clothes," *Queerty*, March 17, 2023, https://www.queerty.com/one-million-moms-throw-temper-tantrum-over-these-adorable-baby-clothes-20230317.
34. Monica Cole, "Hershey's Disturbing New Ad!" American Family Association, March 10, 2023, https://www.afa.net/the-stand/culture/2023/03/hershey-s-disturbing-new-ad/.
35. Greg Owen, "Christian Conservatives Target Netflix for Showing Gay Relationships in Two Cartoons," *LGBTQ Nation*, July 29, 2022, https://www.lgbtqnation.com/2022/07/christian-conservatives-target-netflix-showing-gay-relationships-two-cartoons/.
36. Alex Bollinger, "Christian Conservatives Attack Kay Jewelers for Showing Gay Couple in Ad," *LGBTQ Nation*, April 28, 2022, https://www.lgbtqnation.com/2022/04/christian-conservatives-attack-kay-jewelers-showing-gay-couple-ad/.
37. Bil Browning, "Christian Conservatives Are Livid after Zillow Showed Two Black Women Together in Ad," *LGBTQ Nation*, February 11, 2022, https://www.lgbtqnation.com/2022/02/christian-conservatives-livid-zillow-showed-two-black-women-together-ad/.
38. Dan Avery, "eHarmony's New Inclusive Ads Are Enraging Some on the Right," *NBC News*, February 10, 2021, https://www.nbcnews.com/feature/nbc-out/eharmony-s-new-inclusive-ads-are-enraging-some-right-n1257175.
39. Jamie Burton, "Nike Makes Dylan Mulvaney Sports Bra Model, Days after Bud Light Furor," *Newsweek*, April 6, 2023, https://www.newsweek.com/nike-transgender-dylan-mulvaney-sports-bra-model-days-after-bud-light-furore-1792872.
40. Brian Flood, David Rutz, "Bud Light's Pact with Trans Activist Dylan Mulvaney Sparks Outrage, Praise," *Fox News*, April 5, 2023, https://www.foxnews.com/media/bud-lights-pact-trans-activist-dylan-mulvaney-sparks-outrage-praise.
41. Matt Walsh @MattWalshBlog, *Twitter/X*, April 5, 2023, https://twitter.com/MattWalshBlog/status/1643716618818580483.

42. Michelle Toh, "Bud Light Controversy Cost Parent Company About $395 million in Lost US Sales," CNN, August 3, 2023, https://www.cnn.com/2023/08/03/business/anheuser-busch-revenue-bud-light-intl-hnk/index.html.
43. Eliana Dockterman, "*Barbie* is Officially the Biggest Movie of the Year—And It's Not Going Anywhere," *Time*, August 24, 2023, https://time.com/6304654/barbie-box-office-biggest-movie-2023/.

12. Condom Girl: Persecution Complex

1. History.com Editors, "Columbine Shooting," History A&E Network, November, 9, 2009, https://www.history.com/topics/1990s/columbine-high-school-shootings.
2. Alissa Wilkinson, "After Columbine, Martyrdom Became a Powerful Fantasy for Christian Teenagers," *Vox*, April 17, 2019, https://www.vox.com/culture/2017/4/20/15369442/columbine-anniversary-cassie-bernall-rachel-scott-martyrdom.
3. Dave Cullen, "Inside the Columbine High Investigation," *Salon*, September 23, 1999, https://www.salon.com/1999/09/23/columbine_4/.
4. Kim Severson, "Chick-fil-A Thrust Back into Spotlight on Gay Rights," *New York Times*, July 25, 2012, https://www.nytimes.com/2012/07/26/us/gay-rights-uproar-over-chick-fil-a-widens.html.
5. Amber Roberson, "Timeline: Roy Moore's Political Career, Legal Challenges over the Years," *Montgomery Advertiser*, January 28, 2022, https://www.montgomeryadvertiser.com/story/news/local/2022/01/28/judge-roy-moore-ten-commandments-history-timeline-lawsuits/9211301002/.
6. Roy Moore, "Speech by Judge Roy Moore at Monument Dedication," *WSFA News 12*, December 19, 2002, https://www.wsfa.com/story/1056322/speech-by-judge-roy-moore-at-monument-dedication/.
7. Margaret Hartmann, "Trump's Jesus Court Sketch Is Somehow Way Worse than It Looks," *New York Magazine—Intelligencer*, October 3, 2023, https://nymag.com/intelligencer/2023/10/trumps-jesus-court-sketch-is-even-worse-than-it-looks.html.
8. David Klepper, "Trump Arrest Prompts Jesus Comparisons: 'Spiritual Warfare,'" Associated Press, April 5, 2023, https://apnews.com/article/donald-trump-arraignment-jesus-christ-conspiracy-theory-670c45bd71b3466dcd6e8e188badcd1d.

13. Holy Mosh Pits: Guns, Violence, and Other Christian Things

1. CNN Editorial Research, "Sandy Hook School Shootings Fast Facts," CNN, November 28, 2022, https://www.cnn.com/2013/06/07/us/connecticut-shootings-fast-facts/index.html.
2. Oath Keepers, *Oath Keepers: Guardians of the Republic*, 2010, retrieved from the Library of Congress, https://www.loc.gov/item/lcwaN0003728/.
3. Carrie Johnson, "Stewart Rhodes, Oath Keepers Founder, Sentenced to 18 years for Seditious Conspiracy," NPR, May 25, 2023, https://www.npr.org/2023/05/25/1178116193/stewart-rhodes-oath-keepers-verdict.
4. Tom Gjelten, "Militant Christian Nationalists Remain a Potent Force, Even After the Capitol Riot," NPR, January 19, 2021, https://www.npr.org/2021/01/19/958159202/militant-christian-nationalists-remain-a-potent-force.

5. Fact Sheet, "Armed Extremism Primer: Oath Keepers," Everytown Research & Policy, February 7, 2023, https://everytownresearch.org/report/armed-extremism-primer-oath-keepers/.
6. Samuel L. Perry, "School Shootings Confirm That Guns Are the Religion of the Right," *Time*, May 25, 2022, https://time.com/6181342/school-shootings-christian-right-guns/.
7. Perry, "School Shootings."
8. Chloe Folmar, "Boebert: Jesus Didn't Have Enough AR-15s to 'Keep His Government from Killing Him,'" *The Hill*, June 17, 2022, https://thehill.com/homenews/house/3528049-boebert-jesus-didnt-have-enough-ar-15s-to-keep-his-government-from-killing-him/.
9. Kyle Mantyla, "Former Trump Administration Official William Wolfe Says 'We Are Getting Close' to Christians Taking Up Arms," *Right Wing Watch*, October 31, 2023, https://www.rightwingwatch.org/post/former-trump-administration-official-william-wolfe-says-we-are-getting-close-to-christians-taking-up-arms/.
10. Kyle Mantyla, "From 'Very Biased' to 'Out of Context': William Wolfe Attacks Right Wing Watch for Exposing His Radical Views," *Right Wing Watch*, November 2, 2023, https://www.rightwingwatch.org/post/from-very-based-to-out-of-context-william-wolfe-attacks-right-wing-watch-for-exposing-his-radical-views/.
11. Scott Detrow, Gabriel J. Sánchez, and Sarah Handel, "He Was a Top Church Official Who Criticized Trump. He says Christianity Is in Crisis," NPR, August 8, 2023, https://www.npr.org/2023/08/08/1192663920/southern-baptist-convention-donald-trump-christianity.

14. Rubber Fetus for Jesus: Abortion

1. Michael McAuliff, "Scott DesJarlais Fined $500 For Affairs With Patients," *Huff Post*, May 23, 2013, https://www.huffpost.com/entry/scott-desjarlais-fined_n_3327099.
2. Andy Sher, "DesJarlais Divorce Papers Show Abuse Accusations," *Chattanooga Times Free Press*, September 17, 2010, https://www.timesfreepress.com/news/2010/sep/17/desjarlais-divorce-papers-show-abuse-accusations/.
3. Chas Sisk, "The Biggest Hypocrite in Congress?" *Politico*, August 14, 2014, https://www.politico.com/magazine/story/2014/08/scott-desjarlais-reelection-110028/.
4. Tiana Lowe Doescher, "Do Pro-Life Candidates Belong in Today's Democratic Party? Chris Hale Is Betting on It," *Washington Examiner*, November 3, 2020, https://www.washingtonexaminer.com/opinion/pro-life-democrats-face-two-challenges-gain-acceptance-from-their-own-party-and-gop-voters.
5. Tennessee Statewide Results, "Tennessee Election Results: Fourth Congressional District," *New York Times*, https://www.nytimes.com/interactive/2020/11/03/us/elections/results-tennessee-house-district-4.html.
6. Domenico Montanaro, "Poll: Americans Want Abortion Restrictions, but Not as Far as Red States Are Going," NPR, April 26, 2023, https://www.npr.org/2023/04/26/1171863775/poll-americans-want-abortion-restrictions-but-not-as-far-as-red-states-are-going.

7. Solcyre Burga, "How a 10-Year-Old Rape Victim Who Traveled for an Abortion Became Part of a Political Firestorm," *Time*, July 15, 2022, https://time.com/6198062/rape-victim-10-abortion-indiana-ohio/.
8. Laurie Goodstein, "Falwell: Blame Abortionists, Feminists and Gays," *The Guardian*, September 19, 2001, https://www.theguardian.com/world/2001/sep/19/september11.usa9.
9. Andrew Whitehead and Samuel L. Perry, "White Christian Nationalism Isn't Pro-Life. It's Pro-Order," Religion News Service, January 19, 2023, https://religionnews.com/2023/01/19/white-christian-nationalism-isnt-pro-life-its-pro-order/.
10. Mike Hixenbaugh, "Alabama Justice Who Ruled Embryos Are People Says American Law Should Be Rooted in the Bible," NBC News, February 22, 2024, https://www.nbcnews.com/news/us-news/alabama-justice-embryos-biblical-seven-mountains-rcna139969.
11. Mercedes Schneider, "Roe v. Wade Was Decided by a Republican-Nominated Supreme Court," *HuffPost*, November 6, 2016, https://www.huffpost.com/entry/trump-supporters-roe-vs-wade-was-decided-by-a-republican_b_581fbd44e4b044f827a78f87.
12. Randall Balmer, "The Real Origins of the Religious Right," *Politico*, May 27, 2014, https://www.politico.com/magazine/story/2014/05/religious-right-real-origins-107133/.
13. Balmer, "The Real Origins of the Religious Right."
14. Aimee Picchi, "Texas Abortion Ban Turns Citizens into 'Bounty Hunters,'" *CBS News*, September 3, 2021, https://www.cbsnews.com/news/texas-abortion-law-bounty-hunters-citizens/.
15. Katherine Stewart, "Christian Nationalists Are Excited About What Comes Next," *New York Times*, July 5, 2022, https://www.nytimes.com/2022/07/05/opinion/dobbs-christian-nationalism.html.
16. Alice Miranda Ollstein, "Senate Fails to Pass Abortion Rights Bill—Again," *Politico*, May 11, 2022, https://www.politico.com/news/2022/05/11/senate-doomed-vote-roe-abortion-rights-00031732.
17. Tom Buck @TomBuck, "In light of today's vote by Democrats to legalize abortion until moment of birth, we are rapidly reaching the point that voting for a Democrat should be a matter of church discipline," *Twitter/X*, May 11, 2022, https://twitter.com/TomBuck/status/1524576438950711297.
18. April Ajoy, @aprilajoyr, response to @William_E_Wolfe, "Saying it's better to be racist than to support women's rights is . . . quite the take," *Twitter/X*, June 5, 2023, https://twitter.com/aprilajoyr/status/1665814138768044035?t=eP7k8RA5P8aU0f7GUuNeJg&s=19.
19. Jemar Tisby, *The Color of Compromise: The Truth About the American Church's Complicity in Racism*, Kindle Edition (Grand Rapids, MI: Zondervan, 2020), pp. 160–61.
20. Maggie Fox, "Abortion Rates Go Down When Countries Make It Legal: Report," *NBC News*, March 20, 2018, https://www.nbcnews.com/health/health-care/abortion-rates-go-down-when-countries-make-it-legal-report-n858476.

21. Jason Millman, "Abortions Increased the Year after Roe Was Overturned," *Axios*, October 24, 2023, https://www.axios.com/2023/10/24/abortion-increase-roe-wade-state-ban.
22. Anna Almendrala, "We Already Know How to Safely Reduce Abortions," *HuffPost*, February 14, 2017, https://www.huffpost.com/entry/reducing-abortion-rates-policy_n_589b8ea5e4b09bd304bfd920.
23. Pam Belluck, "They Had Miscarriages, and New Abortion Laws Obstructed Treatment," *New York Times*, July 17, 2022, https://www.nytimes.com/2022/07/17/health/abortion-miscarriage-treatment.html.
24. Jessica Ravitz, "Before Judging 'Late-Term Abortion,' Understand What It Means, Doctors Say," CNN, February 6, 2019, https://www.cnn.com/2019/02/06/health/late-term-abortion-explainer/index.html.
25. Katha Pollitt, "6 Myths About Abortion," *Time*, November 13, 2014, https://time.com/3582434/6-abortion-myths/.

15. Drowning Dinosaurs: Education

1. Hemant Mehta, "These Creationists Learned a Weird Lesson from Sloths," *Friendly Atheist*, January 29, 2021, https://friendlyatheist.patheos.com/2021/01/29/these-creationists-learned-a-weird-lesson-from-sloths/.
2. Bodie Hodge, "What Is the State of the Water Vapor Canopy Model?" *Answers in Genesis*, December 18, 2019, https://answersingenesis.org/environmental-science/state-of-canopy-model/.
3. "The Growing Partisan Divide in Views of Higher Education," Pew Research Center, August 19, 2019, https://www.pewresearch.org/social-trends/2019/08/19/the-growing-partisan-divide-in-views-of-higher-education-2/.
4. Jack Mitchell, "20 Years Ago, the U.S. Warned of Iraq's Alleged 'Weapons of Mass Destruction,'" NPR, February 3, 2023, https://www.npr.org/2023/02/03/1151160567/colin-powell-iraq-un-weapons-mass-destruction.
5. Katherine Schaeffer, "A Year Later, a Look Back at Public Opinion About the U.S. Military Exit from Afghanistan," Pew Research Center, August 17, 2022, https://www.pewresearch.org/short-reads/2022/08/17/a-year-later-a-look-back-at-public-opinion-about-the-u-s-military-exit-from-afghanistan/.
6. Jill Kimball, "Costs of the 20-Year War on Terror: $8 Trillion and 900,000 Deaths," Brown University, September 1, 2021, https://www.brown.edu/news/2021-09-01/costsofwar.
7. "The Seven Mountains of Societal Influence," Generals International, https://www.generals.org/the-seven-mountains.
8. Sarah Schwartz, "Map: Where Critical Race Theory Is Under Attack," *Education Week*, June 13, 2023, https://www.edweek.org/policy-politics/map-where-critical-race-theory-is-under-attack/2021/06.
9. Andrew Atterbury, "DeSantis Defends Banning African American Studies Course as Black Leaders Call for Action," *Politico*, January 23, 2023, https://www.politico.com/news/2023/01/23/desantis-banning-african-american-studies-00079027.

10. Jaclyn Diaz, "Florida Gov. Ron DeSantis Signs a Bill Banning DEI Initiatives in Public Colleges," NPR, May 15, 2023, https://www.npr.org/2023/05/15/1176210007/florida-ron-desantis-dei-ban-diversity.
11. Sarah Schwartz, "The Republican Fight Against 'Critical Race Theory' Continues as Arkansas Enacts New Ban," *Education Week*, January 12, 2023, https://www.edweek.org/policy-politics/the-republican-fight-against-critical-race-theory-continues-as-arkansas-enacts-new-ban/2023/01.
12. Ken Ham, "What Should Christians Think About Critical Race Theory," *Answers in Genesis*, March 23, 2023, https://answersingenesis.org/racism/what-should-christians-think-about-critical-race-theory/.
13. Don Beehler, "Why Critical Race Theory Doesn't Reflect the Values of Christianity," *The Tennessean*, June 29, 2021, https://www.tennessean.com/story/opinion/2021/06/29/critical-race-theory-doesnt-reflect-values-christianity/7789946002/.
14. Jo Yurcaba, "More than 1,600 Books Banned During 2021–22 School Year, Report Finds," *NBC News*, September 19, 2022, https://www.nbcnews.com/nbc-out/out-news/1600-books-banned-2021-22-school-year-report-finds-rcna48367.
15. Jo Yurcaba, "More than 1,600 Books Banned."
16. Lisa Lerer and Patricia Mazzei, "Florida Sex Scandal Shakes Moms for Liberty, as Group's Influence Wanes," *New York Times*, December 18, 2023, https://www.nytimes.com/2023/12/16/us/politics/moms-for-liberty-sex-scandal.html.
17. Laura Clawson, "Book-Banning Advocate Claims 'A Single Kiss' in a Children's Book Led to Her Porn Addiction," *Daily Kos*, November 29, 2023, https://www.dailykos.com/stories/2023/11/29/2208687/-Book-banning-advocate-claims-a-single-kiss-in-a-children-s-book-led-to-her-porn-addiction.
18. Ileana Garnand, "Porn Addiction or PR Stunt? Conroe ISD Bans Book after Anti-Scholastic Testimony," *Lonestar Live*, November 30, 2023, https://www.lonestarlive.com/news/2023/11/porn-addiction-or-pr-stunt-conroe-isd-bans-book-after-anti-scholastic-testimony.html.
19. Anisha Kohli, "Texas Senate Passes Bill to Put the Ten Commandments in Every Classroom," *Time*, April 5, 2023, https://time.com/6269110/texas-bill-10-commandments-schools/.
20. Kohli, "Texas Senate Passes Bill to Put the Ten Commandments in Every Classroom."

16. Uncoordinated Angels: LGBTQ, Part 1

1. Oriana González, "Clarence Thomas Wants SCOTUS to Reconsider Decisions on Gay Marriage, Contraceptives," *Axios*, June 24, 2022, https://www.axios.com/2022/06/24/clarence-thomas-same-sex-marriage-contraception.
2. Brooke Sopelsa, "Trump Cabinet's Bible Teacher Says Gays Cause 'God's Wrath' in COVID-19 Blog Post," *NBC News*, March 25, 2020, https://www.nbcnews.com/feature/nbc-out/trump-s-bible-teacher-says-gays-among-those-blame-covid-n1168981.
3. ABC News, "Falwell Apologizes for Placing Blame," *ABC News*, September 19, 2001, https://abcnews.go.com/GMA/story?id=126698&page=1.

4. Warren J. Blumenfeld, "God and Natural Disasters: It's the Gays' Fault?" *HuffPost*, November 5, 2012, https://www.huffpost.com/entry/god-and-natural-disasters-its-the-gays-fault_b_2068817.
5. The Trevor Project, "National Survey on LGBTQ Youth Mental Health 2020," https://www.thetrevorproject.org/survey-2020/?section=Finding-Support.

17. Walking Dead Demons: LGBTQ, Part 2

1. Kristin Kobes Du Mez, *Jesus and John Wayne: How White Evangelicals Corrupted a Faith and Fractured a Nation* (New York: Liveright Publishing Corporation, 2020), pp. 26–27.
2. Women & the American Story, "Life Story : Phyllis Schlafly (1924–2016)," New-York Historical Society Museum & Library, https://wams.nyhistory.org/growth-and-turmoil/feminism-and-the-backlash/phyllis-schlafly/#resource.
3. James Dobson, "Dr. James Dobson: Why Marriage and Family Matters Now More Than Ever," CBN, October 11, 2020, https://www2.cbn.com/news/us/dr-james-dobson-why-marriage-and-family-matters-now-more-ever.
4. James Dobson, "What Is Happening to America? Can We Stop It?" Dr. James Dobson Family Institute, September 2022, https://www.drjamesdobson.org/newsletters/september-2022-newsletter.
5. Press Office, "U.S. Department of Education Confirms Title IX Protects Students from Discrimination Based on Sexual Orientation and Gender Identity," U.S. Department of Education, June 16, 2021, https://www.ed.gov/news/press-releases/us-department-education-confirms-title-ix-protects-students-discrimination-based-sexual-orientation-and-gender-identity.
6. Dobson, "What Is Happening to America?"
7. Office for Civil Rights, "Exemptions from Title IX," U.S. Department of Education, March 8, 2021, https://www2.ed.gov/about/offices/list/ocr/docs/t9-rel-exempt/index.html.
8. Andrew Stanton, "Pastor Tells Voters to Snub Marjorie Taylor Greene over 'Pathetic' Husband," *Newsweek*, November 7, 2022, https://www.newsweek.com/pastor-tells-voters-snub-marjorie-taylor-greene-pathetic-husband-1757635.
9. David Mikkelson, "Did RNC Speaker Abby Johnson Advocate 'Household Voting'?" *Snopes*, August 28, 2020, https://www.snopes.com/fact-check/abby-johnson-household-voting/.
10. The Transformed Wife @godlywomanhood, "The Women's Suffrage Movement's purpose was to undermine the husband's authority in the home. It was to undermine male leadership in everything and cause division between men and women. Don't be fooled into thinking that it was for anything good. The bad fruit is evident," *Twitter/X*, February 22, 2023, https://twitter.com/godlywomanhood/status/1628388490227613696.
11. Stephen Wolfe, *The Case for Christian Nationalism*, Kindle Edition (Moscow, ID: Canon Press, 2022), pp. 450–451.
12. Ryan Smith, "Marjorie Taylor Greene Thanks Gaetz for Support, Says Women 'Weaker Sex,'" *Newsweek*, April 8, 2022, https://www.newsweek.com/marjorie-taylor-greene-matt-gaetz-support-jimmy-kimmel-spat-gop-republicans-1696337.

13. PatriotTakes @patriottakes, "During a transphobic rant, Marjorie Taylor Greene said women 'are the weaker sex' and more easily defeated by the devil. Greene: 'When the serpent came in the garden, he didn't go to Adam. He went to Eve because the serpent saw the weaker sex and knew he could defeat her,'" video included, *Twitter/X*, June 22, 2023, https://twitter.com/patriottakes/status/1671923121589239808?t=0dkSzN4m8vwaAyAH4rrV4A&s=19.
14. 21 Summit, The Patriarch Convention, 2023, https://21studios.com/21-patriarch/.
15. 21 Summit, The 22 Convention, Make Women Great Again 4.0, https://21studios.com/22-convention/.
16. Virginia Heffernan, "The Crisis over American Manhood Is Really Code for Something Else," *Politico*, July 14, 2023, https://www.politico.com/news/magazine/2023/07/14/josh-hawley-masculinity-crisis-00105436.
17. Trans Legislation Tracker, "Tracking the Rise of Anti-Trans Bills in the U.S.," https://translegislation.com/learn.
18. Rachel Dowd, "Transgender People over Four Times More Likely Than Cisgender People to Be Victims of Violent Crime," UCLA School of Law Williams Institute, March 23, 2021, https://williamsinstitute.law.ucla.edu/press/ncvs-trans-press-release/.

About the Author

April Ajoy is a content creator and podcast host who uses humor to shine light on the harmful, toxic, and sometimes just weird traits of American evangelicalism. Growing up an evangelist's kid entrenched in Christian Nationalism and working in conservative Christian media as an adult, Ajoy saw it all firsthand. Still a Christian, she uses her platform to expose the dangers of Christian Nationalism while promoting a more inclusive faith. April has been featured on Buzzfeed, CNN, *Newsweek,* and more. She's been married to Beecher for ten years, and they have two daughters together.